MW01235608

INTERNATIONAL TRADE LAW

including

TRUMP AND TRADE

IN A NUTSHELL®

SEVENTH EDITION

RALPH H. FOLSOM

Professor of Law

University of San Diego School of Law

A.B. Princeton University, J.D. Yale Law School

LLM London School of Economics

WEST
ACADEMIC
PUBLISHING

Nutshell Series, In a Nutshell and the Nutshell Logo are trademarks registered in the U.S. Patent and Trademark Office.

COPYRIGHT © 1996 WEST PUBLISHING CO.
© West, a Thomson business, 2000, 2004
© 2009, 2012 Thomson Reuters
© 2016 LEG, Inc. d/b/a West Academic
© 2018 LEG, Inc. d/b/a West Academic
      444 Cedar Street, Suite 700
      St. Paul, MN 55101
      1-877-888-1330

West, West Academic Publishing, and West Academic are trademarks of West Publishing Corporation, used under license.

Printed in the United States of America

ISBN: 978-1-64242-292-4

I dedicate this book to the many good souls who have so thoughtfully helped me over the years to improve the successive editions of my international business law books.

PREFACE

Professor Ralph Folsom has completed this seventh edition of *International Trade Law including Trump and Trade.* International trade law is a very broad subject, one which is constantly affected by change, as President Trump has made dramatically clear.

This *Nutshell* focuses on customs and tariff law, regulation of imports and exports, trade remedies against import competition, foreign corrupt practices, technology transfers, free trade agreements and customs unions, the law of the World Trade Organization, and President Trump and his trade policies.

I have also written a much more detailed Concise Hornbook on *Principles of International Trade Law* (West Academic Publishers), which contains numerous trade laws and documents, and can be used as a course book.

For many years I have been graciously aided by academic and professional colleagues in the USA and abroad. I also wish to thank students around the globe for their continuing interest in my international trade classes and writings.

I welcome suggestions for the next edition of this Nutshell.

RALPH H. FOLSOM
RFOLSOM@SANDIEGO.EDU

June 2018

ABOUT THE AUTHOR

Ralph H. Folsom has been a Professor at the University of San Diego School of Law since 1975. A graduate of Princeton University, Yale Law School and the London School of Economics (LLM), Professor Folsom teaches, writes and consults extensively in the field of international business law.

Folsom has been a Senior Fulbright resident scholar in Singapore and a Visiting Professor at the University of Hong Kong, University of Aix-Marseille, University of Brest, University of Paris, University of Toulouse, University of Puerto Rico, Monash University in Australia and Tecnológico de Monterrey in México.

Professor Folsom has authored or co-authored a range of books with West Academic Publishing. These include a popular problem-oriented course book on *International Business Transactions,* soon to be in its Thirteenth Edition.

He is the author of other West Academic Nutshells, including the Nutshells on *International Business Transactions* (co-author), *NAFTA—Free Trade and Foreign Investment in The Americas, Foreign Investment Law,* and *European Union Law including BREXIT.* A revised version of the NAFTA Nutshell is anticipated.

Professor Folsom has also written more extensively than Nutshells permit in the West Concise Hornbook Series: *Principles of International*

Litigation and Arbitration, Principles of European Union Law including BREXIT, Principles of International Trade Law, and Principles of International Business Transactions (co-authored).

OUTLINE

TABLE OF CASES

References are to Pages

INTERNATIONAL TRADE LAW

including

TRUMP AND TRADE

IN A NUTSHELL®

SEVENTH EDITION

INTRODUCTION

Three hypothetical transactions, originally created by Prof. Michael Gordon, illustrate the often unanticipated role of international trade law:

THE STATE TRANSACTION:

PARTS FROM SALEM ARE MADE INTO GOODS IN BOSTON FOR SALE IN BROCKTON

THE UNITED STATES TRANSACTION:

PARTS FROM SAN FRANCISCO ARE MADE INTO GOODS IN BOSTON FOR SALE IN BURBANK

THE INTERNATIONAL TRANSACTION:

PARTS FROM SINGAPORE ARE MADE INTO GOODS IN BOSTON FOR SALE IN BRASILIA AND BOMBAY

The Boston Client

Representing a Boston client who (1) manufactures goods, for example children's clothing and knapsacks, for sale to numerous retail store buyers in the United States, for example in Brockton and Burbank, and who (2) purchases the parts for such products from U.S. sellers, for example in Salem and San Francisco, usually does not involve the application of U.S. trade law governing imports and exports. That is true whether the transaction is exclusively in one state, or involves more than one and perhaps many states.

But if our Boston client is an "international" company—it sells and buys where it can obtain the best price. That means it sells to and buys from parties in foreign nations as well as in the United States. Consequently, U.S. trade law affecting *exports* is applicable when our Boston client sells the goods abroad, for example to buyers in Brasilia and Bombay. U.S. trade law affecting *imports* is applicable when our Boston client purchases parts for the manufacture of its products from Singapore or Sao Paulo.

In each case, importing or exporting, our client must be familiar with the characteristics of competition on an international scale. The client assumes different risks and becomes subject to different laws. Those laws are not only U.S. laws but the laws affecting imports and exports of the foreign nations in which our client does business. Such foreign laws may include rules which appear to exist solely to protect domestic industries. There may be high tariffs, or quotas, or a vast array of nontariff barriers affecting our client's exports, such as packaging or labeling requirements, safety certification or compliance with health standards.

But that also may be how the foreign buyer or seller views the laws of the United States. The United States is not exempt from creating nontariff barriers. The Boston client's importers (buyers) in Brasilia or Bombay may be charged with dumping the Boston sourced goods on the local market, or benefitting from U.S. subsidies. The Boston client may not believe it is acting unfairly in selling to buyers in Brasilia or Bombay, but it has become subject to protective legislation in these foreign nations.

Just as it may be the target in one case, our client may shoot the arrows in another. If the Boston client is unable to sell to its old buyers in Brockton or Burbank, because Singapore or Sao Paulo sellers are not only selling parts to our client, but also selling finished products in competition directly to the Brockton or Burbank buyers, the U.S. trade laws may help our client. This is not because our client is an international trader, but because it is a *domestic* entity which is part of an industry injured or threatened with injury by the foreign goods. The same laws might help a U.S. company which has never engaged and has no intention of engaging in international trade: Enter the Bartow client.

The Bartow Client

Assume that in the small town of Bartow, Florida, a company employs about thirty people and for decades has manufactured a variety of textile products for sale solely in Florida from material produced in North Carolina. It makes children's clothing and knapsacks, just as does the Boston entity described above. But unlike our Boston client, the Bartow entity does not sell abroad. It does not even sell in Georgia! Its owners and employees work hard in meeting the demand for its products in Florida. It pays fair, but not excessive, wages.

Management is very cost conscious, but believes the company can compete with anything produced by companies subject to the same rules of minimum wages, pollution controls, workshop safety, social security, etc.

Two problems have arisen in the past few months, which have involuntarily thrust this small town enterprise into being a participant in international trade. A large Florida department store chain, which had bought its clothing for years from the Bartow entity, informed the company that it was dropping its line of products and replacing them with nearly identical products manufactured by parties in Singapore and Sao Paulo. These are the same foreign sellers that the Boston client has claimed are causing it harm. The foreign made clothing costs the Florida retail chain 40 percent less than they had been paying the Bartow manufacturer.

The second concern arose when the company was asked by a local tourist attraction to bid on the manufacture of 1,000 children's knapsacks in the form of dolphins. The company wanted the job and cut its profit to a narrower margin than it normally accepted. When it presented the design and the bid to the buyer it was told the same knapsacks could be had for half the price in Singapore or Sao Paulo.

Global Trade Law

Although there are significant variations in the trade laws and economic relations of different nations, for most nations there are some accepted norms. Roughly 165 trading nations are members of the World Trade Organization (WTO), the successor to the General Agreement on Tariffs and Trade (GATT 1947). Since its formation at the end of World War II, the GATT/WTO has grown in membership, significantly reduced tariffs, and worked towards abolishing many nontariff trade barriers. The rules noted above of various nations which allow countervailing duty, dumping and safeguard (escape clause) protective remedies all have their roots in the GATT/WTO. Hence, exports by either of the U.S. companies may encounter the same international trade remedies in, say, Brazil or India.

Beyond these areas, the 1995 WTO "package" of agreements covers many other relevant issues: Customs law, trade quotas, agricultural products, health regulation of foods, textiles and clothing (hello Boston and Bartow!), technical product regulations, trade in services, trade-related intellectual property rights and dispute settlement. These agreements are reviewed in Chapter 2.

Our client, whether it is the Boston or Bartow entity, is likely to be more interested in stopping the foreign competition or foreign application of trade remedies than in how it is stopped. Domestically, it may make little difference whether the action chosen is against foreign subsidies, dumping, surges of imports, market disruption, undertaken in the name of national security, or any other actionable activity under any part of U.S. trade law. It is the end result the client wishes to achieve, a reduction or elimination of allegedly "unfair" foreign competition.

The path to that result will be the recommended course of action suggested by the client's counsel. Thus counsel must know about the full array of choices available under the U.S. trade laws, and (if U.S. exports are involved) how to defend against trade remedies in foreign jurisdictions. Trade organizations such as the WTO may grant developing nations like India and Brazil, and more controversially China, special rights to impose barriers against imports, or assist exports.

United States Import Remedies

Why is it possible that the prices could be so low? Both the Boston and the Bartow companies are clearly being injured by these imports. Further inquiry may disclose similar injury to the U.S. children's clothing and knapsack industries as a whole, rather than to just these two domestic companies. Perhaps the products were being subsidized by the foreign governments. That may allow the Boston or Bartow companies to request that the U.S. government commence an investigation under U.S. trade laws, which may conclude that foreign government subsidies were present and there was material injury, or a threat of such injury, consequently calling for the imposition of countervailing tariff duties (CVD).

Or the foreign companies may be dumping the products on the U.S. market. If they are doing so, meaning selling their products for "less than fair value" (the price for which they are sold in the foreign domestic market where they are manufactured), the

U.S. government may begin an investigation. If it is concluded that dumping was present and there was material injury, or a threat of such injury, there may be an imposition of country-specific antidumping duties (AD).

If the source of the foreign goods were Shanghai, where there may be an inadequate market economy cost analysis, it may be very difficult to establish the presence of subsidies, or sales at less than fair value to establish dumping. If China is defined as a nonmarket economy (NME), and that seems less likely with each passing year, "surrogate" countries may be utilized to compute dumping practices. Its status is now under active dispute within the WTO. For more on AD and CVD law, see Chapter 4.

If there is a surge of foreign goods from any of the vast majority of market economy nations, and if they cause or threaten *serious* as opposed to *material* injury to the U.S. industry, the Boston or Bartow company may seek U.S. safeguard or Section 201 "escape clause" action to temporarily limit their entry. But how the U.S. government responds to a domestic company's claim of injury from foreign competition may be based more on relations with foreign nations than an accurate interpretation of the U.S. law. President Trump used Section 201 to temporarily impose global tariffs on solar panels and clothes washers in 2018. See Chapters 4 and 8.

The Boston or Bartow company may correctly feel it is more a pawn in international politics than a player in international business, a perspective some firms certainly shared when President Trump unilaterally imposed in 2018 near-global tariffs on U.S. imports of steel and aluminum in the name of "national security." President Trump has also revived Section 301 of the Trade Act of 1974, which broadly authorizes *unilateral* trade sanctions against nations engaged in discriminatory, unreasonable or unjustifiable activities, think China. Use of Section 301 is limited to trade issues not covered under the WTO package of agreements, such as mandatory technology transfers and IP theft. President Trump has threatened to forcefully use Section 301 against China. See Chapters 5 and 8.

The Bartow company never intended to engage in international trade. It has not. **It still sells nothing abroad.** But it is fearful that soon it will sell nothing in Florida as well. Its officials and lawyers must learn about international business and trade law if the company is to survive, or even if it is not to survive, to provide its former employees with U.S. trade adjustment assistance made available to companies which lose out to foreign competition.

Export Controls

Most of these comments have involved restrictions on imports. U.S. restrictions on imports would help our Boston client in so far as it is a seller of its products within the United States to buyers in Brockton or Burbank, but might hurt that client if it imports components for its production from Singapore or Sao Paulo. Restraints on component imports may cause it to buy higher priced U.S. components from Salem or San Francisco.

Some reference has also been made to controls on exports. To the extent that such controls exist in the United States, and limit our Boston client from exporting to buyers in Brasilia or Bombay, our client would be harmed. If export controls are imposed by the governments in Singapore or Sao Paulo on the components our client needs, it may have to buy them at higher prices from Salem or San Francisco. Unlike import trade remedies, which have been substantially harmonized through the WTO, export control laws tend to be uniquely national in character.

Export controls usually are not imposed for the same reasons as import controls, with the exception that some nations, mainly developing countries, may tax both imports and exports as a revenue raising device. But the United States and many other nations usually limit exports for such reasons as national security, foreign policy goals, or scarcity of certain domestic resources. Most nations encourage exports, often providing incentives, and often engaging in assistance which may constitute unfair trade such as subsidies.

Because export controls often are intended to serve political goals, the executive may be given considerable discretion in imposing export limitations to certain nations. In the United States, conflict between Congress, which believes it has authority over all aspects of foreign commerce, and the President, who believes the executive has control over all aspects of foreign policy, has led to frequent disputes and an inability to enact new export control laws (and also free trade agreements).

Our Boston client may be prohibited from exporting some or all of its products to all nations, or may be prohibited from exporting anything to specific nations. Export controls are thus designed to limit certain goods to any nation, or limit any goods to certain nations, or certain goods to certain nations. To assure compliance, exports may have to be licensed.

The export rules in the United States long divided licenses for the most part between *general* and *validated* licenses. General licenses did not require an application to and approval by the government, only furnishing certain information upon export which was useful for compiling trade statistics. Validated licenses required an application to and permission from the Department of Commerce, often with the scrutiny and sometimes inordinate delay of approval by the Department of Defense.

The end of the Cold War, the movement of many nonmarket economy nations towards democracy and market economics, and the realization by many developing nations that joining the developed world was more promising than leading the third world, encouraged the United States to adopt a simpler export control scheme. The complex matrix of licenses noted above was replaced in 1996 by a scheme intended to be more U.S. exporter-friendly. See Chapter 5 and ask yourself if the new scheme really is exporter friendly.

Regional and Bilateral Trade Law

Suppose your Boston client gets an order to ship its goods to Brussels, and your Bartow client an order to ship its goods to British Columbia. The domestic laws of Belgium and Canada will affect such trading, and so will the laws of the European Union and the NAFTA 1994, assuming the latter survives re-negotiation under President Trump and the former survives BREXIT. Did we mention that Brazil belongs to the MERCOSUR customs union and Singapore now has free trade agreements with the United States, Japan, Korea, China, the EU and others? And India is pushing ahead inside the South Asian Free Trade Area.

The range of laws and economic relations you must consider in advising your clients just expanded beyond domestic and international law to include bilateral and regional law, the framework within which free trade agreements and customs unions frequently operate. Every nation on Earth has at least one such agreement. Naturally there are variations on the theme, with the European Union and NAFTA 1994 serving as prototypes, detailed in my *NAFTA* and *European Union Nutshells*. This Nutshell introduces you to the basics of bilateral and regional trade law in Chapter 7.

What follows in the material ahead is an introduction to the laws and policies, the organizations and entities, and the people involved in international trade and economic relations. This Nutshell covers tariffs, government imposed restrictions on imports and exports, trade remedies, the GATT and the WTO, and the explosion of free trade agreements and customs unions, all in the context of President Trump's highly controversial trade policies summarized in Chapter 8.

CHAPTER 1
WORLD TRADE AND MULTINATIONAL ENTERPRISES

| Trade Deficits and Patterns | Transfer Pricing |
| MNE Operations | MNE Corporate Counsel |

The United States is one of a few central players in the world of international trade. It has engaged in foreign trade from the moment of its independence over two centuries ago. Indeed, one of the reasons independence was sought was England's imposition of severe restrictions on trade between the colonies and foreign nations, intended to preserve the benefits of international trade for England.

Less than two centuries from achieving independence, the United States became a leading trade power in the world. For over a decade after World War II, the United States was in the envious and economically advantageous position of being the major center of production of finished goods for export. But with extraordinary economic growth in Japan and Europe, by the 1980s the United States no longer dominated world trade. It had to compete for sales abroad, and also in the domestic market within the United States. Traditional surpluses in the balance of trade with most nations in some cases began to be reversed. The United States has had to deal with increasingly large trade deficits with Japan, and more recently, the most challenging trade partner—China.

The trade surplus of earlier decades has become a trade deficit of disturbing proportions. The deficit status of U.S. international trade in the 1990s and into the new millennium caused trade to be a topic of common conversation. The U.S. trade deficit is often perceived as threatening jobs for American workers and the consequent diminishment of quality of life of the American people. This has generated annual Congressional proposals of an increasingly restrictive nature. U.S. exports have continued to grow, especially in the service and technology areas, but imports of goods have grown more rapidly. Even the periodic fall of the dollar, making U.S. exports cheaper, has not reversed the trade deficit.

The importance of trade and its underlying economic relations should be apparent. But the huge capacity of the United States to consume foreign products is out of balance with its ability to find reciprocal consumption for its exports. That is due to many reasons, including problems of quality, real and perceived, problems of barriers to trade imposed by every nation, and problems of government leadership. Those who view the United States from abroad continually point to excessive consumption and inadequate savings, and to the budget deficit, as the principal reasons for the deteriorating U.S. trade position. Congress and the administration hear the complaints, but make few corrections. It is easier to blame other nations, a trait President Trump exemplifies. After all, the United States still generates a formidable share of world trade and will continue to do so for a while longer.

Even individual U.S. states have remarkable trade statistics. California alone generates billions of dollars of world trade, making its "gross state product" greater than the gross national products of all but a few nations of the world. In the last few years, however, the per capita standard of living of several other nations has reached and exceeded that in the United States.

TRADE DEFICITS

Some developed nations are unusually dependent on international trade in goods and services. The Netherlands, for example, depends on exports for over 75% of their Gross Domestic Product (GDP). Roughly 50% of the GDPs of Sweden, Germany and Switzerland derive from exports. Canada, New Zealand, France and Britain come in at about 25%, China at 19%, with the United States at approximately 12%.

International trade law has a long and controversial history. Many nations, especially in their early stages of development, are fearful of trade across borders. International trade is a competitive force, one that typically shakes up domestic economic interests and results in trade specialization. It is a powerful engine of change, creating winners and losers in its comparative advantage path. It is now certain, for example, that China's admission to the WTO in 2001 contributed to a significant negative impact on U.S. manufacturing jobs and wages in the Midwest, but also shipment to China of 60% of all U.S. exports of soybeans. Simultaneously, WTO membership helped to lift hundreds of millions of Chinese out of poverty, but also caused the laying off of millions of Chinese state-owned enterprise employees.

Trade is a powerful competitive force increasing the selection of goods and services available in national economies and enhancing domestic market price competition. Wal-Mart's heavy importation of inexpensive Chinese goods, for example, notably reduced U.S. consumer costs, particularly for lower income and displaced Americans. That said, President Trump's America First election revealed deep resentment of the consequences of trade, especially the resulting massive U.S. trade deficit with China, and sizeable trade deficits with Japan, Mexico and Germany. The Trump Administration asserts that China's trade surplus is the product of unfair trade practices and production subsidies. Forgotten in the political dialogue are modest U.S. trade surpluses with Hong Kong, the United Kingdom, Canada, Brazil, Saudi Arabia and Singapore.

There is a need to "unpack" trade deficit data. For example, roughly 65% of the value of iPhones shipped from China originates in the U.S., yet their full value appears in U.S.-China trade data. Roughly 40% of the value all Mexican goods crossing into the United States is American in origin. Furthermore, U.S. trade deficit numbers tend to be portrayed in goods only (especially by the Trump Administration), omitting trade surpluses in services, and not considering foreign investment capital flows.

Many economists maintain that high overall trade deficit countries like the United States reflect substantial consumer and government spending along with low rates of savings. Low overall trade deficit or surplus countries like Germany and China reflect high savings rates and restrained spending patterns. In short, trade deficits and surpluses do not reflect a win/lose zero sum game. They are instead a reflection of internal, notably fiscal, strengths and weaknesses of various countries. Trump Administration tax reductions and unfunded deficit spending thus suggest U.S. trade deficits will increase.

PATTERNS OF WORLD TRADE

Trade traditionally has been measured by the exchange of tangible goods, both raw materials and finished products. This is sometimes referred to as "merchandise trade". The prominence of oil as a trading commodity, and the economic power exerted in the 1970s by the Organization of Petroleum Exporting Countries (OPEC), resulted in a considerable shift of wealth caused by remarkable changes in the price of a single commodity. The power of OPEC diminished in the 1980s and 1990s due to an oversupply of oil and conflict both within the oil industry and within OPEC. Since the millennium, OPEC power and oil prices first rose and then collapsed with the advent of "fracking" techniques that have generated substantial amounts of U.S. oil and gas production.

Energy remains the ultimately important global commodity. It played a critical role in the decision of the United States to commence the Gulf and Iraq Wars, and more recently to become engaged in the war against ISIS in the Middle East. Extractable raw materials remain the principal source of wealth for many nations. Nations which produce many natural and agricultural resources, from tin to bananas, have attempted to create cartels which will give them control of their economic destiny.

Services Trade

In recent years, attention on items of trade and therefore value has shifted from an exclusive focus on tangibles and technology, to an area of trade and economic relations far more difficult to define. That area is trade in services such as advertising, banking, insurance, accounting, consulting, entertainment, construction, tourism, education and the vast area of computer services. For the most part, trade in services is not subject to tariffs. Nontariff barriers (NTBs), often in the form of licenses or permits, predominate. Cross-border trade in legal services also makes a contribution, particularly by large multinational U.S. law firms. U.S. trade in these "invisibles" is measured in billions annually. Trade in tangibles is marred by an increasing deficit, but U.S. trade in services is marked by an increasing surplus.

Many other nations are eager to develop their own services, and to protect them from encroachment by the developed nations. The negotiations in the

Uruguay Round on trade in services were an especially difficult part of the overall trade talks. The industrialized nations, led by the United States, for the most part successfully negotiated lowering trade barriers to services, over the objections of important developing nations such as India and Brazil. These nations fear dominance in ownership of services by the industrialized nations.

The final WTO agreement, the General Agreement on Trade in Services (the GATS), reflected many restrictions and reservations by developing nations determined to establish and maintain their own service sectors. The ability of the WTO to govern trade in services is critical to keeping service-oriented nations like the United States a supporter of this important multilateral trade regulating organization.

The Rise of Asia

Viewing the constantly changing world trade patterns as they have developed to this moment, the dominance of the United States which was prevalent decades ago has diminished substantially and is unlikely to reoccur. This trend is attributable to the prominence of Japan in manufacturing and designing products which meet current consumer demands, to the entry of China and re-entry of India in the world trade arena, to the cooperation of the European nations within the European Union, and to the movement through successive stages of development of many nations, especially the "Four

Dragons" or "Four Tigers" of Asia—Hong Kong, South Korea, Singapore and Taiwan.

Increased "world market share" is the goal of every nation, and nations joust over international trade issues. Asian nations, like others, closely regulate foreign investment coming into the country, and create trade incentives to stimulate greater exports to other countries.

The spectacular success of Japan and China as exporters combined with a creativity to block imports has led to a sequence of protests and threats of sanctions by the United States and the European Union, most notably by President Trump. See Chapters 7 and 8. However accurately Japan or China may be accused of being unfair traders and of using a host of regulatory nontariff trade barriers (NTBs) to keep foreign goods and investment out, the United States often fails to consider that trade imbalances may be as much caused by domestic failures as by foreign intransigence.

Nontariff Trade Barriers

Japan and China are not alone in using nontariff regulatory barriers, such as environmental rules and product and health safety laws. NTBs have arisen to protect domestic industry as the earlier protection by high tariffs has diminished via GATT, WTO and free trade negotiations. Every nation has developed its own methods of keeping imports at bay.

The United States, for example, has employed agricultural quotas and environmental/conservation regulations in this manner. The French provoked a stream of protest by requiring that documentation for imported goods be written in French. France established a "consultative commission for international trade" charged to watch for "abnormal" and excessive imports and unfair export practices of other countries. Meaning, of course, an agency for domestic business to complain to when affected by imports, regardless of their own efficiency in production. In the United States, similar complaints are filed with the Office of the U.S. Trade Representative.

Other nations have responded in various ways to the impact of imports. Restricted by their agreements to specific tariff levels as members of the WTO, they have carried nontariff barriers to a new height of originality. These barriers may assume the form of health or safety standards, packing or labeling requirements, environmental regulations, and many other rules which may in theory seem justified, but in practice are structured or interpreted so as to eliminate or reduce imports and benefit domestic industries.

Lawyers retained to deal with these nontariff barriers, as well as subsidies, dumping or rules of origin, have become the major beneficiaries of these complex trade laws. They alone know how to work through the maze of details in lengthy definitions included in trade laws and multilateral agreements. For example, foreign targets of a U.S. dumping charge must expend enormous resources responding to such charges, thus making these actions themselves another costly form of nontariff barrier.

Trade Incentives

Goods which are sold in one nation are not necessarily either goods produced domestically by locally owned manufacturers, or goods produced abroad by foreign owned manufacturers. They may be goods produced *domestically* by *foreign* owned manufacturers. Or they may be goods produced *abroad* by domestic manufacturers.

Investing abroad is an alternative to exporting goods abroad. Foreign investment shares some benefits of trade. The foreign manufacturer receives the profit, but the host nation of the foreign investment obtains jobs and technology. Raw materials or parts may be sent by the foreign manufacturer, to create what is little more than an assembly plant in the host nation, or raw materials and parts may be purchased in the host nation, adding to the benefits of permitting investment owned by foreign entities. See R. Folsom, *Foreign Investment Law in a Nutshell.*

While trying to hold imports to reasonable levels, every nation wants to be a major exporter. It is, after all, exports that provide the means to pay for imports. The urge to export leads to another scheme of laws. They are usually laws of encouragement in contrast to laws of discouragement which typify the import rules. They may be fashioned in the way of granting tax benefits, offering export financing or insurance, overlooking trade restraint elements of permitted export cartels, or tying permitted imports to the level of exports.

The United States, for example, in enacting the 1982 Export Trading Company Act (ETC), followed the practice of nations such as Japan in assisting exporters. The ETC Act was designed to permit small and medium U.S. firms to gain information about foreign trade opportunities and techniques, and to have easier access to financing for export activity. In 2018, the strident debate over renewing U.S. Export-Import (EXIM) Bank funding continues. Many EXIM export financings have benefited U.S. multinationals such as Boeing and GE.

The Legal Framework of Trade

Every nation which engages in international economic relations develops a legal framework defining its role. That framework will consist of domestic trade laws, including its acceptance of international laws regulating cross-border transactions, and participation in international organizations which also establish trade rules. The United States has developed by legislative and executive action an extensive set of domestic rules governing international trade, many reflecting WTO rules. It has also been a major creator and participant in many organizations which influence or govern trade.

The World Trade Organization, successor to the GATT 1947, is by far the most important such organization. Its "package deal" of about 20 agreements are almost entirely mandatory for its 165 or so members, who must incorporate into their national legal system and obey WTO rules at risk of authorized retaliation if they do not. Roughly 98% of all world trade are covered by the WTO agreements. The United Nations has played a disappointingly minor role in trade, although UNCITRAL, the United Nations Commission on International Trade Law, has become an important forum for the harmonization of rules affecting trade, such as the Convention on International Sale of Goods (CISG).

Regional economic relations have also increased trade among groups of nations. The European Union and NAFTA 1994 are the two most important areas which have reduced barriers to internal trade, although sometimes at the expense of increasing barriers to external trade. Free trade and customs union agreements have been proliferating. See Chapter 7. But however important may be participation in bilateral or multilateral trade agreements or organizations, the will of a single participant to abide by freer trade rules will be expressed in its domestic trade laws and policies. It is under such national laws that multinational enterprises operate.

THE MULTINATIONAL ENTERPRISE (MNE)

One important and controversial business form engaging in international trade is the multinational enterprise (MNE). Indeed, "intra-corporate" trade within MNE companies comprises a very significant share of "international" trade. The most visible MNEs are the largest multinational corporations engaged in business over decades in every sector of the globe. One study revealed that of the top 100 "countries" in the world, MNE comprised almost 70%. MNEs own the bulk of the world's most commercially valuable intellectual property rights.

MNE may be one of several less structured business forms, such as partnerships and joint ventures, used in business of short duration in only a few places in the world. A transaction may be an international business transaction whether the principal players come from private enterprise, from national or local government, or from a combination of both private enterprise and government.

The MNE has aroused concern and prompted new regulatory attempts by governments, acting singly and in concert. Although history may not yet identify the MNE as having been a primary catalyst in pressing diverse and proud countries into a measure of sustained global economic order, the utility and proper role of the MNE have engendered vigorous debate involving much unclear data.

Since 1976 the industrialized member countries within the Organization for Economic Cooperation and Development (OECD) have published a Code of Conduct for Multinationals which sets forth voluntary guidelines for appropriate enterprise behavior. With interpretative assistance of the OECD Investment Committee, MNEs operating within the forty or so OECD member countries are being encouraged to speed compliance with Code provisions dealing with disclosure of enterprise information, employment and industrial relations, and taxation and transfer pricing.

Representatives from the member countries of the International Institute for the Unification of Private Law (UNIDROIT) worked on an international trade law code regarding the formation and interpretation of contracts, especially leasing agreements. The European Union favors regulating MNE activity on a sector basis, such as in areas of company law, taxation, and employment policy.

International regulation of MNEs shows every prospect of increasing, in part due to the role illicit MNE payments play in generating public demand for closer regulation. Often such payments are a fact of international commercial life, whether they are characterized as "advertising expenses", "commissions" "consulting fees", or more simply as "grease" or "bribes". The OECD has reached agreement on rules intended to regulate this kind of behavior, significantly resulting in the U.K. Bribery Act of 2010. This Act in many ways makes the controversial U.S. Foreign Corrupt Practices Act of 1977 look tame. See Chapter 5.

Business enterprises of the United States *and* foreign countries are seriously constrained by the 1977 Foreign Corrupt Practices Act. Amendments to the Act in 1988 removed the controversial basis for liability when the MNE had "reason to know" that some of their payments through intermediaries would end up in the hands of foreign officials. Further amendments in 1998, as a result of signing the OECD Convention on Combating Bribery of

Foreign Officials, tightened definitions of wrongful conduct as has the remarkably stringent British Bribery Act of 2010. See Chapter 5.

TRANSFER PRICING

Affiliated parts of a multinational enterprise often deal with each other across national borders. Since the enterprise as a whole has goals which each part seeks to assist in achieving, intra-corporate dealings may be structured to achieve favorable tax or dividend consequences ("tax efficiency"). The MNE effectively reallocates costs and revenues within its worldwide structure so that profits are increased where tax and exchange controls are considered favorable, and decreased where taxes and controls are considered most severe. This is transfer pricing.

Host nations sometimes impose limits on profits that may be remitted abroad by a foreign investor's local operations. The MNE may seek to offset the effect of these limits on profit remittances. The foreign parent may attempt to charge more for technology transferred to the affiliate, or for raw materials or components sold to the foreign affiliate. Such "trade-based" transfer pricing is estimated to facilitate an outflow of over a trillion dollars annually from developing nations. The core technique is overvaluing import or undervaluing export invoices.

The host nation may respond by limiting amounts which may be paid for technology, or by demanding that the raw materials or components be obtained locally. Developing nations have strongly objected to MNEs' transfer pricing practices when the result appears to be very low or no profits in the developing nation, but the MNE parent appears to be profitable.

Why has the MNE done this? Typically, because the developing nation imposes high taxes on profits, or at least taxes that are higher than in the MNE home nation or tax havens. Another reason to engage in transfer pricing is limits on profit remittances due to exchange controls, which are more lenient or do not exist for technology transfers, or for permitted imports of raw materials or components. What may anger the developing nation even more, and also local shareholders when the MNE has agreed to a joint venture, is when the same transfer pricing practices lead to few profits to distribute as dividends to the local shareholders.

It is not only developing nations which object to artificial transfer pricing practices. Australia, Canada, Japan and the United States formed the Pacific Association of Tax Administrators to combat transfer pricing's possible inter-relationship with tax evasion. Developing country monitoring of transfer pricing has not been very effective, partly because of a reluctance of the developed nations to participate in joint efforts which might transfer tax revenue away from the United States, and partly because much intra-corporate transfer information is regarded as confidential.

The Organization for Economic Cooperation and Development (OECD) has been developing transfer pricing guidelines for multinational companies for decades. Transfer pricing has also been addressed by individual countries. Within the United States, the

IRS has issued regulations under Section 482 of the Internal Revenue Code. These regulations impose penalties for intercompany pricing not conducted under the regulation's arm's-length standards, which adopt a "best method" rule. IRS practices have been criticized as arbitrary and unreasonable. But the IRS claims companies do not properly calculate transfer prices. The Tax Court has had to resolve these conflicts, and is likely to be a frequent player as the IRS steps up its attack on what it considers improper transfer pricing.

Mexico has transfer pricing rules affecting its assembly industries or maquiladoras. Many foreign companies have used fees for services and transfer pricing resulting in almost no Mexican profits. The government has not traditionally enforced provisions of the Mexican Tax Code which would have required maquiladoras to recognize some level of profit. The reason has been to protect jobs and the entire program itself, but the government could demand taxes on an arm's-length basis for the services performed by the maquiladoras.

More recently, Mexico has established minimum maquiladora profit levels as "safe harbors" under its Tax Code. Most firms have moved to take advantage of them, thereby reducing tax risk exposure in Mexico. The experience of the United States and Mexico illustrate how different nations may pursue problems of transfer pricing, from a vigorous attack on the practice to minimal payments to promote social goals, such as job creation.

Finally, a word about illegal multinational enterprises engaged in arms smuggling, drug trafficking, terrorism or public corruption. Like legitimate MNE, these multinationals lace the globe in their operations and extensively engage in trade-related money laundering via transfer pricing on trade in legal goods. One study, for example, suggests that Mexican exports are over-priced by 15 to 20% as a way to move dollars into the country. The Sinaloa cartel laundered some of its dollar profits by exporting toys, food and silk into the USA. Another drug operation charged $970 while exporting plastic buckets to America.

Over-pricing to get money into sanctioned countries like Iran, try $240 for a pound of sugar, helped bring hard currency to Iranian banks and unlock frozen overseas bank accounts. India's official exports to the Bahamas, went up 1000%, yes 1000%, prior to a tax transparency agreement between the two countries as assets were removed from undeclared Bahamian accounts. Exports from China to Hong Kong, and Hong Kong to China, routinely reflect the desire to move money from one to the other.

THE ROLE OF CORPORATE COUNSEL TO A MNE

The role of corporate counsel (in-house counsel) to a MNE is not fundamentally different professionally from that of any other brand of lawyer in relation to a client, though an added emphasis on legal "risk management" is common. Unlike many other lawyers, however, counsel is also in a team member relationship with MNE management personnel. Counsel has an employment obligation to support the MNE management structure. Counsel's corporate legal function may be viewed as one vehicle through which headquarters control is exercised over affiliated, sub-parts of the MNE.

The access to information and exclusive knowledge of information possessed by counsel are visible and substantial parts of the power dimension of MNE global management. For example, counsel's working relationship with foreign assisting counsel in each country where the MNE operates, and that assisting counsel's working relationship with the principal, MNE line management person within each country, play a substantial role in MNE headquarters control and financial success.

If the principal line management person within each country is willing to explore legal aspects of new business ideas with the assisting counsel in that country, and if assisting counsel has a close reporting and consultative relationship with MNE headquarters counsel, chances increase for the "preventive" side of legal practice to help in shaping management decisions and to reduce large, unanticipated legal costs at a later time. The success of counsel's communication with management may generate an ad hoc assignment to a line management function in connection with particular MNE business transactions.

Such closeness can also raise ethical considerations which intersect with counsel's professional responsibilities as a lawyer. For example, currency control measures prevent MNE revenues from being remitted. Moreover, the rate of monetary inflation may be such that revenues left there are subject to substantial devaluation. There is an acute ethical problem for counsel, as a lawyer, who considers the idea that funds might be carried secretly into neighboring countries and then exchanged for hard currency and remitted for deposit in a jurisdiction where inflation is not severe.

Corporate line managers are charged with providing needed revenues. Corporate counsel are engaged principally in minimizing legal "overhead" costs of the corporation. Did they teach you how to be an effective cost or risk manager in law school?

In addition, requests by line management to put recurring types of company agreements into "standard form" contracts must be squared with the reality of enforcing those contracts in different legal systems with divergent views about the sanctity of contracts. Counsel may assist in securing approvals from governmental regulatory bodies or persons charged with overseeing MNE activity, and often must testify on the MNE's behalf before people who need not listen at all or who may only care to listen in an abbreviated way. Many current presidents of corporations in the United States are lawyers and have served as corporate counsel before being appointed president.

You might consider how the following hypothetical day for corporate counsel helps prepare lawyers to become MNE presidents.

A HYPOTHETICAL DAY FOR MNE CORPORATE COUNSEL

By way of hypothetical illustration, a typical office day for corporate counsel to a MNE might include work on problems such as: Senegal has served notice that a MNE's revenues worldwide will be taxed unitarily irrespective of the MNE's tax posture in other countries; the MNE's use of its trade name in Mexico is impeded by a "prior use" problem; a Uruguayan appeals court has held that the MNE's trademark is generic and thus not subject to legal protection; a line management employee of the MNE's Austrian subsidiary company needs an "L" visa to spend some time at the MNE's headquarters offices in the United States; new advertising from the MNE's marketing department has possible legal implications if placed in newspapers throughout Europe; reports of resale price maintenance agreements being made by certain companies in Transylvania and Neverland need to be checked in light of antitrust implications under U.S. and EU law.

Moreover, the MNE's products stolen in Hamburg must be traced through INTERPOL; ways must be explored to get blocked currencies from New Country to the MNE's headquarters in the United States; testimony needs to be prepared for presentation to an environmental control authority in Germany; a presentation must be made to the transportation commissioner of the Province of Ontario to secure permits to increase haulage capacity of the MNE's subsidiary company in Canada; charges of employee discrimination in the Far Islands need to be answered; sale-leaseback agreements need to be negotiated in Sydney; a company needs to be formed for tax protection in the Unusual Islands; and an expropriation in Venezuela requires attention.

The Philippine and Saudi Arabian governments want to increase their equity participation in all existing MNE's joint ventures; certain inquiries by the U.S. Federal Trade Commission need to be answered; someone from the American Bar Association wants counsel to serve on an international trade committee; all standard form contracts used by the MNE and its subsidiary companies are due for another review; line management people are interested in hearing ideas about ways to avoid legal problems, especially transfer pricing and corruption issues, in connection with their proposals for new trade activity.

Trade law compliance programs must be developed for all of the above.

CHAPTER 2
GLOBAL TRADE LAW

Trade Treaties   Smoot-Hawley et al.
GATT 1947   World Trade Organization
WTO Agreements   WTO Disputes

NOTE: For more extensive international trade law and WTO coverage, see R. Folsom, *Principles of International Trade Law* (West Academic Publications). Selected provisions of the GATT 1947 and 1994, various WTO agreements, U.S. trade statutes and the WTO Dispute Settlement Understanding (DSU) are appended in that book.

SMOOT-HAWLEY ET AL.

The United States in its early years sheltered "infant" agricultural and industrial sectors behind protective tariffs and regulatory restraints. When the Great Depression of the 1930s arrived, the United States under President Hoover enacted highly protective tariffs under the Smoot-Hawley Tariff Act of 1930 intended to wall off its economy from foreign competition, in theory "saving American jobs for American citizens." Other nations around the world retreated from international trade through similarly protective laws. Fear of foreign trade (and foreigners) reached a zenith that most economists agree deepened and prolonged the Great Depression. Here is a provocative excerpt from a 1930 letter signed by over 1000 economists opposing Smoot-Hawley:

We are convinced that increased protective duties would be a mistake. They would operate, in general, to increase the prices which domestic consumers would have to pay. By raising prices, they would encourage concerns with higher costs to undertake production, thus compelling the consumer to subsidize waste and inefficiency in industry. At the same time, they would force him to pay higher rates of profit to established firms which enjoyed lower production costs. A higher level of protection, such as is contemplated by both the House and Senate bills, would therefore raise the cost of living and injure the great majority of our citizens.

Few people could hope to gain from such a change. Miners, construction, transportation and public utility workers, professional people and those employed in banks, hotels, newspaper offices, in the wholesale and retail trades, and scores of other occupations would clearly lose, since they produce no products which could be protected by tariff barriers.

The vast majority of farmers, also, would lose. Their cotton, corn, lard, and wheat are export crops and are sold in the world market. They have no important competition in the home market. They cannot benefit, therefore, from any tariff which is imposed upon the basic commodities which they produce. They would lose through the increased duties on manufactured goods, however, and in a double fashion. First, as consumers they would have to pay still higher prices for the products, made of textiles, chemicals, iron, and steel, which they buy. Second, as producers, their ability to sell their products would be further restricted by the barriers placed in the way of foreigners who wished to sell manufactured goods to us.

> Our export trade, in general, would suffer. . . .
> There are already many evidences that such action
> would inevitably provoke other countries to pay us
> back in kind by levying retaliatory duties against our
> goods. There are few more ironical spectacles than
> that of the American Government as it seeks, on the
> one hand, to promote exports through the activity of
> the Bureau of Foreign and Domestic Commerce,
> while, on the other hand, by increasing tariffs it
> makes exportation ever more difficult. President
> Hoover has well said, in his message to Congress on
> April 16, 1929, "It is obviously unwise protection
> which sacrifices a greater amount of employment in
> exports to gain a less amount of employment from
> imports."

Almost ninety years later, a letter from more than
1,100 economists revived this message in the face of
President Trump's protectionist measures. See
Chapter 8.

Despite its economic power and leadership in the
development of modern trade law, the United States
retains some of its early fear and concerns about
international commerce, notably under the Trump
Administration. This is particularly apparent when
U.S. free trade agreements are debated and
undertaken, but also when the U.S. invokes import
trade remedies and controls exports of goods and
technology. Little wonder then that developing
nations, many not much more than 50 years old and
created out of colonial empires, hesitate to embrace
the panoply of modern international trade law.

The need to balance the protection of local
industries from harm by foreign competitors and the

encouragement of trade across national borders is a recurrent theme in the law of international economic relations. There has been a shift in recent years toward freer international trade because of diminished restrictions on imported goods. However, trade problems associated with the movement of goods across national borders still arise because of restrictive trade devices which impede or distort trade. In most countries, "trade adjustment assistance" to adversely damaged workers has been inadequate.

The law of international trade, for better or worse, shapes the scope and direction of the disruptive force of international trade. Common protective devices include tariff barriers (e.g., normal import and export duties, and special antidumping and subsidy countervailing duties), as well as nontariff trade barriers (NTBs) such as quotas, import and export licensing procedures, safety, environmental, health and other regulatory standards, complex customs procedures, and government procurement policies. For example, France once required that all video recorders entering France had to do so through a small customs post at Poitiers and carry documentation written in French. Product distribution practices have been an effective NTB in Japan. The United States has a host of NTB restraints, and the Trump Administration has suggested invocation of protective trade remedies and rules for six "core industries"—steel, aluminum, vehicles, aircraft, shipbuilding and semiconductors.

Commencing in 1932 under President Roosevelt, the United States began to unwind its Smoot-Hawley tariffs, particularly via reciprocal trade agreements, the first of which was with Canada. World War II ultimately rescued the United States from the Depression, but did little to remove high tariffs in Europe and elsewhere. International trade law was at a crossroads.

TRADE TREATIES

Early efforts by countries to limit disruptive trade practices were commonly found in bilateral treaties of friendship, commerce and navigation (FCN). More recently, bilateral and regional trade treaties, open the territory of signatory nations to imports. Such treaties are usually linked to other preferential trade agreements, most often through a reciprocal "most favored nation" (MFN) clause. In a MFN clause, both parties agree not to extend to any other nation trade arrangements which are more favorable than available under the treaty, unless the more favorable trade arrangements are immediately *also* available to the other signatory of the treaty.

At this point, the United States has moved beyond many of its FCN treaties to bilateral Trade and Investment Framework Agreements (TIFAs), Free Trade Agreements (FTAs) and Bilateral Investment Treaties (BITs). Lists of those in force can be found at www.ustr.gov. FCN trade and investment law principles, notably MFN and national treatment, carry over into these agreements. TIFAs are centered on dialogue about trade and investment issues. They often precede the more advanced legal regimes of FTAs and BITs.

The United States has numerous TIFAs with individual countries and regional economic groups. The U.S. has TIFAs with Angola, Ghana, Liberia, Mauritius, Mozambique, Nigeria, Rwanda, South Africa and the Common Market for Eastern and Southern Africa (COMESA), the East African Community, the West African Economic and monetary Union (WAEMU) and the South African Customs Union (titled as a Trade, Investment and Development Agreement).

The U.S. also has TIFAs with Algeria, Bahrain, the Caribbean Common Market (CARICOM), Egypt, the Gulf Cooperation Council, Georgia, Iceland, Iraq, Kuwait, Lebanon, Libya, Oman, Qatar, Saudi Arabia, Switzerland, Tunisia, Turkey, Ukraine, the United Arab Emirates, Uruguay and Yemen. Additional TIFAs have been concluded with Afghanistan, collectively with five Central Asian nations, the Maldives, Nepal, Pakistan, Sri Lanka, the ASEAN group (Association of South East Asian Nations), Brunei, Cambodia, Indonesia, Malaysia, New Zealand, the Philippines, Thailand and Vietnam.

In virtually all parts of the world, countries have joined in customs unions or free trade agreements in order to expand international commerce and to acquire increased bargaining power in international trade negotiations. The European Union is a prime example as is NAFTA 1994. Hundreds of such treaties now operate, covering more than half of world trade. See Chapter 7.

THE GATT (1947)

Participants in the Bretton Woods meetings in 1944 recognized a post-War need to reduce obstacles to freer trade. They envisioned the creation of an International Trade Organization (ITO) to achieve the desired result. Fifty-three countries met in Havana in 1948 to complete drafting the Charter of an ITO that would be the international organizational umbrella underneath which negotiations could occur periodically to deal with tariff reductions on goods. A framework for such negotiations had already been staked out in Geneva in 1947, in a document entitled the General Agreement on Tariffs and Trade (GATT).

Twenty-three nations participated in that first GATT session, India, Chile, Cuba and Brazil representing the developing world. China participated; Japan and West Germany did not. Stringent trading rules were adopted only where there were no special interests of major participants to alter them. The developing nations objected to many of the strict rules, arguing for special treatment justified on development needs, but they achieved few successes in drafting GATT.

The ITO Charter was never ratified. The United States Congress in the late 1940s was unwilling to join more new international organizations, thus U.S. ratification of the ITO Charter could not be secured. By default, and moving by way of the President's power to make executive agreements, the United States joined 21 other countries in signing a Protocol of Provisional Application of the General Agreement on Tariffs and Trade (popularly called the "GATT Agreement").

One notable feature of this protocol was the exemption of existing trade restraints of the Contracting States. The GATT 1947 Agreement evolved from its "provisional" status into the premier international trade body, GATT the organization based in Geneva. It was through this organization that tariffs were steadily reduced over decades by means of increased membership and GATT negotiating Rounds. Today, the GATT 1947 Agreement has been superseded by the substantially similar GATT 1994 Agreement, part of the World Trade Organization "package" of trade agreements that took effect in 1995 (below).

Trade in Goods: Core GATT Principles

One of the core provisions of GATT 1947 and 1994 is Article 1, which makes a general commitment to the long standing practice of "most favored nation treatment" (MFN) by requiring each Contracting Party to accord unconditional MFN status to all other Contracting Parties. Thus, any privilege granted by any Contracting Party to any product imported from any other country (WTO member or not) must also be "immediately and unconditionally" granted to any "like product" imported from any Contracting Parties.

GATT Article 3 incorporates the practice of according "national treatment" to imported goods by providing, with enumerated exceptions, that the products of one Contracting State shall be treated in the same manner regarding taxation and regulation as domestic goods. This Article, for example, requires that the products of the exporting GATT Contracting State be treated no less favorably than domestic products of the importing Contracting State under its laws and regulations concerning sale, internal resale, purchase, transportation and use.

In addition to requiring MFN and national treatment, GATT prohibits use of certain kinds of quantitative restrictions. Article 11 broadly but not completely prohibits the use of other "prohibitions or restrictions" on imports from Contracting Parties. It specifically prohibits the use of "quotas, import or export licenses or other measures" to restrict imports from a Contracting Party. When such measures are authorized, Article 13 requires non-discrimination in quantitative trade restrictions, by barring an importing Contracting State from applying any prohibition or restriction to the products of another Contracting State, "unless the importation of the like product of *all* third countries. . .is similarly prohibited or restricted" (emphasis added).

In the longstanding *Bananas* dispute, for example, the United States joined Ecuador, Guatemala, Honduras and Mexico in successfully challenging EU import restraints against so-called "dollar bananas." The EU failed to comply with the Appellate Body's ruling, and retaliatory measures were authorized and imposed.

The WTO has significantly reduced the number of trade quotas. The Agreement on Textiles eliminated quotas long maintained under the Multi-Fiber Arrangement. Voluntary export restraints (quotas) are severely limited by the Safeguards Agreement. In addition, the WTO removes trade quotas by pressuring for "tariffication," or replacing them with tariffs—sometimes even at extraordinarily high tariff rates. Tariffication is the approach adopted in the WTO Agricultural Agreement. It is expected that high tariff rates will be reduced in subsequent negotiating Rounds. Import licensing schemes are also being phased out under WTO agreements.

GATT Procedures

While the GATT does permit nondiscriminatory "duties, taxes and other charges," the powers of a Contracting Party are limited even as to these devices. First, GATT Article 10 requires that notice be given of any new or changed national regulations which affect international trade, by requiring the prompt publication by any Contracting Party of those "laws, regulations, judicial decisions and administrative rulings of general application." Second, the Contracting Parties commit themselves, under GATT Article 28 to a continuing series of multilateral trade negotiations MTN ("from time to time") to seek further reductions in tariff levels and other barriers to international trade.

Such negotiations are to be "on a reciprocal and mutually advantageous basis." GATT negotiated tariff rates (called "concessions" or "bindings"), which are listed in the "tariff Schedules", are deposited with GATT by each participating country. These concessions must be granted to imports from any Contracting Party, both because of the GATT required MFN treatment, and also because Article 2 specifically requires use of the negotiated rates.

Framers of GATT were well aware that a commitment to freer trade could cause serious, adverse economic consequences from time to time within part or all of a country's domestic economy, particularly its labor sector. The GATT contains at least seven safety valves (in nine clauses of the Agreement) to permit a country, in appropriate circumstances, to respond to domestic pressures while remaining a participant in GATT. Two prominent safety valves contained in Article 6 deal with antidumping and countervailing duties. In a nutshell, these special tariffs are authorized against what the GATT deems unfair international trade practices. They are detailed in Chapter 4.

GATT MULTINATIONAL TRADE NEGOTIATION ROUNDS

Under the auspices of GATT Article 28, the Contracting Parties committed themselves to hold periodic multinational trade negotiations (MTN or "Rounds"). They have completed eight such Rounds to date. While the first five Rounds concentrated on item by item tariff reductions, the "Kennedy Round"

(1964–1967) was noted for its achievement of across-the-board tariff reductions.

The GATT regularly held multilateral trade negotiations (MTN) seeking open up international trade. These periodic GATT "Rounds" cumulatively reduced average tariff barriers to 80 percent below those existing in the post WWII era. After the most recent multilateral negotiations, the Uruguay Round finalized in 1994, average tariff rates of developed countries on dutiable manufactured imports were cut from 6.3 percent to 3.9 percent.

The GATT completed eight such Rounds with the GATT membership steadily increasing:

Geneva (1947) with 19 countries

Annecy (1948) with 27 countries

Torquay (1950) with 33 countries

"Dillon Round" Geneva (1960–62) with 36 countries

"Kennedy Round" Geneva (1964–67) with 74 countries

"Tokyo Round" Geneva (1973–79) with 85 countries

"Uruguay Round" Geneva (1986–94) with 128 countries

The WTO Doha Round (2001–15) with 164 countries is dead

Tariff reductions are one of the success stories of the GATT. But not all nations participated in the GATT Rounds, or are members of its replacement, the WTO. For example, Iran is still seeking membership in the WTO. China and Chinese Taipei (Taiwan) did not join until 2001, Vietnam in 2007, and Russia in 2012.

In 1961, GATT began to consider how to approach the increasing trade disparity with the developing world. In 1964, GATT adopted Part IV, which introduced a principle of "diminished expectations of reciprocity". Reciprocity remained a goal, but developed nations would not expect concessions from developing nations which were inconsistent with developmental needs. For the developing nations, non-reciprocity meant freedom to protect domestic markets from import competition. Import substitution was a major focus of developmental theory in the 1960s, and developing nations saw keeping their markets closed as a way to save these domestic industries. Although they also sought preferential treatment of their exports, that was a demand which would remain unsatisfied for another decade.

The "Tokyo Round" (1973–1979) engendered agreements about several areas of nontariff barrier (NTB) trade restraints. Nearly a dozen major (but optional) agreements on nontariff barrier issues were produced in the Tokyo Round. In the early 1970s, national and regional generalized preference schemes (GSP) developed to favor the exports of developing nations. The foreign debt payment problems of the developing nations suggested that they need to generate revenue to pay these debts, and that developmental theory must shift from import substitution to export promotion.

In 1986, the "Uruguay Round" of multilateral trade negotiations began at a Special Session of the GATT Contracting States. This Uruguay Round included separate negotiations on trade in goods and on trade in services, with separate groups of negotiators dealing with each topic. Subtopics for negotiation by subgroups included nontariff barriers, agriculture, subsidies and countervailing duties, intellectual property rights and counterfeit goods, safeguards, tropical products, textiles, investment policies, and dispute resolution. The negotiating sessions were extraordinarily complex, but were able to achieve a successful conclusion, giving birth to the World Trade Organization in 1995.

Doha Dies

The latest Round failed to start as scheduled late in 1999. An array of "anti-globalization" interests and street protests in Seattle led by labor and environmental groups caused the delay. Regrouping in remote Qatar, the Doha Round was launched in 2001 was scheduled for completion in 2005.

Agriculture, services, intellectual property, antidumping duties, tariffs, export subsidies, market access, implementation, electronic commerce, dispute settlement, trade and the environment, trade, debt and finance, and special and differential treatment and assistance for developing countries were on the Doha agenda. Developed WTO countries pushed the so-called "Singapore" issues of investment, competition policy, transparency in procurement, and trade facilitation.

At Cancun in 2003, the WTO developing nations rejected these issues while focusing on agricultural trade protectionism by industrial nations. Marathon talks in July of 2008 failed to resolve agricultural trade issues, suggesting that the Doha round is dead. This has caused many nations to accelerate their participation in bilateral and regional free trade agreements. See Chapter 7. WTO trade initiatives since Doha have been limited to *optional* trade facilitation, information technology and agricultural export subsidy agreements.

CREATING THE WORLD TRADE ORGANIZATION (WTO)

Creating the rules-based World Trade Organization, despite the leading role of the United States, was not easy. Eight years in negotiation, the major issue was trade in agricultural goods, with the EU maintaining a strongly protective position and the Cairns Group led by the USA seeking to reduce agricultural trade barriers and subsidies. In the end, a modest compromise was achieved in the WTO Agreement on Agriculture, discussed below.

What drove that compromise? In this author's opinion, the United States played two critical cards: First, it aggressively undertook unilateral, totally unauthorized trade actions against "foreign country practices" under Section 301 of the Trade Act of 1974, outlined in Chapter 6, and revitalized by President Trump against China in 2018. See Chapter 8. Under considerable pressure, these actions primarily opened up foreign markets to U.S. exports. Second, the United States played the NAFTA card, commencing negotiations and reaching an extensive free trade and foreign investment agreement with Mexico and Canada. NAFTA 1994 negotiations ran more or less one year ahead of the Uruguay Round, influencing the content of and pushing forward the creation of the WTO and its package of agreements.

That said, significant differences between the WTO Agreements and NAFTA 1994 exist. A chart comparing NAFTA and WTO coverage is presented below. For example, NAFTA covers business visas, state trading, competition policy, and has an entire chapter dedicated to energy, all of which are absent from the WTO package. The WTO Agreements cover customs valuation and pre-shipment inspection, which NAFTA 1994 does not. Nothing in the WTO package of agreements touches on labor or the environment, NAFTA's two side agreements.

On market access, procurement, investment and most services, NAFTA 1994 went further and faster than the Uruguay Round WTO agreements. There is significant overlap on intellectual property where NAFTA's leading edge was particularly influential. The WTO Agreement on Agriculture, on the other hand, exceeded by a good measure NAFTA's trade opening initiatives. The WTO package also addressed basic telecommunications, which was mostly omitted from NAFTA 1994. The WTO has (since 1997) fostered an information technology tariff reduction agreement, but Mexico does not participate.

These differences may help explain why the basic rule of NAFTA 1994 dispute settlement is that the complaining country normally has the prerogative of choosing as between NAFTA and WTO procedures. For details and examples, see my *NAFTA Nutshell*.

WTO AGREEMENTS

The WTO is the product of the Uruguay Round of GATT negotiations, which was successfully completed in 1994. The Uruguay Round produced a package of agreements. These are the Agreement Establishing the World Trade Organization and its Annexes, which include the General Agreement on Tariffs and Trade 1994 (GATT 1994) and a series of Multilateral Trade Agreements (the Covered Agreements), and a series of optional Plurilateral Trade Agreements.

GATT 1947 and GATT 1994 are two distinct agreements. GATT 1994 incorporates the provisions of GATT 1947, except for the Protocol of Provisional Application, which is expressly excluded. Thus, problems created by exempting existing national laws at the time of the adoption of the Protocol are avoided by this exclusion in the Covered Agreements. Otherwise, in cases involving a conflict between GATT 1947 and GATT 1994, GATT 1947 controls. The WTO is guided by the decisions, procedures and customary practices developed under GATT 1947.

Annexed to the WTO Agreement are several Multilateral Trade Agreements. As to trade in goods, they include Agreements on Agriculture, Textiles, Antidumping, Subsidies and Countervailing

Measures (SCM), Safeguards, Technical Barriers to
Trade, Sanitary and Phytosanitary Measures (SPS),
Pre-shipment Inspection, Rules of Origin, and Import
License Procedures. In addition to trade in goods,
they include a General Agreement on Trade in
Services (GATS) and Agreements on Trade-Related
Aspects of Intellectual Property Rights (TRIPS) and
Trade-Related Investment Measures (TRIMS).

Affecting all of these agreements is the
Understanding on Rules and Procedures Governing
the Settlement of Disputes (DSU). Most importantly,
all of the Multilateral Trade Agreements are binding
on *all* Members of the World Trade Organization,
now about 165 nations. Each WTO member state is
obliged to incorporate these WTO legal into their
national legal regimes. Hence, unlike international
investment law, international trade law is
reasonably harmonized.

In addition to the Multilateral Trade Agreements,
there are also Plurilateral Trade Agreements which
are also annexed to the WTO Agreement. These
agreements, however, are not binding on all WTO
Members, and Members can choose to adhere to them
or not. They include Agreements on Government
Procurement, Trade in Civil Aircraft, International
Dairy (rescinded) and an Arrangement Regarding
Bovine Meat (rescinded). States which do not join the
plurilateral trade agreements do not receive benefits
under them.

THE WTO AGREEMENTS PACKAGE

AGREEMENT ESTABLISHING THE WORLD
TRADE ORGANIZATION (WTO)

Agreements on Trade in Goods

1   General Agreement on Tariffs and Trade
     (GATT) 1994

     (a)   Understanding on the Interpretation
           of Article II:1(b) (tariff concessions)

     (b)   Understanding on the Interpretation
           of Article XVII (state trading
           enterprises)

     (c)   Understanding on Balance-of-
           Payments Provisions

     (d)   Understanding on the Interpretation
           of Article XXIV (free trade areas and
           customs unions)

     (e)   Understanding on the Interpretation
           of Article XXV (waivers)

     (f)   Understanding on the Interpretation
           of Article XXVIII (modification of tariff
           schedules)

     (g)   Understanding on the Interpretation
           of Article XXXV (non-application of
           GATT)

2   GATT 1994

3   Agreement on Agriculture

4   Agreement on Sanitary and Phytosanitary Measures (SPS)

5   Agreement on Textiles and Clothing

6   Agreement on Technical Barriers to Trade (TBT)

7   Agreement on Trade-Related Investment Measures (TRIMS)

8   Agreement on Implementation of Article VI (antidumping and countervailing duties)

9   Agreement on Implementation of Article VII (customs valuation)

10   Agreement on Pre-Shipment Inspection

11   Agreement on Rules of Origin

12   Agreement on Import Licensing Procedures

13   Agreement on Subsidies and Countervailing Measures (SCM)

14   Agreement on Safeguards

General Agreement on Trade in Services (GATS) and Annexes

Agreement on Trade-Related Aspects of Intellectual Property Rights (TRIPS), including Trade in Counterfeit Goods

Understanding on Rules and Procedures Governing the Settlement of Disputes (DSU)

Trade Policy Review Mechanism

Plurilateral Trade Agreements

4(a) Agreement on Trade in Civil Aircraft

4(b) Agreement   on   Government Procurement

4(c) International   Dairy   Arrangement (rescinded)

4(d) Arrangement Regarding Bovine Meat (rescinded)

ADMISSION TO THE WTO, WITHDRAWAL

Admission to the World Trade Organization is by "consensus." In theory, this gives each member a veto over applicant countries. In reality, no nation wishing to join has ever formally been vetoed, though many have been long delayed. It took, for example, well over a decade to negotiate acceptable terms of entry for the People's Republic of China. Such negotiations are handled individually by member states, not by the WTO as an organization. United States negotiations with China were particularly lengthy and difficult, one principal issue being whether China should be admitted as a developing or developed nation. (The issue was fudged, with China treated differently within the WTO package of agreements.)

Essentially, applicant counties make an offer of trade liberalization commitments to join the WTO. This offer is renegotiated with interested member nations, some 40 nations regarding China including the European Union which negotiates as a unit

(NAFTA does not). Regarding China, the last member to reach agreement on WTO admission was Mexico, which extracted stiff promises against the dumping of Chinese goods. The various commitments made by the applicant in these negotiations are consolidated into a final accession protocol which is then approved by "consensus", meaning essentially every member has a veto. Russia completed this negotiation process in 2012, Vietnam in 2007. Iran's desire to join has basically been frustrated by U.S. refusal to negotiate on its WTO entry.

The existing 130 or so members of the GATT in 1994 became the founding members of the WTO. At this writing, there are approximately 165 WTO member states. Belarus and Uzbekistan, along with Iran and Sudan and 17 other countries, are in the accession process to the WTO. Belarus applied in 1993 and Turkmenistan a year later. As of 2018, Belarus' accession is characterized by the WTO as "work in progress" but not at an advanced stage. Uzbekistan's accession working party is described by the WTO's web site as inactive.

Any member may withdraw with six months' notice, something to remember with President Trump.

WTO AGREEMENTS AND U.S. LAW

The WTO Covered Agreements concern not only trade in goods, but also trade in services (GATS), and trade-related aspects of intellectual property (TRIPS). The basic concepts that GATT applied to trade in goods (described above) are now applied to these areas through GATS and TRIPS. In the WTO Covered Agreements, the basic concepts of GATT 1947 and its associated agreements are elaborated and clarified. In addition, there is an attempt to transform all protectionist measures relating to agriculture (such as import bans and quotas, etc.) into only tariff barriers, which can then be lowered in subsequent MTN Rounds (a process known as "tariffication"). WTO also contains some superficial provisions on trade-related investment measures (TRIMS). Some of the WTO provisions, particularly those concerning trade in goods, will be discussed in more detail below, in relation to United States trade law.

The United States enacted legislation to implement WTO and the Covered Agreements on December 3, 1994, but did not ratify them as a treaty. The Uruguay Round Implementation Act legislation was submitted to Congress under "fast track" procedures, which required that the agreement and its implementing legislation be considered as a whole, and prohibited Congressional amendments to the implementing legislation. The Congressional authority for "fast track" procedures also required that the President give ninety days' notice of his intention to enter into such an agreement.

Neither GATT 1947 nor the WTO Agreement, GATT 1994, and the other Covered Agreements have been ratified as treaties, and therefore comprise international obligations of the United States only to the extent that they are incorporated in United States' implementing legislation. GATT 1947 was not considered controlling by the courts of the United States, and these courts have always held themselves bound to the U.S. legislation actually enacted. The WTO Covered Agreements are considered to have a non-self-executed status, and therefore are likely to be regarded in the same manner as GATT 1947.

GATT/WTO NONTARIFF TRADE BARRIER CODES (NTBs)

There are numerous nontariff trade barriers applicable to imports. Many of these barriers arise out of safety and health regulations. Others concern the environment, consumer protection, product standards and government procurement. Many of the relevant rules were created for legitimate consumer and public protection reasons. They were often created without extensive consideration of their international impact as potential nontariff trade barriers. Nevertheless, the practical impact of legislation of this type is to ban the importation of nonconforming products. Thus, unlike tariffs which can always be paid, and unlike quotas which permit a certain amount of goods to enter the market, nontariff trade barriers have the potential to totally exclude foreign exports.

Multilateral GATT negotiations since the end of World War II have led to a significant decline in world tariff levels, particularly on trade with developed nations. As steadily as tariff barriers have disappeared, nontariff trade barriers (NTBs) have emerged. Health and safety regulations, environmental laws, rules regulating products standards, procurement legislation and customs procedures are often said to present NTB problems.

Negotiations over nontariff trade barriers dominated the Tokyo Round of the GATT negotiations during the late 1970s. A number of optional NTB "codes" (sometimes called "side agreements") emerged from the Tokyo Round. These concerned subsidies, dumping, government procurement, technical barriers (products standards), customs valuation and import licensing. In addition, specific agreements regarding trade in bovine meats, dairy products and civil aircraft were also reached. The United States accepted all of these NTB codes and agreements except the one on dairy products. Most of the necessary implementation of these agreements was accomplished in the Trade Agreements Act of 1979.

Mandatory GATT codes were agreed upon under the Uruguay Round ending in late 1993. They revisit all of the NTB areas covered by the Tokyo Round Codes and create new codes for sanitary and phytosanitary measures (SPS), trade-related investment measures (TRIMS), pre-shipment inspection, rules of origin, escape clause safeguards and trade-related intellectual property rights (TRIPS). The United States Congress approved and implemented these Codes in December of 1994 under the Uruguay Round Agreements Act.

One problem with nontariff trade barriers is that they are so numerous. Intergovernmental negotiation intended to reduce their trade restricting impact is both tedious and difficult. There are continuing attempts through the World Trade Organization to come to grips with additional specific NTB problems. Furthermore, various trade agreements of the United States have been undertaken in this field. For example, the Canada-United States Free Trade Area Agreement and the NAFTA 1994 built upon the existing GATT agreements to further reduce NTB problems between the United States, Canada and Mexico.

WTO AGREEMENT ON AGRICULTURE

Agricultural issues played a central role in the Uruguay Round GATT negotiations. More than any other issue, they delayed completion of that Round from 1990 to 1993 and threatened the Doha Round. The agreement finally reached was a trade liberalizing, market-oriented effort. Each country promised a number of commitments on market access, reduced domestic agricultural support levels and export subsidies. The United States Congress approved of these commitments by adopting the Uruguay Round Agreements Act.

Broadly speaking nontariff trade barriers to international agricultural trade are replaced by tariffs that provide substantially the same level of protection. This is known as "tariffication." It applies to virtually all NTBs, including variable levies, import bans, voluntary export restraints and import quotas. Tariffication applies specifically to U.S. agricultural quotas adopted under Section 22 of the Agricultural Adjustment Act. All agricultural tariffs, including those converted from NTBs, were reduced by 36 and 24 percent by developed and developing countries, respectively, over 6 and 10 year periods.

Certain minimum access tariff quotas apply when imports amount to less than 3 to 5 percent of domestic consumption. An escape clause exists for tariffed imports at low prices or upon a surge of importation depending upon the existing degree of import penetration. The efficacy of these "liberalizations" was severely challenged by developing nations led by Brazil and India in the Doha Round. They claim that agricultural trade restraints combined with export subsidies from surplus producers like the U.S. and the EU undermine their agricultural production and exports.

Regarding domestic support for agriculture, some programs with minimal impact on trade are exempt from change under the WTO Agreement. These programs are known as "green box policies." They include governmental support for agricultural research, disease control, infrastructure and food security. Green box policies were also exempt from GATT/WTO challenge or countervailing duties until 2004. Direct payments to producers that are not linked to production are also generally exempt. This will include income support, adjustment assistance, and environmental and regional assistance payments. Furthermore, direct payments to support crop reductions and *de minimis* payments are exempted in most cases.

After removing all of the exempted domestic agricultural support programs, the Agreement on Agriculture arrives at a calculation known as the

Total Aggregate Measurement of Support (Total AMS). This measure is the basis for agricultural support reductions under the agreement. Developed nations promised to reduce their Total AMS by 20 percent over 6 years, developing nations by 13.3 percent over 10 years.

Agricultural export subsidies of developed nations had to be reduced by 36 percent below 1986–1990 levels over six years and the quantity of subsidized agricultural exports by 21 percent. Except for a handful of developed members, agricultural export subsidies were subsequently reduced to zero by WTO developed nations, including the United States. Developing nations had to meet corresponding 24 and 14 percent reductions over 10 years. Late in 2015, with relatively few exceptions, developed and developing WTO members agreed to eliminate direct farm export subsidies. They also imposed rules on export credits, international food aid and state trading enterprises in the agricultural sector.

Under the 1995 agreement on agriculture, all conforming tariffications, reductions in domestic support for agriculture and export subsidy alterations were essentially exempt from challenge until 2004 within the GATT/WTO on grounds such as serious prejudice in export markets or nullification and impairment of agreement benefits. However, countervailing duties could be levied against all unlawfully subsidized exports of agricultural goods except for subsidies derived from so-called national "green box policies" (discussed above). In *U.S.-Upland Cotton,* the Appellate Body affirmed that member states must not only conform to the Agreement on Agriculture, but also the Subsidies and Countervailing Measures (SCM) Agreement. In that decision, U.S. compliance with the Agriculture Agreement was acknowledged, but its "Step-2" payments to cotton users favoring domestic over imported cotton (local content subsidies) were held to violate the SCM Agreement.

WTO AGREEMENT ON TEXTILES

One critical reason why developing nations opted into the WTO package is the Agreement on Textiles. It eliminated as of 2005 the quotas long maintained under the Multi-Fiber Arrangement (MFA). The demise of MFA textile quotas in 2005, as widely expected, dramatically accelerated Chinese and other Asian textile exports to the United States. Responding to domestic pressures, the United States repeatedly invoked special safeguard protections against textile and clothing imports during the ten-year phase-out period that ended in 2005. Since then the average U.S. bound and applied tariff on textile products has been around 8 percent, and consumers must search very hard to find Made-in-the-USA clothing.

GENERAL AGREEMENT ON TRADE IN SERVICES (GATS)

Market access for services is a major focus of the WTO General Agreement on Trade in Services (GATS). Since the United States is the world's largest exporter of services, including for example tourism, education, computer and professional services, it has a special interest in GATS. The U.S. Congress approved and implemented the GATS agreement in 1994 under the Uruguay Round Agreements Act. Subsequently, early in 1995, the United States refused to extend most-favored-nation treatment to financial services. The European Union, Japan and other GATS nations then entered into an interim two-year agreement which operated on MFN principles.

Financial services were revisited in 1996–97 with further negotiations aimed at bringing the United States into the fold. These negotiations bore fruit late in 1997 with 70 nations (including the United States) joining in an agreement that covers 95 percent of trade in banking, insurance, securities and financial information. This agreement took effect March 1, 1999.

A general right of most-favored-nation treatment in the services sector has been established. National laws that restrict the number of firms in a market that are dependent upon local "needs tests" or that mandate local incorporation are regulated by the GATS. Various "transparency" rules require disclosure of all relevant laws and regulations, and these must be administered reasonably, objectively and impartially. Certain mutual recognition of education and training for service-sector licensing will occur. State monopolies or exclusive service providers may continue, but must not abuse their positions. Detailed rules are created in annexes to the GATS on telecommunications and air transport services. Under the Telecommunications annex, for example, the United States successfully argued that Telmex had abused its monopoly position in Mexico by charging discriminatory, non-cost-oriented connection fees for foreign calls.

In addition, each WTO member state made under GATS Article 16 specific schedule of commitments (concessions) on opening up their markets in services' sectors negotiated using the WTO Services Sectoral Classification List. They further agreed under Article 16 to provide national treatment to their services' commitment schedule. For example, to what degree may foreign banks or foreign economic consultants provide services, and are they entitled to national treatment?

The answers to those questions will be found in the GATS specific commitments of each member. The European Union, for example, has refused to make commitments in the audio-visual sector. These commitments may be modified or withdrawn after three years, subject to a right of compensation that can be arbitrated.

Much to its consternation, the United States was found to have failed to exclude Internet gambling services under its GATS commitments' schedule. This caused Antigua-Barbuda to prevail in a dispute that alleged U.S. gambling laws discriminatorily prohibited its right to export such services to the U.S. market. The United States also lost the argument that its Internet gambling services' restraints were justifiable on public morals' grounds. This argument failed as discriminatory under the "chapeau" of the

GATS Article 16 general exceptions (similar to GATT Article 20 general exceptions).

The GATS has reduced unilateral U.S. action under Section 301 of the Trade Act of 1974 to gain access to foreign markets for U.S. service providers. This reduction flows from U.S. adherence to the Dispute Settlement Understanding (DSU, see below). The DSU obligates its signatories to follow streamlined dispute settlement procedures under which retaliation is restrained until the offending nation has failed to conform to a WTO ruling.

WTO DECISION-MAKING

The World Trade Organization is structured in three tiers. One tier is the Ministerial Conference, which meets biennially and is composed of representatives of all WTO Members. Each Member has an equal voting weight, which is unlike the representation in the IMF and World Bank where there is weighted voting, and financially powerful states have more power over the decision-making process.

The Ministerial Conference is responsible for all WTO functions, and is able to make any decisions necessary. It has the power to authorize new multilateral negotiations and to adopt the results of such negotiations. The Ministerial Conference, by a three-fourths vote, is authorized to grant waivers of obligations to Members in exceptional circumstances. It also has the power to adopt interpretations of Covered Agreements. When the Ministerial

Conference is in recess, its functions are performed by the General Council.

The second tier is the General Council which has executive authority over the day to day operations and functions of the WTO. It is composed of representatives of all WTO Members, and each member has an equal voting weight. It meets whenever it is appropriate. The General Council also has the power to adopt interpretations of Covered Agreements.

The third tier comprises the councils, bodies and committees which are accountable to the Ministerial Conference or General Council. Ministerial Conference committees include Committees on Trade and Development, Balance of Payment Restrictions, Budget, Finance and Administration. General Council bodies include the Dispute Settlement Body, the Trade Policy Review Body, and Councils for Trade in Goods, Trade in Services and Trade-Related Intellectual Property Rights. The Councils are all created by the WTO Agreement and are open to representatives of all Member States. The Councils also have the authority to create subordinate organizations. Other committees, such as the Committee on Subsidies and Countervailing Measures are created by specific individual agreements.

Of the General Council bodies, the two most important are the Dispute Settlement Body (DSB) and the Trade Policy Review Body (TPRB). The DSB is a special meeting of the General Council, and therefore includes all WTO Members. It has responsibility for resolution of disputes under all the Covered Agreements, and is discussed in more detail below under Dispute Resolution.

The purpose of the Trade Policy Review-Mechanism (TPRM) is to improve adherence to the WTO agreements and obligations, and to obtain greater transparency. Individual Members of WTO each prepare a "Country Report" on their trade policies and perceived adherence to the WTO Covered Agreements. The WTO Secretariat also prepares a report on each Member, but from the perspective of the Secretariat. The Trade Policy Review Body (TPRB) then reviews the trade policies of each Member based on these two reports. At the end of the review, the TPRB issues its own report concerning the adherence of the Member's trade policy to the WTO Covered Agreements. The TPRB has no enforcement capability, but the report is sent to the next meeting of the WTO Ministerial Conference. It is then up to the Ministerial Conference to evaluate the trade practices and policies of the Member.

WTO Consensus Rules

The process of decision-making in the WTO Ministerial Conference and General Council relies upon "consensus" as the norm, just as it did for decision-making under GATT 1947. "Consensus", in this context means that no Member formally objects to a proposed decision. Thus, consensus is not obtained if any one Member formally objects, and has often been very difficult to obtain, which proved to be a weakness in the operation of GATT 1947. However, there are many exceptions to the consensus formula under WTO, and some new concepts (such as "inverted consensus", discussed below) which are designed to ease the process of decision-making under WTO.

Article 9(1) of the WTO Agreement first provides that "the practice of decision-making by consensus" followed under GATT shall be continued. The next sentence of that provision, however, states that "where a decision cannot be arrived at by consensus, the matter at issue shall be decided by voting", except where otherwise provided. The ultimate resolution of the conflict between these two sentences is not completely clear.

There are a number of exceptions to the requirement for consensus that are expressly created under the WTO Agreement. One such exception is decisions by the Dispute Settlement Body, which has its own rules (see below). Another set of exceptions concerns decisions on waivers, interpretations and amendments of the Covered Agreements. Waivers of obligations may be granted and amendments adopted to Covered Agreements only by the Ministerial Conference. Amendments of Multilateral Trade Agreements usually require a consensus, but where a decision on a proposed amendment cannot obtain consensus, the decision on that amendment is to be made in certain circumstances by a two-thirds majority vote.

In "exceptional circumstances", the Ministerial Conference is authorized to grant waivers of obligations under a Covered Agreement by a three-fourths vote. Another exception to the consensus requirement allows procedural rules in both the Ministerial Conference and the General Council to be decided by a majority vote of the Members, unless otherwise provided.

Operationally speaking, the WTO membership rarely meets in its entirety. Alliances and groups within the membership meet to undertake WTO decisions. For example, the "Cairns Group" of 18 member-states has focused on agricultural trade issues and endured as a group for some time. Groups and alliances often shift depending upon the subject matter.

DISPUTE-SETTLEMENT UNDER THE WTO

The WTO provides a unified intergovernmental system for settling international trade disputes through the Dispute Settlement Understanding (DSU) using the Dispute Settlement Body (DSB). The DSB is a special assembly of the WTO General Council, and includes all WTO Members. There are seven stages in the resolution of disputes under WTO:

1) Consultation;

2) Panel establishment, investigation and report;

3) Appellate review of the panel report;

4) Adoption of the panel and appellate decision;

5)   Implementation of the decision adopted;

6)   Settlement by compensation; and

7)   Authorized retaliation.

There is also a parallel process for binding arbitration, if both parties agree to submit this dispute to arbitration, rather than to a DSB panel. In addition, during the implementation phase (5), the party subject to an adverse decision may seek arbitration as a matter of right.

Three further points are worthy of emphasis concerning proceedings before the DSB. First, since the WTO came into being in 1994, dispute settlement before the DSB, once initiated, is compulsory and binding. Second, this dispute settlement option is not open to private litigants, for only member state governments may file an action before the DSB. Finally, although formally binding, the WTO has no direct power to compel compliance with its decisions. Nonetheless, it may order compensation for the aggrieved state(s) or authorize retaliatory trade sanctions, and these often provide a significant incentive for an offending state to bring its domestic law into compliance.

Although the DSU offers a unified dispute resolution system that is applicable across all sectors and all WTO Covered Agreements, there are many specialized rules for disputes which arise under them. Such specialized rules appear in the Agreements on Textiles, Antidumping, Subsidies and Countervailing Measures, Technical Barriers to Trade, Sanitary and Phytosanitary Measures,

Customs Valuation, General Agreement on Trade in Services, Financial Services and Air Transport Services. The special provisions in these individual Covered Agreements govern, where applicable, and prevail in any conflict with the general provisions of the DSU.

Under the WTO, unlike under GATT 1947, the DSU practically assures that panels will be established upon request by a Member. Further, under WTO, unlike under GATT 1947, the DSU virtually ensures the adoption of unmodified panel and Appellate Body decisions. It accomplishes this by requiring the DSB to adopt these decisions automatically and without amendment unless they are rejected by a consensus of all Members. This "inverted consensus" requires that all Members of the DSB, including the Member who prevailed in the dispute, decide to reject the dispute resolution decision. Such an outcome is very unlikely. This inverted consensus requirement is imposed on both the adoption of panel reports or Appellate Body decisions and also on the decision to establish a panel.

The potential resolutions of a dispute under DSU range from a "mutually satisfactory solution" agreed to by the parties under the first, or consultation phase, to authorized retaliation under the last, or implementation, phase. The preferred solution is always any resolution that is mutually satisfactory to the parties. After a final decision, there are three types of remedies available to the prevailing party if a mutually satisfactory solution cannot be obtained.

One is for the respondent to bring the measure found to violate a Covered Agreement into conformity with the Agreement. A second is for the prevailing Member to receive compensation from the respondent which both parties agree is sufficient to compensate for any injury caused by the measure found to violate a Covered Agreement.

Finally, if no such agreement can be reached, a prevailing party can be authorized to suspend some of its concessions under the Covered Agreements to the respondent. These suspended concessions, called "retaliation," are normally authorized within the same trade sector and agreement (say goods or services). If that will not create sufficient compensation, retaliation can be authorized across trade sectors and agreements, which has proven to be a powerful incentive to achieve compliance by the offending WTO member.

The entire WTO dispute resolution process, from filing a complaint to authorized retaliation, can take roughly three years. One perspective on WTO dispute settlement seeks a rule-oriented use of the "rule of law". The other seeks a power-oriented use of diplomacy. The United States and less developed countries have traditionally sought to develop a rule-oriented approach to international trade disputes. The European Union and Japan have traditionally sought to use the GATT/WTO primarily as a forum for diplomatic negotiations, although the EU now ranks second in number of WTO dispute proceedings.

These different views created part of the conflict at the December 1999 Seattle WTO meeting (which failed to launch the Millennium Round). If the DSB is a court, its proceedings should be open and "transparent." However, if it is just another form of government-to-government diplomacy, that has always been held in secret.

Phase 1: Consultation

Any WTO Member who believes that the Measures of another Member are not in conformity with the Covered Agreements may call for consultations on those measures. The respondent has ten days to reply to the call for consultations and must agree to enter into consultation within 30 days. If the respondent does not enter into consultations within the 30-day period, the party seeking consultations can immediately request the establishment of a panel under DSU, which puts the dispute into Phase 2.

Once consultations begin, the parties have 60 days to achieve a settlement. The goal is to seek a positive solution to the dispute, and the preferred resolution is to reach whatever solution is mutually satisfactory to the parties. If such a settlement cannot be obtained after 60 days of consultations, the party seeking consultations may request the establishment of a panel under DSU, which moves the dispute into Phase 2.

Third parties with an interest in the subject-matter of the consultations may seek to be included in them. If such inclusion is rejected, they may seek their own consultations with the other Member.

Alternatives to consultations may be provided through the use of conciliation, mediation or good offices, where all parties agree to use the alternative process. Any party can terminate the use of conciliation, mediation or good offices and then seek the establishment of a panel under DSU, which will move the dispute into Phase 2.

Phase 2: Panel Establishment, Investigation and Report

If consultations between the parties fail, the party or parties seeking the consultations (the complainant) may request the DSB to establish a three-person panel to investigate, report and resolve the dispute. It is not uncommon to have several member states, sometimes a dozen or more, join together as complainants. This often creates high profile WTO disputes. The DSB must establish such a panel upon request, unless the DSB expressly decides by consensus not to establish the panel. Since an "inverted consensus" is required to reject the establishment of the panel and the complainant Member must be part of that consensus, it is very likely that a panel will be established. Hundreds of panels have been established since 1995.

The WTO Secretariat maintains a list of well-qualified persons who are available to serve as panelists. The panels are usually composed of three individuals from that list who are not citizens of either party. If the parties agree, a panel can be composed of five such individuals. The parties can also agree to appoint citizens of a party to a panel.

Panelists may be either nongovernmental individuals or governmental officials, but they are to be selected so as to ensure their independence. Thus, there is a bias towards independent individuals who are not citizens of any party. If a citizen of a party is appointed, that government may not instruct that citizen how to vote, for the panelist must be independent. By the same reasoning, a governmental official of a non-party Member who is subject to instructions from a home government would not seem to fit the profile of an independent panelist.

The WTO Secretariat proposes nominations of the panelists. Parties may not normally oppose the nominations, except for "compelling reasons." The parties are given twenty days to agree on the panelists and the composition of the panel. If such agreement is not forthcoming, the WTO Director-General is authorized to appoint the panelists, in consultation with other persons in the Secretariat.

The disputes brought to DSB panels can involve either violations of Covered Agreements or non-violation nullification and impairment of benefits under the Covered Agreements. A prima facie case of nullification impairment arises when one Member infringes upon the "obligations assumed under a Covered Agreement." Such infringement creates a presumption against the infringing Member, but the presumption can be rebutted by a showing that the complaining Member has suffered no adverse effect from the infringement.

The panels receive pleadings and rebuttals and hear oral arguments. Panels can also engage in fact development from sources outside those presented by the parties. Thus, the procedure has aspects familiar to civil law courts. A panel can, on its own initiative, request information from anyone, including experts selected by the panel. It can also obtain confidential information in some circumstances from an administrative body which is part of the government of a Member, without any prior consent from that Member. Finally, a panel can establish its own group of experts to provide reports to it on factual or scientific issues.

A panel is obligated to produce two written reports—an interim and a final report. A panel is supposed to submit a final written report to the DSB within six months of its establishment. The report will contain its findings of fact, findings of law, decision and the rationale for its decision. Before the final report is issued, the panel provides an interim report to the parties. The purpose of this interim report is to apprise the parties of the panel's current analysis of the issues and to permit the parties to comment on that analysis. The final report of the panel need not change any of the findings or conclusions in its interim report unless it is persuaded to do so by a party's comments. However, if it is not so persuaded, it is obligated to explain in its final report why it is not so persuaded.

The decisions in WTO panel reports are final as to issues of fact. The decisions in panel reports are not necessarily final as to issues of law. Panel decisions on issues of law are subject to review by the Appellate Body, which is Phase 3, and explained below. Any party can appeal a panel report, and appeals are usually taken.

Phase 3: Appellate Body Review of the Panel Report

Appellate review of panel reports is available at the request of any party, unless the DSB rejects that request by an "inverted consensus." There is no threshold requirement for an appellant to present a substantial substantive legal issue. Thus, most panel decisions are appealed as a matter of course unless there is fear of creating adverse Appellate Body (AB) "precedent". However, the AB can only review the panel reports on questions of law or legal interpretation.

The WTO Appellate Body was created as a new institution. GATT 1947 had nothing comparable to it. It is composed of seven members ("judges") who are appointed by the DSB to four year terms. Each judge may be reappointed, but only once, to a second four-year term. Each judge is to be a recognized authority on international trade law and the Covered Agreements. Appointments to the Appellate Body have included a number of distinguished judges, law professors, government trade officials and trade lawyers from a range of developed and developing countries.

The review of any panel decision is performed by three judges out of the seven. The parties do not, however, have any influence on which judges are selected to review a particular panel report. There is a schedule, created by the Appellate Body itself, for the rotation for sitting of each of the judges. Thus, a party might try to appear before a favored judge by timing the start of the dispute settlement process to arrive at the Appellate Body at the right moment on the rotation schedule, but even this limited approach has difficulties.

The Appellate Body receives written submissions from the parties and has 60, or in some cases 90, days in which to render its decision. The Appellate Body review is limited to issues of law and legal interpretation. The panel decision may be upheld, modified, or reversed by the AB decision. Appellate Body decisions are anonymous, and ex parte communications are not permitted, which makes judge-shopping by parties difficult. *Appellate Body decisions do not represent binding precedent.* That said, many have observed a desire on the part of the Appellate Body to achieve consistency and a willingness to discuss its prior rulings when rendering decisions.

Phase 4: Adoption of the Panel or Appellate Body Decision

Appellate Body determinations are submitted to the DSB. Panel decisions which are not appealed are also submitted to the DSB. Once either type of decision is submitted to the DSB, the DSB must automatically adopt them without modification or amendment at its next meeting unless the decision is rejected by all Members of the DSB through the form of "inverted consensus" discussed previously.

An alternative to Phases 2 through 4 is arbitration, if both parties agree. The arbitration must be binding on the parties, and there is no appeal from the arbitral tribunal's decision to the DSB Appellate Body.

Phase 5: Implementation of the Decision Adopted

Once a panel or Appellate Body decision is adopted by the DSB, implementation is a three-step process. In the first step, the Member found to have a measure which violates its WTO obligations has "a reasonable time" (usually 15 months) to bring those measures into conformity with the WTO obligations. That remedy is the preferred one, and this form of implementation is the principal goal of the WTO dispute settlement system. To date, most disputes have resulted in compliance in this manner.

Phase 6: Settlement by Compensation

If the violating measures are not brought into conformity within a reasonable time, the parties proceed to the second step. The parties negotiate to reach an agreement upon a form of "compensation" which will be granted by the party in violation to the injured party. Such "compensation" will usually comprise trade concessions, which are over and above those already available under the WTO and Covered Agreements. The nature, scope, amount and duration of these additional concessions is at the negotiating parties' discretion, but each side must agree that the final compensation package is fair and is properly related to the injury caused by the violating measures.

Few such compensation agreements have ever been achieved, though the United States compensated most of the membership after losing a dispute to Antigua about whether it had "reserved" (excepted) Internet gambling from coverage under the GATS. The United States also compensated the EU in a copyright dispute involving small business use of music and in the HAVANA CLUB trademark dispute, as well as Brazil after losing a subsidies dispute concerning cotton.

Phase 7: Authorized Retaliation

If the parties cannot agree on an appropriate amount of compensation within twenty days, the complainant may proceed to the third step. The party or parties injured by the violating measures seek authority from the DSB to retaliate against the party whose measures violated its WTO obligations (the respondent). Thus, complainant seeks authority to suspend some of its WTO obligations benefitting the respondent. The retaliation proposed must ordinarily be within the same sector and agreement as the violating measure. "Sector" is sometimes broadly defined, as all trade in goods, and sometimes narrowly defined, as in individual services in the Services Sectoral Classification List. "Agreement" is also broadly defined. All the agreements listed in Annex IA to the WTO Agreement are considered to be a single "agreement." If retaliation within the sector and agreement of the violating measure is considered insufficient compensation, the complainant may seek suspension of its obligations across sectors and agreements.

Within 30 days of the complainant's presentation of the request to retaliate, the DSB must grant the request, unless the request is rejected by all the members through an "inverted consensus." However, the respondent may object to the level or scope of the retaliation. Upon such an objection, the issues raised by the objection will be examined by either the Appellate Body or by an arbitrator. The respondent has a right, even if arbitration was not used in Phases 2 through 4, to have an arbitrator review in Phase 5 the appropriateness of the complainant's proposed level and scope of retaliation. The arbitrator will also examine whether the proper procedures and criteria to establish retaliation have been followed. The Phase 5 arbitration is final and binding and the arbitrator's decision is not subject to DSB review.

In addition to objecting to the level of authorized retaliation, the responding WTO member may simultaneously challenge the assertion of noncompliance. This challenge will ordinarily be heard by the original panel and must be resolved within 90 days. Thus the request for authorized retaliation and objections thereto could conceivably be accomplished before noncompliance is formally determined. In practice, WTO dispute settlement has melded these conflicting procedures such that compliance and retaliation issues are decided together, typically by the original panel.

Retaliation in Action

Retaliation has rarely been authorized, and even less rarely imposed. The amount of a U.S. retaliation permitted after the WTO *Bananas* and *Beef Hormones* decisions (above) were not implemented by the EU was contested. The arbitration tribunals for this issue were the original WTO panels, which did not allow the entire amount of the almost $700 million in retaliatory tariffs proposed by the United States. The U.S. was authorized and levied retaliatory tariffs amounting to about $100 million (*Bananas*) and $200 million (*Beef Hormones*) against European goods because of the EU failure to implement those WTO decisions. Since 2000, Congress has authorized rotating retaliatory tariffs in "carousel" fashion upon different goods. The threat of carousel retaliation contributed to an April 2001 settlement of the *Bananas* dispute and a 2009 settlement of the *Beef Hormones* dispute.

Perhaps the most dramatic use of retaliation occurred in a tax subsidy dispute concerning Internal Revenue Code extraterritorial export tax preferences (FISCs). The amount of EU retaliation permissible after the U.S. lost (for the second time) under WTO subsidy rules was disputed. A WTO panel, serving as an arbitrator, authorized approximately $4 *billion* in EU retaliation against U.S. exports. This retaliation commenced in March of 2004 and escalated monthly until the U.S. capitulated by amending the I.R.C. late in 2004.

Cross-Sector Retaliation

In a landmark ruling, a WTO panel acting as an arbitrator authorized Ecuador to remove protection of intellectual property rights regarding geographical indicators, copyrights and industrial designs on European Union goods for sale in Ecuador. This authorization was part of Ecuador's $200 million compensation in the *Bananas* dispute. The WTO panel acknowledged that Ecuador imports mostly capital goods and raw materials from the European Union and that imposing retaliatory tariffs on them would adversely harm its manufacturing industries. This risk supported "cross-retaliation" outside the sector of the EU trade violation (goods) and likewise contributed to a rapid settlement of the *Bananas* dispute. Cross-sector retaliation has also been authorized against the U.S. after losing a GATS dispute to Antigua on Internet gambling restraints, and losing a cotton subsidy dispute with Brazil.

U.S. INVOLVEMENT IN WTO DISPUTE RESOLUTION

The WTO dispute resolution process has been invoked more frequently than many expected. The United States has been the leading complainant and respondent in WTO disputes. Early on, the U.S. lost a dispute initiated by Venezuela and Brazil concerning U.S. standards for reformulated and conventional gasoline. The offending U.S. law was amended to conform to the WTO ruling. It won on a complaint initiated jointly with Canada and the European Union regarding Japanese taxes on alcoholic beverages. Japan subsequently changed its law. When Costa Rica complained about U.S. restraints on imports of underwear, the U.S. let the restraints expire prior to any formal DSB ruling at the WTO. Similar results were reached when India complained of U.S. restraints on wool shirts and blouses. A patent law complaint by the U.S. against India prevailed in the DSB and ultimately brought changes in Indian law regarding pharmaceuticals and agricultural chemicals.

The U.S. won a panel decision against Mexico's exorbitant telecom interconnection rates. The United States also won a major dispute with Canada concerning trade and subsidies for periodicals. This celebrated *Sports Illustrated* dispute proved that WTO remedies can be used to avoid Canada's cultural industries exclusion under NAFTA 1994. See my *NAFTA Nutshell* for details.

The United States prevailed against Argentina regarding tariffs and taxes on footwear, textiles and apparel. It lost a challenge (strongly supported by Kodak) to Japan's distribution rules regarding photo film and paper. In this dispute the U.S. elected *not* to appeal the adverse WTO panel ruling to the Appellate Body. In contrast, the European Union took an appeal which reversed an adverse panel ruling on its customs classification of computer equipment. The U.S. had commenced this proceeding. Opponents in many disputes, Japan, the United States and the European Union united to complain that Indonesia's National Car Program was discriminatory and in breach of several WTO agreements. The complainants prevailed in a WTO proceeding against local content and trade balancing requirements for foreign auto manufacturers. These requirements violated the TRIMS agreement. Indonesia altered its program.

India, Malaysia, Pakistan and Thailand teamed up to challenge U.S. shrimp import restraints enacted to protect endangered sea turtles. The WTO Appellate Body generally upheld their complaint and the U.S. has moved to comply. The adequacy of U.S. compliance was unsuccessfully challenged by Malaysia. The European Union and the United States jointly opposed Korea's discriminatory taxes on alcoholic beverages. This challenge was successful and Korea now imposes flat non-discriminatory taxes. The United States also complained of Japan's quarantine, testing and other agricultural import rules. The U.S. won at the WTO and Japan has changed its procedures.

In a semiconductor dumping dispute, Korea successfully argued that the U.S. was not in compliance with the WTO Antidumping Agreement. The United States amended its law, but Korea has instituted further proceedings alleging that these amendments are inadequate. The United States did likewise after Australia lost a subsidies dispute relating to auto leather exports. The reconvened WTO panel ruled that Australia had indeed failed to conform to the original adverse DSB decision. A U.S. challenge concerning India's quotas on imports of agricultural, textile and industrial products was upheld. India and the United States subsequently reached agreement on a timeline for removal of these restraints. Closer to home, New Zealand and the United States complained of Canada's import/export rules regarding milk. Losing at the WTO, Canada agreed to a phased removal of the offending measures.

The U.S. lost a "big one" when the DSB determined that export tax preferences granted to "Foreign Sales Corporations" of U.S. companies were illegal. The United States expanded the FSC regime by removing the requirement that eligible goods be manufactured in the U.S. It claimed that this change made the FSC program not contingent upon exports, and thus WTO-legal. The European Union challenged this assertion of compliance before the WTO and won. Retaliation finally brought U.S. compliance. In March of 2004, the European Union commenced raising tariffs against U.S. goods under the WTO retaliation authorized out of the FSC/export tax subsidy dispute noted above. Monthly increments were planned until either the U.S. complied or the EU reached the maximum of roughly $4 billion annually it was authorized to retaliate. In the Fall of 2004, the United States repealed the extraterritorial income exclusion and the EU subsequently removed its retaliatory tariffs.

Another "big one" went in favor of the United States. The European Union challenged the validity under the DSU of unilateral retaliation under Section 301 of the Trade Act of 1974. See Chapters 6 and under President Trump Chapter 8. Section 301 has been something of a *bete noire* in U.S. trade law, but the WTO panel affirmed its legality in light of President Clinton's undertakings to administer it in accordance with U.S. obligations to adhere to multilateral WTO dispute settlement. To be sure, this ruling will be cited in WTO challenges by China against President Trump's Section 301 tariffs. See Chapters 6 and 8.

The WTO Appellate Body ruled against the United States regarding the legality of the Antidumping Act of 1916 and the royalty free provisions of the 1998 Fairness in Music Licensing Act. The Appellate Body also ruled against Section 211 of the Omnibus Appropriations Act of 1998 denying trademark protection in connection with confiscated assets (the "Havana Club" dispute). U.S. compliance with these rulings has been slow in forthcoming, although the Antidumping Act of 1916 has been repealed and compensation was paid in the Havana Club and Music Licensing disputes.

A WTO Panel ruled that the Byrd Amendment violates the WTO antidumping and subsidy codes. The Byrd Amendment (Continued Dumping and Subsidy Act of 2000) authorizes the Customs Service to forward AD and CVD duties to affected domestic producers for qualified expenses. Eleven WTO members including the EU, Canada and Mexico challenged the Amendment. This ruling was affirmed by the WTO Appellate Body and retaliation was authorized. Late in 2005, the U.S. repealed the Byrd Amendment, subject to a contested two-year phase-out.

U.S. involvement in WTO dispute settlement continues to be extensive. The Appellate Body ruled that U.S. countervailing duties against British steel based upon pre-privatization subsidies were unlawful. U.S. complaints against Korean beef import restraints and procurement practices were upheld. Canada's patent protection term was also invalidated by the WTO under a U.S. complaint. European Union complaints concerning U.S. wheat gluten quotas have been sustained. The *Wheat Gluten* dispute questions the legality of U.S. "causation" rules in Safeguard (escape clause) proceedings under Section 201 of the Trade Act of 1974. See Chapter 4. Major U.S. Section 201 tariffs against steel adopted by President George W. Bush were invalidated 18 months later by the Appellate Body in 2003. Is this a harbinger for President Trump's solar panel and clothes washer Safeguard tariffs of 2018? See Chapter 8.

A WTO panel ruled that Airbus had received $20 billion in illegal EU "launch" subsidies. That same panel found Boeing the recipient of $5 billion in federal research contract subsidies that violated the WTO Subsidies Code. These disputes, long in the making, remain ongoing.

The Mexico-United States "sugar war" came to a head before the Appellate Body. Mexico's 20% soft drink tax on beverages not using cane sugar, its 20% distribution tax on those beverages, and related bookkeeping requirements were found to violate GATT Article III and not exempt under Article XX(d). Subsequently, the two countries settled their dispute by agreeing to free trade in sugar and high fructose corn syrup. This agreement does not bar AD or CVD duties on either sweetener, subject now to managed quota trading under another U.S.-Mexico settlement. Sugar remains one of the most highly protected sectors of the U.S. economy sheltered behind quotas dating back to the 1930s. Commonly triple the world commodity price of sugar, U.S. sugar quotas drove Hershey Chocolates among others to move its factories abroad. The CIA reports that sugar producers in Jamaica switched to marijuana as a consequence of U.S. sugar import quotas.

The United States continued to lose WTO disputes about its zeroing methodology (see Chapter 4) in antidumping proceedings. Despite over 12 decisions against zeroing, the U.S. moved slowly to alter its rules to comply with WTO rulings, finally eliminating zeroing in new AD investigations, but not reviews of existing AD duties. The U.S. repealed the Byrd Amendment distributions of antidumping and countervailing duty revenues to U.S. industries, subject to a contested two-year phase out. As the U.S. wound down its "Byrd Amendment" (repealed in 2006), Japan and the EU continued retaliatory tariffs that correspond in amount to those distributions, $8 million and $95 million in 2010 respectively.

Little Antigua-Barbuda won a WTO panel ruling under the GATS against certain U.S. Internet gambling restraints. Retaliation was authorized, and the U.S. settled with nearly all members save Antigua-Barbuda by offering compensation. The U.S. failed to persuade the Appellate Body to require the

European Union under GATT Article 10(3) to undertake a major overhaul of its customs law system targeting inconsistencies therein among the member states. The U.S. lost a country of origin labeling (COOL) dispute raised by Mexico and Canada challenging mandatory retail meat origin packaging rules. Over $1 billion in annual retaliatory tariffs on U.S. exports to Canada and Mexico were authorized. The U.S. moved swiftly towards repeal of its COOL regulations.

The U.S. lost a cotton subsidy challenge by Brazil. The United States agreed to pay $147 million annually to provide technical assistance to Brazilian cotton farmers. In return, Brazil suspended retaliatory tariffs and cross-sector IP sanctions authorized by the WTO because of the U.S. cotton subsidy violations.

Beef Hormones NTB Dispute

The *Beef Hormones* case illustrates NTB issues and a relatively rare outcome in WTO dispute settlement. The EU banned imports of growth enhancing hormone-treated beef from the U.S. and Canada as a health hazard. The WTO Appellate Body ruled that, since the ban was stricter than international standards, the EU needed scientific evidence to back it up. However, the EU had failed to undertake a scientific risk assessment, and its scientific reports did not provide any rational basis to uphold the ban. In fact, the primary study had found no evidence of harm to humans from the growth-enhancing-hormones.

The Appellate Body ruled that the ban violated the WTO Sanitary and Phytosanitary Standards (SPS) Code and required the EU to produce scientific evidence to justify the ban within a reasonable time, or to revoke the ban. Arbitrators determined that 15 months was a reasonable time, but the EU failed to produce such evidence and the U.S. retaliated with over $200 million annually in tariffs on EU exports.

The United States maintained that the European Union must eliminate their ban on hormone-treated beef in order to conform to the ruling. Naturally, the Europeans saw things a bit differently. If they could come up with solid scientific evidence that the administration of hormones to beef in the U.S. and Canada poses risks to human health, they hoped to escape retaliation. The EU claimed on the basis of post-dispute studies that one beef hormone was proven harmful to human health, and five others ought to be banned as a precautionary principle. The EU petitioned the WTO to seek removal of the U.S. sanctions. This petition was rejected in 2008 by the Appellate Body, again for want of scientific justification.

Finally, in 2009, a phased four-year settlement of the *Beef Hormones* dispute was reached. The U.S. got a higher quota to export hormone-free beef to the EU in return for phasing out its retaliatory tariffs on EU goods. The U.S. threat of carousel sanctions, i.e., rotating goods subject to retaliation, was instrumental to this settlement. Meanwhile, because the U.S. beef industry failed to timely ask for a continuation of the retaliatory tariffs, the Federal

Circuit ruled in 2010 that they expired in 2007. Refunds were given to importers of EU products who paid those tariffs. Thus the EU ban on hormone-treated beef continues.

The United States has also settled a number of disputes prior to WTO panel decisions, and remains in consultation on other disputes that may be decided by a WTO panel. For the latest summary of all WTO disputes, including many not involving the United States, see www.wto.org.

CHINA INVOLVEMENT IN WTO DISPUTES

China, a member since 2001, is involved in a growing number of WTO disputes. Here is a sampling of those disputes.

Canada, the European Union and the United States complained against Chinese duties on imported Auto Parts (10 percent) that rose to those on complete autos (25 percent) if the imported parts exceeded a fixed percentage of the final vehicle content or price, or if specific combinations of imported auto parts were used in the final vehicle. In addition, extensive record keeping, reporting and verification requirements were imposed when Chinese auto companies used imported parts. In July of 2008, a WTO panel ruled that these "internal charges" violated Articles 3(2) and 3(4) of the GATT and China's accession commitments.

The core Panel ruling, affirmed by the Appellate Body, found China's Auto Parts measures discriminatory in favor of domestic producers, a violation of the national treatment standard for taxes and regulations. This ruling marked the first time after China's admission in 2001 that it was held in breach of its WTO commitments and obligations.

Less than one month after losing this dispute, China enacted a "green tax" on gas-guzzling autos, most of which just happened to be imported. The sales tax on cars with engine capacities over 4.1 litres has been doubled to 40%. Autos with engines between 3 and 4.1 litres were taxed at 25%, up from 15%. At that time, most Chinese-made cars had engines with 2.5 litres or less. Autos with engines between 1 and 3 litres remained taxed at 8% and 10%. The smallest cars with engines below 1 litre had their sales tax reduced from 3 to 1 percent. This green tax achieved protective results similar to China's Auto Parts tariff structure.

Other disputes challenging China's compliance with WTO law have been reviewed. They concern China's auto export subsidies and CVDs on auto imports, protection and enforcement of intellectual property rights (2009 WTO panel ruled against China), trade and distribution of publications and audiovisual entertainment products and services (2009 Appellate Body ruled against China), commodity export tariffs and restrictions (2012 WTO Appellate Body ruled against China), application of Chinese AD to U.S. grain-oriented flat rolled steel (GOES) (2012 WTO Appellate Body ruled against China), discriminatory treatment of foreign electronic payment services (2012 WTO panel ruled against China, but compliance remains outstanding), rare earth export controls (2014 Appellate Body rules against China) and AD and CVD duties on U.S. electrical steel exports (2015 WTO panel rules against China). The United States has been a complaining party to all of these disputes.

China, in turn, has challenged U.S. safeguard measures applied to Chinese steel exports (2010 WTO Panel rejected challenge) and tires (2011 WTO Panel rejected challenge). It has challenged U.S. antidumping and countervailing duties on paper products from China (2011 WTO Panel ruled against U.S. dual assessment of AD and CVD duties), as well as U.S. AD and CVD on Chinese solar panels.

In a major dispute, China challenged in 2017 continued U.S. and EU application of nonmarket economy rules in antidumping disputes. See Chapter 4. China has also challenged President Trump's solar panel and clothes washers Safeguard tariffs, as well as Trump's "national security" steel and aluminum tariffs. See Chapter 8. Numerous U.S. CVDs against a range of Chinese goods were successfully challenged in 2018 on procedural grounds by China before a WTO panel. Meanwhile, the United States is challenging Chinese export restrictions on raw materials and alleged unlawful subsidization of aluminum, rice, wheat and corn.

The Trump Administration notably filed in 2018 a WTO complaint, joined by Japan and the European Union, against alleged patent violations of Articles 3 and 28 of TRIPS. These allegations assert that foreign patent holders are unable to stop Chinese licensees from continuing to use patented technology after licenses expire. They also assert Chinese discrimination against and less favorable mandatory adverse contract terms for imported foreign technology. The U.S. specifically cites four Chinese laws as the source of these TRIPS violations: The PRC Foreign Trade Law, Contract Law, Chinese-Foreign Equity Joint Venture Law, and the PRC Regulations on the Administration of the Import and Export of Technologies. See Chapters 6 and 8.

THE INTERNATIONAL
MONETARY FUND (IMF)

Most nations have a national currency and pursue an internal monetary policy to meet their own political and economic goals. Fifteen EU nations have joined in a common currency, the Euro, managed by the European Central Bank. No central authority controls a world monetary system; monetary policy is decentralized. Since 1944, nations have coordinated national monetary policies principally through the International Monetary Fund (IMF).

Both the IMF and the International Bank for Reconstruction and Development (the "World Bank") arose out of the Bretton Woods Conference in 1944. The World Bank was to facilitate loans by capital surplus countries (e.g., then the United States) to countries needing foreign investment for economic redevelopment after World War II. The IMF was to stabilize currency exchange rates, assist countries in their balance of payments, and repair other war damage to the international monetary system. Twenty-nine countries including the United States became party to the IMF Articles of Agreement in 1945. Today, over 150 countries are members of the IMF.

IMF Operations

The IMF goals are to facilitate the expansion and balanced growth of international trade, to assist in the elimination of foreign exchange restrictions which hamper the growth of international trade, and to shorten the duration and lessen the disequilibrium in the international balances of payments of members. The mitigation of wide currency fluctuations is achieved through a complex lending system which permits a country to borrow money from other Fund members or from the Fund (by way of "Special Drawing Rights" or "SDRs") for the purpose of stabilizing the relationship of its currency to other world currencies. These monetary drawing arrangements permit a member country to support its national currency's relative value when compared with national currencies of other countries, especially the "hard" ("reserve") currencies such as the Swiss franc, the Euro, Japanese yen, and United States dollar.

IMF loans have traditionally been "conditioned" upon adoption of specific economic reforms by debtor states, especially in Asia and Latin America. This has led to the perception that the IMF is the world's "sheriff", setting the terms for refinancing national debts and protecting the interests of commercial bank creditors. The IMF has functioned as the first line of negotiation in an international "debt crisis," and commercial and national banks often conform their loans to IMF conditions. These IMF conditions can have dramatic political and social repercussions in debtor nations.

From 2006 onwards, nations paid their IMF debt in record numbers. Argentina did so with an assist from Venezuela. Brazil, Russia, Bolivia, Uruguay, Indonesia, the Philippines and others joined in the flight from IMF loan conditions. The IMF's loan portfolio stood at $100 billion in 2003. By 2009, that portfolio was approaching zero, the IMF was running a budget deficit, and proposing sales of gold to make up the difference. Many commentators wondered aloud, what is the role of the IMF without loans? Then the world financial and economic meltdown arrived in the fall of 2008. By year's end and thereafter the IMF was back in the loan business, with increased funds and notable participation in conditioned bail-outs of Iceland, Greece, Portugal, Ireland and other European nations. In 2018, the IMF strictly conditioned a crisis loan to Argentina.

The IMF, like any bureaucracy in search of a mission, drafted a Code of Best Practices for "Sovereign Wealth Funds" (SWFs). Such Funds are said to hold over $3 trillion, and are expanding rapidly. Abu Dhabi, Saudi Arabia, Kuwait, Singapore, Russia, China and Norway (for example) all have large SWFs, many of which played an important role in bailing out U.S. banks and securities firms during the 2007–08 sub-prime lending crisis. The primary concern is that SWFs might use their power for political purposes. Their emergence further diminishes the need for IMF loans. As yet the SWFs have not "conditioned" their lending or investment decisions.

Special Drawing Rights (SDRs)

The International Monetary Fund has established a form of international money which is not a national currency and is called a Special Drawing Right (SDR). Certificates of deposit are denominated in SDRs; short-term SDR loans may be obtained commercially; and some OPEC nations have begun to value their national currencies in SDRs. Mechanically, an SDR is an international medium of exchange having a 2016 composite value based 42% percent on the U.S. dollar, 31 percent on the Euro, 11% on the Chinese yuan, 8 percent on the Japanese yen, and 8 percent on the British pound. Each exchange rate fluctuation in any one of these "basket currencies" produces commensurately only a smaller, fractional fluctuation in the value of an SDR.

Although the SDR has been talked about as if it is a supranational currency, and China has advocated as much, the SD "Right" is more technically a "unit of account" created by an IMF process. When an IMF member country, having a negative balance of payments position, runs short of its currency "reserves" (which may be its stocks of "hard" "reserve" currencies or gold), the member country may exercise its "Right" to make a "Special Drawing" from the IMF (e.g., the country may ask the IMF to arrange for that country to receive $40 million worth of currency). Upon receipt of the Drawing "request", the IMF approaches another member country having a fuller stock of "reserves" (which "back up" its national currency), and requests that country to provide currency to the requesting country (e.g., to provide $40 million worth of currency other than gold). In return for having supplied the currency, the supplying country acquires additional Special Drawing Rights (e.g., worth $40 million) which it may revoke if ever its currency "reserves" get too low.

Each IMF Member Country participating in the SDR scheme has a finite allocation of SDRs available for its possible use. A net result of the SDR scheme is that countries "swap" currencies to help other countries from time to time in maintaining existing, relative values between their national currency and other currencies of the world. Greece in 2015, for example, used its SDR quota to "repay" IMF debt associated with its bailouts.

CHAPTER 3
IMPORTS

Tariffs and Quotas	U.S. Trade and Import Laws
Product Standards	Nontariff Trade Barriers
U.S. Trade Agencies	Duty Free Entry
Customs Law	Procurement Trade Protections

Virtually all governments regulate the entry of goods into their jurisdiction. Customs tariffs may be collected, and conformity of the imported goods to local product standards will be reviewed. Much of the law related to restrictions on imports is derived from agreements governing international economic relations, notably those of the World Trade Organization. In this chapter, we will focus on United States law, which is broadly representative of the regulation of imports.

UNITED STATES TRADE AGENCIES AND ACTORS

The international trade of the United States is regulated by a number of different governmental bodies. The International Trade Administration (ITA) is part of the Commerce Department, which in turn is part of the Executive Branch of the federal government. The Commerce Department also contains the Office of Export Licensing and the Office of Anti-Boycott Compliance. The International Trade Commission (ITC) is an independent federal government agency that measures domestic injury in trade remedy proceedings. The specialized Court of International Trade (CIT), with substantial, exclusive judicial review powers in trade matters, is part of the Judicial Branch of the United States government. Lastly, the Office of the United States Trade Representative (USTR) works directly under the President, representing the country in trade negotiations and trade agreement disputes (Chapter 7), and administers Section 301 actions. (Chapter 6).

U.S. International Trade Administration (ITA)

The Commerce Department's International Trade Administration (ITA) is an administrative agency. In broadest terms, the ITA is to foster, promote and develop world trade, and to bring U.S. companies into the business of selling overseas. At a practical level, the ITA is designed to be helpful to the individual business by providing it with information concerning the "what, where, how and when" of imports and exports, such as information sources, requirements for a particular trade license, forms for international license agreement or procedures to start a business in a foreign country. The ITA provides business data and educational programs to United States businesses.

In addition to these duties, the ITA also decides whether there are subsidies in countervailing duty (CVD) cases, sales at less than fair value in antidumping duty (AD) cases, and national security import controls. Prior to 1980, such decisions were made by the Treasury Department. The ITA is not, however, involved in decision-making in safeguard

(Section 201), market disruption (Section 406) and unfair import practices (Section 337) proceedings. See Chapter 4.

U.S. International Trade Commission (ITC)

The United States International Trade Commission (ITC) is an independent bipartisan agency created by an act of Congress. The ITC is the successor to the United States Tariff Commission. In 1974, the name was changed and the ITC was given additional authority, powers and responsibilities. The Commission's present powers and duties include preparing reports pertaining to international economics and foreign trade for the Executive Branch, the Congress, other government agencies and the public. To carry out this responsibility, the ITC conducts investigations which entail extensive research, specialized studies and a high degree of expertise in all matters relating to the commercial and international trade policies of the United States.

Statutory investigations conducted by the ITC include unfair import trade practice determinations (Section 337 proceedings), domestic industry injury determinations in antidumping and countervailing duty cases, and safeguard and market disruption import relief recommendations. See Chapter 4. The ITC also advises the President about probable economic effects on domestic industries and consumers of modifications on duties and other trade barriers incident to proposed trade agreements with foreign countries.

The ITC is intended to be a quasi-judicial, bipartisan, independent agency providing trade expertise to Congress and the Executive. Congress went to great lengths to create a bipartisan body to conduct international trade studies and provide reliable expert information. The six Commissioners of the ITC are appointed by the President and confirmed by the United States Senate for nine year terms, unless appointed to fill an unexpired term. The presence of entrenched points of view is inhibited because a Commissioner who has served for more than five years is not eligible for reappointment. Not more than three Commissioners may be members of the same political party.

The Chairman and Vice-Chairman are designated by the President for two year terms. No Chairman may be of the same political party as the preceding Chairman, nor may the President designate two Commissioners of the same political party as Chairman and Vice-Chairman. Congress further guaranteed the independence of the ITC from the Executive Branch by having its budget submitted directly to the Congress. This means that its budget is not subject to review by the Office of Management and Budget.

U.S. Court of International Trade (CIT)

The United States Court of International Trade (CIT) is an Article III court under the United States Constitution for judicial review of civil actions arising out of import transactions and certain federal statutes affecting international trade. It grew out of the Board of General Appraisers (a quasi-judicial administrative unit within the Treasury Department which reviewed decisions by United States Customs officials concerning the amount of duties on imports in actions arising under the tariff acts) and the United States Customs Court which had essentially the same jurisdiction and powers. The President, with the advice and consent of the Senate, appoints the nine judges who constitute the Court of International Trade. Not more than five of the nine judges may belong to any one political party.

The geographical jurisdiction of the Court of International Trade extends throughout the United States, and it is also authorized to hold hearings in foreign countries. The court has exclusive subject matter jurisdiction to decide any civil action commenced against the United States, its agencies or its officers arising from any law pertaining to revenue from imports, tariffs, duties or embargoes or enforcement of these and other customs regulations. This includes disputes regarding trade embargoes, quotas, customs classification and valuation, country of origin determinations and denials of protests by the U.S. Customs Service.

The court's exclusive jurisdiction also includes any civil action commenced by the United States that arises out of an import transaction, and authority to review final agency decisions concerning antidumping and countervailing duty matters, the eligibility of workers, firms and communities who are economically harmed by foreign imports for trade adjustment assistance, disputes concerning the release of confidential business information, and decisions to deny, revoke or suspend the licenses of customs brokers. However, the CIT does not have jurisdiction over disputes involving restrictions on imported merchandise where public safety or health issues are raised. This limitation on CIT jurisdiction arises because such issues involving domestic goods would be determined by other regulatory bodies, and only referral to United States District Courts can ensure uniform treatment of both imports and domestically produced goods.

The standard for the judicial review exercised by the CIT varies from case to case. In some instances, such as confidentiality orders, a de novo trial is undertaken. In others, notably antidumping and countervailing duty cases, the standard is one of substantial evidence, or arbitrary, capricious or unlawful action, or an abuse of discretion. In trade adjustment assistance litigation, the administrative determinations are considered conclusive absent substantial evidentiary support in the record with the CIT empowered to order the taking of further evidence. Unless otherwise specified by statute, the Administrative Procedure Act governs the judicial review by the CIT of U.S. international trade law.

The CIT possesses all the remedial powers, legal and equitable, of a United States District Court, including authority to enter money judgments for or against the United States, but with three limitations. First, in an action challenging a trade adjustment ruling, the court may not issue an injunction or writ of mandamus. Second, the CIT may order disclosure of confidential information only as specified in Section 777(c)(2) of the Tariff Act of 1930. Third, the CIT may order only declaratory relief for suits brought under the provision allowing the court accelerated review because of a showing of irreparable harm.

The CIT must ordinarily give substantial due deference to Customs Service regulations under *Chevron* rules (467 U.S. 837 (1984) even when undertaking de novo review. However, the Supreme Court has ruled that *Chevron* does not apply to product classification decisions by the Customs Service. *United States v. Mead Corp.*, 533 U.S. 218 (2001). CIT decisions are first appealed to the Court of Appeals for the Federal Circuit (formerly to the Court of Customs and Patent Appeals), and ultimately to the United States Supreme Court.

The United States Trade Representative (USTR)

In response to Section 1104 of the Trade Agreements Act of 1979, the President reviewed the structure of the international trade functions of the Executive Branch. Although this did not lead to the establishment of a new Department of International Trade and Investment, it did lead to enhancement of the Office of the Special Representative for Trade Negotiations, which has since been renamed the United States Trade Representative (USTR). The powers of the USTR were expanded and its authority given a legislative foundation. The USTR is appointed by the President, with the advice and consent of the Senate. The Office of the USTR has been the principal vehicle through which tariff and trade negotiations have been conducted on behalf of the United States. Among other things, the USTR has had continuing responsibility in connection with implementation of the WTO Agreements and U.S. free trade agreements. The USTR is the contact point for persons who desire an investigation of instances of noncompliance with any trade agreement.

In 1988, the duties of the USTR were significantly expanded in conjunction with an overhaul of Section 301 of the Trade Act of 1974. Section 301 creates a controversial unilateral trade remedy which principally has been used to obtain foreign market access for U.S. exports, but can also be used to control imports, as President Trump plans to do with Chinese exports. See Chapter 8 . Prior to 1988, the President directly administered Section 301. Thereafter, as amended by the Omnibus Trade and Competitiveness Act, the USTR assumed this role along with new duties governing the Super 301 and Special 301 procedures created in 1988. Moreover, since the 1988 Act expanded the coverage of Section 301 and introduced mandatory (not discretionary) remedies, the USTR became centrally involved in many domestic industry complaints about foreign governments. See Chapter 4.

UNITED STATES TRADE LAWS

Rules and sources of law for United States international trade are mostly found in a sequence of specific trade acts which make up the basic framework for import and export trade. To these, however, must be added numerous provisions of other laws which are directed to specific trade issues. For example, the Export Administration Act of 1979 details U.S. export controls, the subject of Chapter 5. United States trade case law tends to be limited. Trade rules have evolved in legislative chambers and multilateral organizations rather than in the courts. There is really no common law of trade; the decisions which do exist are almost exclusively interpretations of the statutory rules.

For U.S. international trade law, there is no easy single statutory source of law. New trade statutes do two things. They create some new trade rules and thus have some permanency standing alone. But they also modify earlier trade statutes. Thus a search often requires checking several U.S. trade laws, although certain subjects tend to be identified with a single trade Act. For example, the Tariff Act of 1930 is where the tariff schedules are located along with several U.S. "trade remedies" for domestic interests impacted by imports.

The Trade Act of 1974 is where rules governing trade with less favored nations, those not benefitting from "normal" MFN status, are found. It is a source of trade rules for more than most favored nations, for example those benefitting duty free entry under the Generalized System of Preferences (GSP) program. The Trade Agreements Act of 1979, the Omnibus Trade and Competitiveness Act of 1988, the Uruguay Round Implementation Act of 1994, the Trade Act of 2002 and the Trade Preferences Extension Act of 2015 cover a number of GATT/WTO trade rules.

Trade is thus governed principally by a matrix of separate U.S. trade laws ranging from the Tariff Act of 1930 to the Trade Preferences Extension Act of 2015.

These are not the only laws which govern United States trade. There are many other acts which regulate trade, some of which appear as amendments to other laws. For example, the Foreign Corrupt Practices Act of 1977, intended to reduce the making of improper payments to government officials abroad, is a relatively brief Act which modifies trade and the securities laws. See Chapter 5. The Caribbean Basin Economic Recovery Act of 1983, and the Africa Growth and Opportunity Act of 2000 extend special duty free import rights to goods from those developing areas. The Buy American Act of 1933 grants government procurement preferences to U.S. manufacturers and service providers to the exclusion of many foreign suppliers.

All of these laws provide the basic domestic law framework governing United States trade. When combined with United States obligations in international and regional organizations and agreements such as the WTO and NAFTA 1994, along with U.S. free trade agreements, one begins to understand the complexity and diversity of United States international trade and economic relations law.

U.S. IMPORT LAWS

The first of the principal laws regulating imports to the United States is the *Tariff Act of 1930*. This is the famous Smoot-Hawley Tariff Act, which raised tariff walls to substantial heights and worsened the world depression of the 1930s. The severe tariffs of Smoot-Hawley have since been largely diminished for those nations which benefit from most favored nation (MFN) "normal" tariff status, but remain on the books for a few less favored countries. One reason the 1930 Act remains in force is that it is the location of the hundreds of pages of tariffs—the U.S. Harmonized Tariff Schedules.

In addition to tariffs, the 1930 Act includes the organization and functions of the International Trade Commission. It controls some of the actions which the Commission may take, including of considerable importance, what are commonly referred to as Section 337 actions challenging unfair practices in import trade. There are extensive provisions for the promotion of foreign trade, and also a major provision protecting American trademarked goods from the entry of counterfeit products, Section 526. Finally, the Tariff Act of 1930 includes the United States rules governing country-specific countervailing (CVD) and antidumping (AD) tariff duties, retained under NAFTA 1994. For example, President Trump quickly imposed CVD on Canadian softwood lumber exports.

Other trade acts were enacted subsequent to the 1930 Act, notably the *Trade Expansion Act of 1962* allowing U.S. imposition of tariffs and other trade restraints in the name of "national security". President Trump employed this rarely used trade remedy to impose broad U.S. tariffs on steel and aluminum in 2018. See Chapter 7.

The next major statute important to U.S. international trade law is the *Trade Act of 1974*. This Act includes executive negotiating authority for trade agreements with other countries, the creation of the office of the United States Trade Representative, and provisions governing the interrelationship of Congress and the President with regard to trade relations. Furthermore, it includes global provisions regulating relief from injury caused by surging import competition, particularly Section 201 actions, known as "escape clause" or "safeguards" actions, used by President Trump in 2018 against solar panel and clothes washer imports. Part of the relief from safeguard injury includes adjustment assistance for workers, renewed in 2015.

Another title of the 1974 Act addresses the enforcement of United States rights under trade agreements, and beyond that, against discriminatory, unreasonable or unjustifiable foreign country practices, reflected in Section 301. President Trump revived this dormant unilateral trade remedy in 2018, focusing on Chinese technology transfer practices perceived to lie outside mandatory WTO dispute settlement jurisdiction.

A separate title governs trade relations with communist countries. These provisions include the little used but potentially important Section 406, allowing "market disruption" actions. Finally, the 1974 Trade Act includes the generalized system of preferences (GSP) scheme, which gives to certain developing nations duty free tariff status.

The *Trade Agreements Act of 1979* is the third important trade act. This Act was passed principally to implement several of the NTB codes negotiated in the Tokyo Round of the GATT, concluded in the mid-1970s. Thus, it has sections dealing with government procurement and technical barriers to trade (standards). Changes to the rules governing countervailing and antidumping duties, and to customs valuation, both part of newly adopted GATT codes, were implemented by this Act, but as amendments to the Tariff Act of 1930 rather than enduring provisions identified with the 1979 Act.

The fourth important act is the *Trade and Tariff Act of 1984.* In addition to making amendments to the earlier acts, this Act extended "fast track" negotiating authority (discussed below) to the President, which provided for the development of free trade agreements with Israel and Canada. The fifth act is the *Omnibus Trade and Competitiveness Act of 1988.* This Act authorized the President to enter into the Uruguay Round of GATT negotiations that led to the creation of the WTO. It also implemented the Harmonized Tariff Schedule of the United States. Special attention was devoted in the 1988 Act to amending Section 301 of the 1974 Trade Act. It is the source of the "Special 301" procedures whereby the United States targets nations with which it has major intellectual property disputes.

When the United States became a signatory to the North American Free Trade Agreement in 1993,

Congress soon thereafter enacted the *North American Free Trade Implementation Act*, which made NAFTA 1994 part of U.S. trade law. Similarly, when the United States became a signatory to the Agreement Establishing the World Trade Organization in 1994, and its extensive package of agreements and understandings, Congress enacted the *Uruguay Round Agreements Act of 1995*, which made the WTO a part of U.S. trade law. See Chapter 2.

The *Trade Act of 2002* renewed, after a notable lapse during the Clinton administration, "fast track" international trade negotiating authority for the President. It is under this authority that President George W. Bush concluded free trade agreements with Chile, Singapore, five Central American nations and the Dominican Republic (CAFTA-DR), Oman, Bahrain, Peru, Colombia, Panama, Morocco, South Korea and Australia. He also pursued agreement on other bilateral free trade deals, a Free Trade Area of the Americas, and the Doha Round of World Trade Organization negotiations, none of which were completed prior to the expiration of fast track in July 2007.

After a lapse, President Obama received fast track authority in 2015, notably to pursue negotiations on the Trans-Pacific Partnership (TPP) and the Transatlantic Trade and Investment Partnership (TTIP). In addition, the *Trade Preferences Extension Act of 2015* renewed various U.S. duty free entry programs, and also reauthorized trade adjustment assistance for impacted U.S workers and firms. A product of bipartisan efforts in Congress, the 2015 Act extended until June 30, 2018, well into the Trump Administration. In March of 2018, President Trump requested a three-year extension of fast track authority, which will happen automatically under the 2015 Act absent Congressional passage of a resolution rejecting the extension.

THE ORIGINS OF UNITED STATES TARIFFS

Article I, Section 8, of the United States Constitution authorizes Congress to levy uniform tariffs on imports. Tariff legislation must originate in the House of Representatives. Although tariffs were primarily viewed as revenue-raising measures at the founding of the nation, it was not long before tariffs became used for openly protectionist purposes. The Tariff Act of 1816 initiated this change in outlook.

During much of the 19th Century, the United States legislated heavy protective tariffs. These were justified as necessary to protect the country's infant industries and to force the South to engage in more trade with the North (not with Europe). Exceptions were made to the high level of tariffs for selected United States imports. These typically flowed from conditional most-favored-nation reciprocity treaties. The first of these treaties involved Canada (1854) and Hawaii (1875).

As the United States moved into the 20th Century, additional tariffs in excess of the already high level of protection were authorized. "Countervailing duty" tariffs were created in 1890 to combat export subsidies of European nations, particularly

Germany. After 1916, additional duties could also be assessed if "dumping practices" were involved. Early American dumping legislation was largely a reaction to marketplace competition from foreign cartels.

Throughout all of these years the constitutionality of protective tariffs was never clearly resolved. In 1928, however, the United States Supreme Court firmly ruled that the enactment of protective tariffs was constitutional. This decision, followed by the crash of the stock market in 1929, led to the enactment of the Smoot-Hawley Tariff Act of 1930. This Act set some of the highest rates of tariff duties in the history of the United States. It represents the last piece of tariff legislation that Congress passed without international negotiations. These tariffs remain part of the United States law and are generally referred to as "Column 2 Tariffs" under the U.S. Harmonized Tariff Schedule (HTS).

Since 1930, changes in the levels of tariffs applicable to goods entering the United States have chiefly been achieved through international trade agreements negotiated by the President and affirmed by Congress. During the 1930s and 40s, the Smoot-Hawley tariffs generally applied unless altered through bilateral trade agreements. The Reciprocal Trade Agreements Act of 1934 gives the President the authority to enter into such agreements, and under various extensions this authority remains in effect today. An early agreement of this type was the Canadian Reciprocal Trade Agreement of 1935.

UNITED STATES TARIFF RATES

United States tariffs generally take one of three forms. The most common is an *ad valorem* rate. Such tariffs are assessed in proportion to the value of the article. Tariffs may also be assessed at specific rates or compound rates. Specific rates may be measured by the pound or other weight. A compound rate is a mixture of an *ad valorem* and specific rate tariff. Tariff rate quotas involve limitations on imports at a specific tariff up to a certain amount. Imports in excess of that amount are not prohibited, but are subject to a higher rate of tariff. Thus tariff rate quotas tend to restrict imports that are in excess of the specified quota for the lower tariff level.

These are three sets of United States tariff rates:

Column 1 General,

Column 1 Special, and

Column 2.

Column 1 General tariff rates, known as most favored-nation (MFN) or "normal" tariffs, are the lower and most likely to be applicable. Column 2 tariff rates, originating in the Smoot-Hawley Tariff Act of 1930, are the higher and least likely to be applicable.

In addition, there are a variety of selective Column 1 Special provisions, usually duty free entry programs to which the U.S. subscribes. These include the Generalized System of Tariff Preferences of the United States (GSP), the Caribbean Basin Initiative, the Africa Growth and Opportunity Act, the Hope for

Haiti program, and Section 9802.00.80 of the HTS. The North American Free Trade Agreement (NAFTA 1994), the Central American Free Trade Agreement (CAFTA 2005) and a growing number of bilateral U.S. free trade agreements, also generally provide for duty free access. See Chapter 7.

Column One "Normal" Tariffs and the GATT

The Trade Agreements Extension Act of 1945 authorized the President to conduct multilateral negotiations in the trade field. It was out of this authority that the General Agreement on Tariffs and Trade (GATT 1947) was negotiated. The GATT became effective on January 1, 1948 and was implemented in the United States by executive order. Indeed, despite a wide-ranging impact on United States tariff levels between 1948 and 1994, GATT 1947 was never ratified by the United States Congress. It was replaced in 1995 with GATT 1994, one of the many WTO agreements ratified by Congress.

GATT is the source of the principal tariffs assessed today on imports into the United States. These duties, known as most-favored-nation (MFN) tariffs or "Column 1 tariffs," have been dramatically reduced over the years through successive rounds of GATT/WTO trade negotiations. See Chapter 2. They are unconditional MFN tariffs, meaning that reciprocity is not required in order for them to apply to WTO member nations.

The term "most-favored-nation" is misleading in its suggestion of special tariff arrangements. It is more appropriate and officially correct to think of MFN tariffs as the "normal" level of U.S. tariffs, to which there are exceptions resulting in the application of higher, lower or zero tariffs. At this point, the average MFN tariff applied to manufactured imports into the United States is approximately 3.5 percent.

Column 1 (MFN) tariff status for exports to the United States can also be obtained under U.S. bilateral trade agreements. Chinese goods enjoyed such status long before WTO membership, but were subject to the "Jackson-Vanik Amendment." This provision of the 1974 Trade Act requires tolerably liberal emigration policies of nonmarket economy nations for U.S. Column 1 tariff status to apply. Chinese and Vietnamese goods qualified under the Jackson-Vanik for normal MFN treatment prior to WTO membership for China in 2001 and Vietnam in 2007. Each year the President issued a "waiver" to facilitate these outcomes.

As of 2018, Jackson-Vanik still applies to most Central Asian nations, including Kazakstan, Uzbekistan, Turkmenistan, and Tjikistan, as well as Belarus, although all receive MFN tariff treatment on an annual basis through biannual compliance reports or waivers.

Additional U.S. Tariffs

In addition to its GATT/WTO negotiated MFN normal tariffs, the United States and other WTO member states are authorized in appropriate circumstances to assess special tariffs. Antidumping duties (AD) are authorized to counteract dumping practices (sales of goods abroad at prices below those in the country of export). Countervailing tariffs (CVD) are authorized in response to selected foreign government subsidies that benefit their exports. Occasionally, as well, additional tariffs may be assessed under Safeguard (escape clause) proceedings when imports surge. U.S. tariffs can be applied in the name of "national security", and under unilateral Section 301 proceedings against foreign government conduct. These special, additional U.S. tariffs are covered in Chapter 4 on Trade Remedies and have risen in prominence under President Trump's protective America First programs (Chapter 7).

Additional U.S. tariffs can also be levied as "authorized retaliation" under WTO (Chapter 2) and U.S. free trade agreement (Chapter 6) rules.

Foreign Trade Zones

"Free trade zones" are located throughout the U.S., many of them near ports and airports. While imported goods remain in the zones, they are not subject to U.S. tariffs. The imported goods are subject to U.S. tariffs when they leave the zones, but only if they are then brought into the United States. If they are exported from the free trade zone to another country, they will never be subjected to U.S. tariffs.

Such zones serve as distribution centers, encourage assembly of certain manufactured items for export, provide local employment, and may lessen overall tariffs which must be paid before an assembled item crosses the zone for routine importation into the country. In the U.S., these zones are supervised by the Foreign Trade Zones Board (located within the Commerce Department) and by the Customs Service.

U.S. CUSTOMS LAW

Trillions of dollars of imports enter the United States each year. To calculate U.S. import duties, you must first determine the classification, country of origin and the customs valuation of imported goods. In other words, what is it, where is it from, and what is its customs value?

Customs Classification

Imported goods must "pass customs". Usually, the passage through customs and physical entry into a country occur simultaneously. When goods arrive at the United States border, the consignee (or an agent, such as a customs broker) files both "entry" and "entry summary" forms which are used to determine the classification, valuation, origin and conformity to product standards of the imported goods. At the same time, a deposit of the amount of estimated customs duties is made with customs officials. A procedure for immediate release of imported goods is available, as is the use of consolidated periodic statements for all entries made during a billing period.

The classification problem may be illustrated as follows: Are parts of a wooden picture frame, imported piece by piece in separate packages for later assembly within a country, to be assessed duties prescribed for wood picture frames or for strips of wood molding? Is "wood picture frame" even an appropriate nomenclature, or should what is commonly known to be a wood picture frame have a tariff nomenclature of "art object" or "forest product" or simply "personal belonging"?

For decades, most of the countries in the world, except the United States and Canada, classified imports according to the Brussels Tariff Nomenclature (BTN), which identifies items along a progression from raw materials to finished products. The United States had its own system of classification set out in the Tariff Schedule of the United States (TSUS). However, beginning in 1982, the United States initiated steps to convert the TSUS into a Harmonized Commodity Description and Coding System (HS) of classification, in common with the classification system developed by the World Customs Organization in Brussels.

The United States adopted the Harmonized System as the Harmonized Tariff Schedule (HTSUS) for classification of all imports by enactment of the Omnibus Trade and Competitiveness Act of 1988, with an effective date of Jan. 1, 1989. Most nations have adopted HTS and use it to classify U.S. exports.

The HTS "nomenclature" has twenty sections, the majority of which group articles from similar branches of industry or commerce. For example, Section I covers live animals and animal products, Section II vegetable products, Section III animal or vegetable fats, Section IV prepared foodstuffs, and Section V mineral products. The twenty sections are subdivided into 99 chapters, which in total list approximately 5,000 article descriptions in the heading and sub-heading format. These provisions apply to all goods entering the customs territory of the United States.

Most problems arise when it is possible to classify imported goods under more than one heading. For example, the U.S. tariff on autos (including SUVs) is 2.5%, but 25% on pick-up trucks and cargo vans. Ford produced cargo vans in Turkey, temporarily adding a second row of seats, windows and foot-wells for passage through U.S. customs as an auto. These items were removed and recycled, and the cargo van became itself again, once the U.S. border was crossed. What classification applies? Can Ford game the customs classification system?

If the importer and the United States customs officials disagree about the proper classification of an imported item, and appeals within the U.S. customs service fail to resolve the dispute, the United States Court of International Trade (CIT) has exclusive jurisdiction. The CIT ruled Ford's vehicles from Turkey were autos not cargo vans!

In cases decided under the prior Tariff Schedule of the United States (TSUS), the CIT followed its own logic, without reference to decisions of other courts, because the approach of the U.S. TSUS was so unique. In the cases decided under HTSUS, the CIT has continued this tradition in its decisions under the new classification system, rather than viewing the decisions of foreign courts or the Rules accompanying the HTS as persuasive.

The U.S. Supreme Court notably held in *United States v. Mead Corp.*, 533 U.S. 218 (2001) that Customs Service classification rulings are not entitled to full administrative deference. Rather, such rulings are entitled to limited deference depending on their "thoroughness, logic and expertness, fit with prior interpretations, and any other sources of weight."

Rules of Origin for Goods

Tariff schedules often provide that duties on an imported item vary depending upon the country from which the item comes. Hence, where goods are from, legally speaking, matters. To resolve this issue, "rules of origin" come into play. Two common situations raising questions of origin involve products shipped to the United States from Country "X" that have been manufactured in Country "Y", and products shipped to the United States from Country "X", in which the product was made, but certain component parts of the product have originated in Country "Y".

Under U.S. "rules of origin" an article is a product of a country if it is *wholly* the growth, product, or manufacture of that country. Minerals, farm products and timber are classic examples of clear national origin.

When an article which consists in whole or in part of materials from another country, U.S. rules of origin vary. The base line U.S. rule of origin is that a product originates where it has been last "substantially transformed" into a new and different article of commerce with a name, character, or use distinct from that of the article or articles from which it was so transformed. This core "substantial transformation" test is relevant, for example, in determining the rate at which U.S. customs duty is charged (MFN or not). The substantial transformation test is generally the fallback rule of origin for goods, absent specific U.S. provisions to the contrary, which are numerous.

Special rules of origin apply to the various U.S. duty free entry programs (see below) which rely principally on changes in tariff classifications and regional value content to determine which goods may freely be traded. The Court of International Trade requires importers seeking preferential or duty free tariff treatment to verify the country of origin of their goods. "Reasonable care" must be exercised, not just simple reliance on the exporter's assertions of origin. Failures in this regard can result in collection of lost duties and penalties.

Under the 1995 WTO Agreement on Rules of Origin, there is an effort to harmonize the rules of origin on a world-wide basis. A committee of experts was charged with creating rules which are "objective, understandable, and predictable." More than 20 years later, no WTO agreement on rules of origin has emerged. *This leaves each nation in charge of developing its own rules of origin for goods.* Not surprisingly, there are significant, frequently contested differences.

Customs Valuation

Even though an imported item may be classified, have an ascertainable legal origin, and a clear-cut percentage rate of duty, difficulty may still arise in getting the importer and customs authorities to agree upon the item's value to which that percentage applies. For decades, United States customs valuation of an imported item was gauged by the American Selling Price (ASP) of the item—i.e., the usual wholesale price at which the same item manufactured in the United States was offered for sale.

However, Article 7 of GATT 1947 requires that "value for customs purposes. . .should not be based on the value of merchandise of national origin or on arbitrary or fictitious values." The 1979 Tokyo Round produced a Customs Valuation Code, which established the details of an approach which was quite different from ASP. This approach was incorporated into the U.S. Trade Agreements Act of 1979.

United States customs valuation is now generally calculated as the arms-length "transaction value" of the imported item. "Transaction value" is "the price actually paid or payable for the merchandise when sold for exportation to the United States" plus "certain amounts reflecting packing costs, commissions paid by buyer, any assist, royalty or license fee paid by buyer, and any resale, disposal, or use proceeds that accrue to seller." Normally, transaction value can be easily determined from the invoice. But problems can arise when "double invoicing" (customs fraud) occurs: There is one true invoice and another lower priced invoice to reduce tariff duties. In addition, when the transaction is between affiliated businesses, that is to say not arms-length, valid invoice prices will not suffice to clear customs.

If an arms-length transaction value cannot be determined, certain fallback methods are used. In descending order of eligibility these methods are: The transaction value of identical merchandise, the transaction value of similar merchandise, the resale price of the merchandise with allowances for certain factors, or the cost of producing the imported item.

These approaches to valuation form the core of the new Agreement on Implementation of Article 7 of GATT 1994 (WTO Customs Code). Hence, unlike rules of origin, WTO member states have adopted a uniform approach to customs valuation law.

U.S. IMPORT QUOTAS, VOLUNTARY EXPORT RESTRAINTS

Goods imported into the United States may have to qualify within numerical quota limitations imposed on that item or upon that kind of item. "Tariff-rate quotas" admit a specified quantity of goods at a preferential rate of duty. Once imports reach that quantity, tariffs are normally increased.

The United States has employed import quotas for many years. Tariff-rate quotas have been applied to dairy products, olives, tuna fish, anchovies, brooms, and sugar, syrups and molasses. Quite a few absolute quotas originate under Section 22 of the Agricultural Adjustment Act. These quotas are undertaken when necessary to United States farm price supports or similar agricultural programs. They have been used on animal feeds, dairy products, chocolate, cotton, peanuts, and selected syrups and sugars.

Some U.S. agricultural quotas have been converted into tariffs under the WTO Agreement on Agriculture. Some quotas imposed by the U.S. are sanctions for unfair trade practices, as was the case against tungsten from China. Major quota restraints on textile imports were achieved as a result of the GATT-authorized international Multi-Fiber Arrangement, which expired in 2005 under the WTO Textiles Agreement. Global trade in textiles and apparel is now normally quota free, significantly benefitting China and other Asian producers.

The Agricultural Act of 1949 requires the President to impose global import quotas on Upland Cotton. Whenever the Secretary of Agriculture determines that its average price exceeds certain statutory limits, unlike the ordinary restrictive import quota, the importation of Upland Cotton is duty free. Like the U.S. Meat Import Act, this provision tends to be countercyclical to market forces for cotton in the United States. A U.S. cotton subsidy system was ruled invalid by the WTO Appellate Body in a dispute brought by Brazil, but the U.S. is essentially paying Brazil not to retaliate as authorized.

Lastly, the United States sometimes imposes import restraints for national security or foreign policy reasons. Many of these restraints originate from Section 232 of the Trade Expansion Act of 1962. This provision authorizes the President to "adjust imports" whenever necessary to the national security of the country. President Trump invoked Section 232 in 2018 to impose tariffs (not quotas) on U.S. steel and aluminum imports. Chapter 8.

Trade embargoes (zero quotas) are sometimes imposed on all the goods from politically incorrect nations (e.g., North Korea, Cuba). Product-specific import bans also exist for selected goods, e.g., narcotic drugs and books urging insurrection against the United States. The importation of "immoral" goods is generally prohibited, even for private use, and the obscenity of such items is decided by reviewing the community standards at the port of entry. Generally, goods produced with forced, convict, indentured or the "worst forms" of child labor are excluded from the United States. For example, the ban against goods produced by convicts has been applied to certain items from the People's Republic of China.

If a quota system is created, a fundamental subsidiary issue is: How will the quotas be allocated? The U.S. Customs Service generally administers quotas on a first-come, first-served basis. This approach creates a race to enter goods into the United States. The President is authorized to sell import licenses at public auctions. One advantage of an auction system is its revenue raising potential. Instead of an auction system, the U.S. has ordinarily used a Presidentially-managed system of import allocations, especially in regard to agricultural import quotas.

In the past, quotas were often part of a "voluntary export restraint" (VER) or orderly market agreement (OMA) between the U.S. and one or more foreign governments, and represented adherence by those governments to U.S. initiatives. The negotiations typically concentrated on obtaining foreign government agreement to limitations on exportation of their products into the U.S. market, and did not pursue rules on who might use the resulting allocations. A classic example for many years was Japanese "voluntary" restraints on exporting autos to the United States negotiated by President Reagan at a time when U.S. producers were lagging behind Japanese car styling, fuel efficiency and quality. Korea's 2018 re-negotiated free trade agreement with the United States includes voluntary export restraints on steel. The WTO Agreement on Safeguards severely limits the use of VERs and OMAs. See Chapters 4 and 8.

U.S. PUBLIC PROCUREMENT

Where public procurement is involved, and the taxpayer's money is at issue, virtually every nation has some form of legislation or tradition that favors buying from domestic suppliers. In federal nations like the United States, these rules can also be found in state and local purchasing requirements.

The principal United States statute affecting imports in connection with government procurement is the Buy American Act of 1933. This Act requires the government to buy American unless the acquisition is for use outside the U.S., there are insufficient quantities of satisfactory quality available in the U.S., or domestic purchases would be inconsistent with the public interest or result in unreasonable costs.

Buy American

As currently applied, the United States Buy American Act requires federal agencies to treat a domestic bid as unreasonable or inconsistent with the public interest only if it exceeds a foreign bid by more than six percent (customs duties included) or ten percent (customs duties and specific costs excluded). Exceptions to this general approach exist for reasons of national interest, certain designated small business purchases, domestic suppliers operating in areas of substantial unemployment and demonstrated national security needs. Bids by small businesses and companies located in labor surplus areas are generally protected by a 12 percent margin of preference. Bids from U.S. companies are considered foreign rather than domestic when the materials used in the products concerned are below 50 percent American in origin. These rules apply to civil purchasing by the United States government, but are suspended for purchasing subject to the WTO Procurement Code.

The Department of Defense has its own Buy American rules. Generally speaking, a 50 percent price preference (customs duties excluded) or a 6 or 12 percent preference (customs duties included) whichever is more protective to domestic suppliers is applied. However, intergovernmental "Memoranda of Understanding" (MOU) on defense procurement provide important exceptions to the standard Department of Defense procurement rules.

A practice known as "unbalanced bidding" has arisen in connection with the Buy American Act. Unbalanced bidding involves the use of United States labor and parts by foreigners in sufficient degree so as to overcome the bidding preferences established by law for U.S. suppliers. This occurs because the United States value added is *not* included in the calculations of the margin of preference for the U.S. firms. Thus foreign bids minus the value of work done in the U.S. are multiplied by the 6, 12 or 50 percent Buy American Act preference. If the U.S. bids are above the foreign bids but within the margin of preference, the U.S. firm gets the contract. If the U.S. bids are higher than the foreign bids plus the margin of preference, the foreigners get the contract.

Additional procurement preferences are established by the Small Business Act of 1953. Under this Act, federal agencies may set aside certain procurement exclusively for small U.S. businesses. In practice, the federal government normally sets aside about 30 percent of its procurement needs in this fashion. Special set-aside rules apply to benefit socially and economically disadvantaged minority-owned businesses. These preferences are generally not altered by U.S. adherence to the WTO Procurement Code.

A number of federal statutes also contain specific Buy American requirements. These include various GSA, NASA and TVA appropriations bills, the AMTRAK Improvement Act of 1978, the Public Works Employment Act of 1977, various highway and transport acts, the Clean Water Act of 1977, and the Rural Electrification Acts of 1936 and 1938. Many of these statutes involve federal funding of state and local procurement. All are generally excluded from the WTO Procurement Code as applied by the United States.

In addition to the Buy American Act, state and local purchasing requirements may inhibit import competition in the procurement field. For example, California once had a law which made it mandatory to purchase American products. This law was declared unconstitutional as an encroachment upon the federal power to conduct foreign affairs. A Massachusetts ban on contracting with companies with investments in Myanmar (Burma) was likewise struck down. See *Crosby v. National Foreign Trade Council,* 530 U.S. 363 (2000).

State statutes which have copied the federal Buy American Act, on the other hand, and incorporated public interest and unreasonable cost exceptions to procurement preferences, have generally withstood constitutional challenge. For example, courts have upheld New Jersey laws fashioned in this manner. Courts have also declared lawful a Pennsylvania statute that requires state and local agencies to ensure that contractors do not provide products containing foreign steel.

GATT 1947 Procurement Code and U.S. Response

The Buy American Act was conformed to the optional GATT 1947 Procurement Code negotiated during the Tokyo Round. That Code did not apply to state and local purchasing. Congress expressed its displeasure with the degree to which that Code opened up sales opportunities for United States firms abroad. It therefore amended the Buy American Act in 1988 to deny the benefits of the GATT Procurement Code when foreign governments are not in good standing under it. United States government procurement contracts are also denied to suppliers from countries whose governments "maintain. . .a significant and persistent pattern of practice or discrimination against U.S. products or services which results in identifiable harm to U.S. businesses."

Presidential waivers of these statutory denials may occur in the public interest, to avoid single supply situations or to assure sufficient bidders to provide supplies of requisite quality and competitive prices.

The European Union was one of the first to be identified as a persistent procurement discriminator by the USTR. This identification concerned longstanding heavy electrical and telecommunications disputes that were partly settled by negotiation with the EU. The remaining disputes led to U.S. trade sanctions and EU retaliation. This did not occur with Greece, Spain and Portugal (where the EU procurement rules did not apply), and with

Germany which broke ranks and negotiated a path breaking bilateral U.S. settlement. Japan has also been identified as a persistent procurement discriminator in the construction, architectural and engineering areas.

The Tokyo Round GATT Procurement Code was not particularly successful at opening up government purchasing. Only Austria, Canada, the twelve European Union states, Finland, Hong Kong, Israel, Japan, Norway, Singapore, Sweden, Switzerland and the United States adhered to that Procurement Code. This was also partly the result of the 1979 Code's many exceptions. For example, the Code did not apply to contracts below its threshold amount of $150,000 SDR (about $171,000 since 1988), service contracts, and procurement by entities on each country's reserve list (including most national defense items).

Because procurement in the European Union and Japan is often decentralized, many contracts fell below the SDR threshold and were therefore GATT exempt. By dividing up procurement into smaller contracts national preferences were retained. United States government procurement tended to be more centralized and thus more likely to be covered by the GATT Code. This pattern may help explain why Congress restrictively amended the Buy American Act in 1988.

WTO Procurement Code

The WTO Procurement Code took effect in 1996 and replaced the 1979 Tokyo Round Code. It remains optional for WTO members and again participation is generally limited to developed nations. The WTO Code expanded the coverage of the prior Code to include procurement of services, construction, government-owned utilities, and some state and local (sub-central) contracts. The U.S. and the European Union applied the new Code's provisions on government-owned utilities and sub-central contracts as early as 1994.

Various improvements to the procedural rules surrounding procurement practices and dispute settlement under the WTO Code attempt to reduce tensions in this difficult area. For example, an elaborate system for bid protests is established. Bidders who believe the Code's procedural rules have been abused will be able to lodge, litigate and appeal their protests. The Procurement Code became part of U.S. law in 1994 under the Uruguay Round Agreements Act.

The United States has brought, with few exceptions, all procurement by executive agencies subject to the Federal Acquisition Regulations under the Code's coverage. This has the effect of suspending application of the normal Buy American preferences to such procurement. That said, thirteen U.S. states have not conformed to the WTO Procurement Code.

Further, the United States, amid considerable controversy, adopted "Buy American" steel rules in the Obama administration economic stimulus plan (the American Recovery and Reinvestment Act of 2009), exempting WTO Procurement Code participants and U.S. free trade agreements.

Additional Buy American preferences were created by the Obama administration auto bail-out plans and other legislation. This pattern has continued under President Trump, who for example mandated U.S.-made pipes in approved pipeline projects.

U.S. PRODUCT STANDARDS

There are numerous nontariff trade barriers applicable to United States imports. Many of these barriers arise out of federal or state safety and health regulations. Others concern the environment, consumer protection, product standards and government procurement. Many of the relevant rules were created for legitimate consumer and public protection reasons. They were often created without extensive consideration of their international impact as potential nontariff barriers. Nevertheless, the practical impact of legislation of this type is to ban the importation of nonconforming products from the United States market. Thus, unlike tariffs which can always be paid and unlike quotas which permit a certain amount of goods to enter the United States market, nontariff barriers have the potential to totally exclude foreign exports.

The diversity of U.S. regulatory approaches to products and the environment makes it extremely difficult to generalize about nontariff trade barriers. In 2008, all imports of plants and wood products (even toothpicks) were subjected to new disclosure duties that may inhibit trade. All foods imported into the United States are subject to inspection for their wholesomeness, freedom from contamination, and compliance with labeling requirements (including the 1993 nutritional labeling rules). This examination is conducted by the Food and Drug Administration using samples submitted to it by the United States Customs Service. If these tests result in a finding that the food products cannot be imported into the United States, they must be exported or destroyed.

The Consumer Products Safety Act bars the importation of consumer products which do not comply with the standards of the Consumer Products Safety Commission. Exporters of consumer products must certify that their goods conform to applicable United States safety and labeling standards. Any product that has a defect which is determined to constitute a "substantial product hazard" or is imminently hazardous may be banned from the United States market. The Customs Service may seize any such nonconforming goods. These goods may be modified in order to conform them to U.S. Consumer Products Safety Commission requirements. Otherwise, such goods must be exported or destroyed, an end result notably applied in 2007 to children's toys from China.

The Bioterrorism Act of 2002 requires all U.S. and foreign food companies selling in the United States to register with the Food and Drug Administration. Importers must notify the FDA in advance and in detail of food shipments, and keep records of suppliers and customers. The FDA can detain any food deemed a risk, including late or missing notice items.

Generally speaking, the United States maintains an open market for competitive trade in services. One major exception is maritime transport. In this area, the U.S. protects its domestic industry from import competition under the Merchant Marine Act of 1920 ("Jones Act") and other statutes. For example, the shipment of Alaskan oil is reserved for U.S.-flag vessels as is the supply of offshore drill rigs. The Jones Act most notably prohibits foreign vessels from transporting goods or passengers between U.S. ports and on U.S. rivers, lakes and canals. The reservation of goods for U.S.-flag ships (such trade is known as cabotage) is very significant economically, amounting to some billions annually with a heavy concentration in petroleum products.

United States environmental or conservation laws notably affecting international trade include:

- The Endangered Species Act of 1973 prohibiting import/export of endangered species.

- The "Pelley Amendment" authorizing import restraints against fish products of nations undermining international fisheries or wildlife conservation agreements.

- The High Seas Driftnet Fisheries Enforcement Act of 1992 banning imports of fish, fish products and sport fishing gear from countries violating the United Nations driftnet moratorium.

- The Sea Turtle Conservation Act prohibiting shrimp imports harvested with adverse effects on sea turtles first used in 1993 against shrimp from several Caribbean nations and now applicable globally to Thailand, India, China and Bangladesh among others.

- The Wild Bird Conservation Act banning imports of tropical wild birds.

- The Antarctic Marine Living Resources Convention Act prohibiting import/export of living resources.

- The African Elephant Conservation Act restricting ivory imports.

- The Lacey Act prohibiting imports of fish, wildlife, plant and wood that violate foreign laws.

WTO Product Standards Law

Under United States law, state and federal agencies may create standards which specify the characteristics of a product, such as levels of quality, safety, performance or dimensions, or its packaging and labeling. However, in accordance with the WTO Technical Barriers to Trade Agreement (Standards Code), these "standards-related activities" must not create "unnecessary obstacles to U.S. foreign trade," and must be demonstrably related to "a legitimate domestic objective" such as protection of health and safety, security, environmental or consumer interests.

Sometimes there is a conflict between federal and state standards. For example, federal law licensing endangered species' articles preempted California's absolute ban on trade in such goods. The Office of the USTR is charged with responsibility for implementation of the WTO Standards Code within the United States.

United States standards have been attacked as nontariff trade barriers violating international obligations. Sometimes the standards have been upheld, sometimes not. For example, a binational arbitration panel established under Chapter 18 of the Canada-U.S. FTA issued a decision upholding a United States law setting a minimum size on lobsters sold in interstate commerce. The panel found that, since the law applied to both domestic and foreign lobsters, it was not a disguised trade restriction.

In 2012, the WTO Appellate Body determined that the United States ban on flavored cigarettes, as applied to clove cigarettes from Indonesia, breached the WTO Technical Barriers to Trade (TBT) Code national treatment standard. The Appellate Body noted particularly the discriminatory allowance for sale in the U.S. of menthol flavored cigarettes.

Tuna, Shrimp and Beef Disputes

In 1991, a GATT panel found that United States import restrictions designed to protect dolphin from tuna fishers violated GATT 1947. The panel ruled that GATT did not permit any import restrictions based on extraterritorial environmental concerns, whether they were considered disguised trade restrictions or not. This decision suggested difficulty with a number of United States laws which concern health, safety and environmental conditions in exporting nations.

A 1994 decision by a second GATT 1947 panel recognized the legitimacy of environmental regulations, but ruled against the tuna boycott by the U.S. because of its focus on production methods and the unilateral imposition of standards by the U.S. In 1997, Congress enacted legislation that replaced the domestic controls on imported tuna with international restrictions stated in the Declaration of Panama. This Declaration, with internationally accepted standards, finally placed U.S. tuna legislation in conformity with its GATT/WTO obligations.

Nevertheless, in 2008, Mexico initiated WTO proceedings against U.S. "dolphin-safe" label rules and a Ninth Circuit decision requiring zero use of purse seine nets for such labels. In 2010, the U.S. commenced NAFTA 1994 proceedings seeking to force Mexico to withdraw its WTO complaint and re-file it under NAFTA. "Standards" disputes are supposed to be resolved exclusively under NAFTA Chapter 20 procedures and trade rules that strongly favor national laws. In 2011, a WTO panel held in favor of Mexico's complaint, which Mexico declined to re-file under NAFTA. The WTO Appellate Body affirmed, ruling that the U.S. dolphin-safe label rules violated the national treatment standard of the WTO TBT Code.

In 1998 the WTO Appellate Body ruled against a U.S. ban on shrimp imports from nations that fail to use turtle exclusion devices comparable to those required under U.S. law. The Appellate Body found the U.S. ban undermined the multilateral GATT 1994 trading system because the security and predictability of the system would be compromised if other Members adopted similar measures. The unilateral use of extraterritorial measures to protect exhaustible natural resources was not "justifiable." The Appellate Body believed international agreement on the subject should be sought.

The standards of other nations have also been challenged as violations of WTO obligations. For example, the United States has challenged European Union bans of imports of meat from the United States, first for containing certain hormones, later for unsanitary conditions in U.S. meatpacking facilities. In the former controversy, the United States retaliated. In 1997 and again in 2008, the WTO Appellate Body ruled against the EU ban on hormone-treated beef, citing the lack of an adequate scientific basis for the ban as required under the WTO Sanitary and Phytosanitary (SPS) Agreement.

Import Labeling Disputes

The United States requires clear markings of countries of origin on imports. This can be perceived, especially by those abroad, as a nontariff trade barrier intended to promote domestic purchases. Section 304 of the Tariff act of 1930 establishes the basic rules for origin markings. Every imported article of foreign origin (or its container) must be marked conspicuously, legibly, indelibly and as permanently as practical in English so as to indicate to ultimate purchasers its country of origin. Violation of these rules can result in additional tariffs of up to 10 percent. Intentional removal or alteration of markings is a crime.

In 2008, as part of the Farm Bill, new Lacey Act import disclosure and country of origin requirements were broadly created for plants and wood products. Additional import disclosure and origin "COOL" rules for meat and meat products were also legislated in the 2008 Farm Bill. The COOL rules were successfully challenged by Canada and Mexico before the WTO. The Appellate Body declared them discriminatory, and violations of TBT Code national treatment obligations. The U.S. subsequently repealed the COOL rules.

TRANSBORDER DATA FLOWS

Because information transfers are linked with employment and trade patterns, many countries have taken a keen interest in regulating transborder data flows (TBDFs). Technical strides in satellite communications and the digital age make regulation a challenge. In 1981, the OECD approved fourteen principles as Guidelines on the Protection of Privacy and TransBorder Flow of Personal Data. In 1998, Europe finalized a data privacy directive that was noticeably more protective of individual privacy than U.S. law. Any information relating to natural persons must be secure, current, relevant and not excessive in content. In most cases, personal data may be processed only with individual consent. Individuals have broad rights of disclosure, access, correction and erasure of data, particularly before it is used in direct marketing.

Transfers of data to non-EU countries are prohibited unless the recipient jurisdiction provides an "adequate level of protection." Whether the United States does so is hotly debated. To remove risks of liability under the European law, "safe harbors" have been created by EU-USA agreements for firms willing to abide by the *EU* rules on data privacy enforced by *U.S.* authorities. The primary safe harbor involves participation in self-regulating privacy groups (e.g., BBB Online) supervised by the U.S. Federal Trade Commission. EU law on data privacy has thus become a global standard.

The EU enacted tighter revisions to its data privacy rules with major penalties in 2018 after an adverse European Court of Justice (ECJ) ruling suggested the initial "safe harbor" cooperation agreement with the United States was void. A new U.S.-EU safe harbor agreement on data exchanges, known as the Privacy Shield, is now in place and sure to be challenged before the ECJ. See R. Folsom, *European Union Law including BREXIT in a Nutshell.*

U.S. DUTY FREE GENERALIZED TARIFF PREFERENCES (GSP)

The Generalized System of Preferences (GSP) recognizes that economic development of the third world requires the assistance of industrialized nations, and grants preferences to products of developing countries without demanding reciprocity. In addition to obtaining MFN tariff rates, developing countries can ship goods *duty free* into U.S. and other major industrial markets under GSP. These special arrangements for developing countries are permitted by the provisions of GATT/WTO. They have been implemented by the U.S., the EU, Japan and other major "donor" nations, although each GSP program differs in structure and approach.

It was not until the Trade Act of 1974 that a GSP system was incorporated into United States tariff law. The Trade Act authorized GSP tariff preferences for ten years. Various GSP renewals have followed, including through 2020 at present. The United States GSP system, as presently operated, designates certain nations as "beneficiary developing countries." Unless a country is so designated, none of its imports can enter duty free under the GSP program. In addition, only selected goods are designated "eligible articles" for purposes of the GSP program. Thus, for duty free entry under the GSP program to occur, the goods must originate from a beneficiary nation and qualify as eligible articles.

Any United States producer of an article that competes with GSP imports can file a petition with the United States Trade Representative (USTR) to have a country or particular products withdrawn from the program. This petitioning procedure can also be used in the reverse by importers and exporters to obtain product or beneficiary country status under the United States GSP program. The

President is given broad authority to withdraw, suspend or limit the application of duty free entry under the GSP system.

Tens of billions worth of goods from well over 100 countries typically enter the U.S. market duty free under the GSP program, but it is estimated that more imports could achieve this status if traders better understood the GSP.

GSP Country Eligibility, Graduation

The designation of developing countries as eligible for the GSP benefits has always been to some extent politicized—e.g., by declaring all communist states and all but three OPEC member states to be ineligible. In addition, under 1984 amendments, the President must evaluate whether a country recognizes "internationally recognized worker's rights" and adequately protects intellectual property rights before that country can be designated as a GSP beneficiary. the President must also evaluate whether nations give more preferential treatment to imports from other developed nations than to U.S. products, assist terrorists, expropriate U.S. owned investments, refuse to cooperate in drug enforcement, or deny recognition of international arbitration awards.

In applying these country eligibility criteria, past Presidents have disqualified a variety of nations from the U.S. GSP program. For example, Romania, Nicaragua, Paraguay, Chile, Burma, the Central African Republic and Liberia have all been disqualified in the past for failure to meet the workers' rights standards. Argentina and Honduras have lost GSP benefits for perceived failures to adequately protect U.S. pharmaceutical patents. Panama under General Noriega was rendered ineligible because of the failure to cooperate on narcotics. Intellectual property piracy led to the suspension of Ukraine's country eligibility in the GSP program.

The President's review of a country's eligibility under the GSP program is ongoing. This led to the reinstatement of GSP beneficiary nations. Russia was made a GSP beneficiary by President Clinton, later removed by President Obama. China is not a GSP beneficiary. Any country designated as a beneficiary nation under the GSP program that is subsequently disqualified by exercise of Presidential discretion, or "graduated" (see below), must receive 60 days' notice from the President with an explanation of this decision. This, in effect, presents the opportunity to reply and negotiate.

1984 amendments required the President to complete a general review of all GSP products to determine whether they were "sufficiently competitive" to graduate. Graduation has had its greatest impact on so-called "newly industrialized countries." In 1989, South Korea, Taiwan, Hong Kong and Singapore were graduated entirely from the GSP list. At the same time, Bahrain, Brunei, Nauru and Bermuda were dropped from the list because their per capita GNP exceeded the statutory "competitive need" limit for country eligibility. In 2015, Seychelles, Uruguay and Venezuela were excluded for the same reason from GSP benefits. In 1995, the Bahamas and Israel were similarly dropped, and in 1997 Malaysia was entirely graduated. Russia was likewise graduated in 2014.

All developing nation U.S. free trade partners, for example Mexico, Jordan, Morocco, Colombia and Peru, have been removed from the GSP list of eligible countries.

GSP Product Eligibility, Removal

For each designated GSP beneficiary country, the President also issues a list of products from that country eligible for duty free entry into the United States. The statutory authorization for the United States GSP program generally excludes leather products, textiles and apparel, watches, selected electronics and, certain steel, footwear and categories of glass from being designated as eligible articles. All these goods are thought to involve particular "import sensitivity."

Products of particular GSP beneficiary countries can be added or removed to the list of GSP qualified goods by petition of interested persons. The petitions, and the resultant certification or de-certification, are determined by the U.S. Trade Representative, with the advice of the U.S. International Trade Commission (ITC). The criterion used is "import sensitivity," which means that American industry or labor must actively seek protection from this foreign competition. The tendency of the decisions has been not to displace American interests, and to regard the GSP benefits as a "gift" to developing countries.

The GSP rule of origin requires that the product be shipped directly from the beneficiary developing country to the United States. Where the goods are locally produced from local resources, there is no further problem. However, where the goods exported by the beneficiary country are produced from materials imported into the developing country, further analysis is necessary.

In such cases, the present GSP rule of origin requires that at least 35 percent of the value of an item be added within a developing country for the item to be considered as "originating" in that developing country. Thus, Toyotas manufactured in Japan, but shipped to the U.S. through a GSP beneficiary country, would not qualify for GSP duty free treatment. But Toyotas manufactured in the GSP beneficiary country from parts manufactured in Japan could so qualify, if the value of the parts aggregated only 60 percent of the value of the final product. In addition, the Federal Circuit Court of Appeals has ruled that the processing of goods in the GSP country must create two substantial transformations in the identity of the goods for GSP treatment to be available. See *Torrington Company v. United States,* 764 F.2d 1563 (Fed.Cir.1985).

Specific products from specific countries can be removed from the GSP list to the MFN list. In one case, for example, the President's decision to withdraw GSP benefits for "buffalo leather and goat and kid leather (not fancy)" from India was affirmed. See *Florsheim Shoe Co. v. United States,* 744 F.2d 787 (Fed.Cir.1984). In another decision, the

President's discretionary authority to deny GSP benefits to cut flowers from Colombia was similarly upheld. See *Sunburst Farms, Inc. v. United States*, 797 F.2d 973 (Fed.Cir.1986).

U.S. DUTY FREE CARIBBEAN AND AFRICAN TRADE PREFERENCES

In addition, and sometimes overlapping with the GSP, the United States grants duty free entry under a number of other special programs.

Caribbean Preferences

The European Union has had for many years a policy which grants substantial duty free entry into its market for goods originating in Mediterranean Basin countries. The United States has duplicated this approach for the Caribbean Basin. This is accomplished through the Caribbean Basin Economic Recovery Act of 1983 (CBI). For these purposes, the Caribbean Basin is broadly defined to include nearly all of the islands in that Sea, and a significant number of Central and South American nations bordering the Caribbean. So defined, there are 28 nations (not including Cuba) which could qualify for CBI treatment.

As with the GSP program, the Caribbean Basin Initiative (CBI) involves presidential determinations to confer beneficiary status upon any of these eligible countries. U.S. Presidents have typically required of each potential beneficiary a concise written presentation of its policies and practices directly related to the issues raised by the country designation criteria listed in the Caribbean Basin Economic Recovery Act. Wherever measures were in effect which were inconsistent with the objectives of these criteria, U.S. presidents have sought assurances that such measures would be progressively eliminated or modified. For example, the Dominican Republic promised to take steps to reduce the degree of book piracy and the Jamaican and Bahamian governments promised to stop the unauthorized broadcast of U.S. films and television programs.

Unlike the GSP, there are no presidential determinations as to which specific products of these countries shall be allowed into the United States on a duty free basis. All Caribbean products except those excluded by statute are eligible for duty free entry. Moreover, there are no "competitive need" or annual per capita income limits under the CBI.

Lastly, unlike the GSP program which must be renewed periodically, the Caribbean Basin Initiative is a permanent part of the U.S. tariff system. For U.S. free trade partners in the region, Panama and CAFTA/DR for example, the CBI and GSP duty free regimes are no longer applicable.

Special duty free U.S. treatment has been granted to Haitian apparel under the Hope for Haiti program, renewed in 2015.

Andean Preferences

The Andean Trade Preference Act (ATPA) of 1991, renewed in the Trade Act of 2002, authorizes the

President to grant duty free treatment to imports of eligible articles from Colombia, Peru, Bolivia and Ecuador. Venezuela is not included as a beneficiary under this Act. The Andean Trade Preference Act is patterned after the Caribbean Basin Economic Recovery Act of 1983. Goods that ordinarily enter duty free into the United States from Caribbean Basin nations will also enter duty free from these four Andean countries. The same exceptions and exclusions discussed above in connection with the Caribbean Basin Initiative generally apply.

While the CBI is a permanent part of United States Customs law, the ATPA was only authorized initially for a period of ten years. Furthermore, the guaranteed access levels for Caribbean Basin textile products, separate cumulation for antidumping and countervailing duty investigations, and the waiver of the Buy American Act for procurement purposes are not authorized by the ATPA. Broadly speaking, the passage of the ATPA represents assistance to these nations in return for their help in containing narcotics. U.S. free trade agreements with Peru and Colombia supersede the ATPA, whose continued application to Ecuador and Bolivia is in doubt.

African Preferences

The Africa Growth and Opportunity Act of 2000 (AGOA) granted duty-free and quota-free access to the U.S. market for apparel made from U.S. fabric and yarn. Apparel made from African fabric is capped for duty free entry. The least developed sub-Saharan countries enjoy duty-free and quota-free apparel access regardless of the origin of the fabric. The Act also altered U.S. GSP rules to admit certain previously excluded African products on a duty-free basis, including petroleum, watches and flat goods.

Sub-Saharan countries can export almost all products duty-free to the United States. These countries are encouraged to create a free trade area with U.S. support. African exports are subject to import surge (escape clause) protection and stringent rules against transshipments between countries for purposes of taking advantage of U.S. trade benefits.

AGOA was renewed in 2015 subject to eligibility rules concerning market-based economies, poverty reduction, rule of law, and anti-corruption and human rights efforts, including internationally recognized workers' rights.

GOODS INCORPORATING UNITED STATES COMPONENTS

Section 9802.00.80 of the Harmonized Tariff Schedule of the United States (formerly Section 807.00 of the Tariff Schedule of the United States) is an unusual "duty free" provision. This section allows for the duty free importation of United States fabricated components that were exported ready for assembly abroad. If qualified, goods assembled abroad containing U.S. components are subject only to a duty upon the value added through foreign assembly operations.

In order for this to be the case, Section 9802.00.80 requires that the components be fabricated and a product of the United States, that they be exported in a condition ready for assembly without further fabrication, that they not lose their physical identity by change in form, shape or otherwise, and that they not be advanced in value or improved in condition abroad except by being assembled and except by operations incidental to the assembly process such as cleaning, lubricating and painting.

If all of the Section 9802.00.80 criteria are met, the tariff that will be assessed upon the imported assembled product will be limited to a duty upon the full value of that product less the cost or value of U.S. made components that have been incorporated into it. Those who seek to take advantage of Section 9802.00.80 must provide the United States Customs Service with a Foreign Assembler's Declaration and Certification. The assembly plant operator certifies that the requirements of Section 9802.00.80 are met, and the importer declares that this certification is correct.

Billions of dollars of ordinarily tariffed value have been excluded as a result of this Customs law provision. Motor vehicles, semiconductors, office machines, textiles and apparel, and furniture are good examples of the kinds of products assembled abroad with fabricated U.S. components so as to meet the requirements of Section 9802.00.80. Historically, many of these products were assembled in Japan, Germany or Canada. In recent times, the assembly operations (maquiladoras) to which Section 9802.00.80 frequently applies have more commonly been found in the developing world. The Section does not apply to U.S. free trade partners.

DUTY FREE ACCESS TO
MULTIPLE MARKETS

The end-game so far as exporters to and importers are concerned is unlimited duty free access. Except for raw materials (oil and gas for example) and goods from U.S. free trade partners, few foreign exports will ordinarily qualify for such treatment. However, products of GSP-eligible developing nations, and especially Caribbean or African countries, may significantly achieve this goal. This is possible because of United States adherence to the duty-free entry programs discussed above.

There are, of course, exceptions and controls (quotas, NTBs) that may apply under these duty free programs. Nevertheless, the United States market is so lucrative that careful study of these external trade rules is warranted. Such studies can realize unusually advantageous trade situations. For example, many developing nations have duty free rights of entry into the European Union under the Lomé/Cotonou Conventions, the Union's Mediterranean Basin Policy or the EU version of the GSP program. See R. Folsom, *European Union Law including BREXIT in a Nutshell.* The goods of some of these nations may also qualify for duty free access to the United States market.

A producer strategically located in such a nation (e.g., Jamaica) can have the best of both worlds, duty free access to the European Union and the United

States. Mexico, which in addition to NAFTA 1994 has free trade agreements with the European Union, Japan and dozens of other countries, is another premier duty-free export location.

CHAPTER 4

TRADE REMEDY RESPONSES TO IMPORT COMPETITION

Antidumping Duties	Countervailing Duties
National Security	Gray Market Trading
Trade Safeguards	IP Infringing Imports
Trade Adjustment Assistance	Counterfeit Goods
U.S. Trade Remedy Procedures	

The core of the GATT (1947) and (1994) agreements is the principle of binding tariffs applied equally to all WTO member states, the most-favored-nation (MFN) principle. These tariffs, negotiated in the various GATT/WTO Rounds, are commonly referred to as MFN or normal tariffs. See Chapter 2. The national tariff levels of the approximately 165 WTO member states reflect these negotiated tariffs. In the United States tariff code, MFN tariffs are referenced as Column 1 "normal" tariffs. See Chapter 3.

TRADE REMEDIES

The GATT/WTO system allows exceptions to MFN tariff levels. Two of the most important are country-specific "antidumping duties" (ADs) and "countervailing duties" (CVDs). Such duties are intended to "remedy" what the GATT/WTO has agreed are unfair international trade practices. Global GATT/WTO "safeguard" tariffs and restraints, on the other hand, are temporarily permitted in response to import surges that are not considered unfair. President Trump has demonstrated a fourth potential source of GATT/ WTO lawful trade remedy import tariffs, those undertaken as a matter of self-assessed "national security". Think of all these options as special tariffs which, in authorized circumstances, are *additional* to MFN normal tariffs.

None of the "trade remedies" in favor of domestic producers is based on any notion of reciprocity. That is, none has any relation to restricting goods from a country that does not allow or restrains entry of goods into its markets. Antidumping and countervailing duties deal only with unfair selling prices for dutiable imported goods, and the Safeguard "escape clause" mechanism deals only with temporarily protecting a domestic industry from unexpected surges in competition arising from imported goods. National security tariffs are asserted to be unilaterally determined. President Trump has controversially invoked Safeguard tariffs on imported solar panels and clothes washers, and national security tariffs on steel and aluminum. See Chapter 7.

Coverage of President Trump's threatened unilateral, Section 301 tariffs against China and others, and their responses, is presented in Chapter 6. These tariffs are not authorized by the WTO.

AD and CVD Basics

Antidumping duties are a permissible trade response where an enterprise prices its goods for sale in the country of importation at a level that is less than that charged for comparable sales in the home country (i.e., at "less than fair value" (LTFV)). Hence AD generally counteract private sector discriminatory pricing. Countervailing duties are a permissible response to certain "subsidies" given in another country that favor its exports in the international marketplace. Hence CVD counteract governmental subsidies. AD and CVD cannot simultaneously be applied.

The WTO system recognizes and permits both antidumping duties and countervailing duties, providing of course the respective requirements are satisfied. Each "trade remedy" also is governed by a separate Agreement ("Code") that provides more detail on the circumstances under which member states may impose these exceptional duties. Because the AD and CVD Codes are mandatory in the WTO system, they provide the foundation for a reasonably uniform body of legal rules for trade remedies among the roughly 165 WTO member states.

Under the WTO Antidumping Agreement (AD Code) and the WTO Subsidies and Countervailing Measures Agreement (CVD Code), a country may impose a special duty on products of another WTO member state only if two requirements are met. First, the country must find sufficient evidence of an unfair trade practice, either dumping (sales at less than fair value) or prohibited or actionable subsidies.

Second, the practice must *cause* a sufficiently significant injury to a domestic industry. In the case of dumping or subsidies, this requires proof that the practice has caused or threatens to cause "*material injury*" to a domestic industry, or that it has "materially retarded" the establishment of such an industry. Thus, the substantive grounds for the determination of the existence of "dumping" and of a "countervailable (actionable) subsidy" are different, but the domestic injury standard is essentially the same.

Safeguard Basics

Under the WTO Safeguards Agreement, the imposition of temporary protective relief from imports does not require a showing of any unfair trade practice, such as dumping or subsidies. As a result, the injury standard is higher: Under U.S. law, "safeguard" duties or other protective measures authorized by the President are only permitted when increased imports ("surges") are a "*substantial cause*" of "*serious* injury, or threat of serious injury" (emphasis added) to a domestic industry.

National Security Basics

GATT Article 21 reserves the right of all WTO members to prevent any member from taking any action which "it considers necessary for the protection of its essential security interests" *relating to* fissionable materials, traffic in arms, and implements of war and other goods for the purpose of supplying a military establishment, or taken in a time of war or other emergency in international relations. The *relating to* language of Article 21 suggests national security tariffs are WTO justiciable, though the United States asserts not. Other members argue that invocation of Article 21 can only occur "in good faith", a reviewable WTO standard. They also assert that the economic welfare of nations is not an essential security interest, and that invocation of Section 232 (below) by the U.S. is a protectionist tactic inconsistent with WTO obligations.

Section 232 of the Trade Expansion Act of 1962 authorizes the Secretary of Commerce, consulting with the Secretary of Defense, to conduct investigations to determine the effects of imports on the national security of the United States. The Commerce Secretary reports, with recommendations, to the President who is empowered to "adjust the imports". President Trump utilized this largely self-judging and rarely invoked remedy in 2018 to place tariffs on U.S. steel and aluminum imports and is studying their use against auto imports. See Chapter 8.

Nearly all free trade agreements contain "national security" reservations, utilizing a mixture of language that may differ from GATT Article 21. See Chapter 7.

DUMPING AND ANTIDUMPING DUTIES

The economics of dumping arise from a producer's opportunity to compartmentalize the overall market for its product, thus permitting it to offer the product for sale at different prices in different geographic areas. Only if trade barriers or other factors insulate each market sector from others is there opportunity to vary substantially the product's price in different sectors of the global market. For example, a producer can securely "dump" products in an overseas market at cheap prices and high volume only if it can be sure that the market in its home country is immune from return of these products. The objectives of dumping range include increasing marginal revenues, ruining a competitor's market position, and developing a new market on an expeditious basis.

On the other hand, a sale at less than the home price may not necessarily represent an unfair trade practice. It may instead merely result from a short-term need to introduce new products, sell off excess inventory, or conduct a distress sale in difficult financial circumstances. Indeed, "dumping" products in order to establish a foothold in a new foreign market or to raise brand awareness may make sense as a marketing technique. Consumers, at least in the short term, are typically enthusiastic about obtaining goods at "dumped" prices.

Hence there is considerable debate about the economic rationality of categorizing dumping an unfair trade practice and invocation of AD tariffs can backfire. Early in the 1990s, for example, U.S. computer makers succeeded in obtaining a 63%

antidumping tariff on flat-panel screens from Japan. Toshiba USA, Apple and IBM all moved their computer production out of America. Nevertheless, a substantial body of international trade law seeks to identify dumping and counteract it through AD tariffs.

WTO ANTIDUMPING AGREEMENT

GATT Article VI grants WTO member states the right to impose antidumping duties. But the more detailed standards for such duties are set forth in a separate WTO Agreement: "The Agreement on Implementation of Article VI of GATT 1994." This "Antidumping Agreement" provides that a member state may impose antidumping duties if a product's export price is less than the "normal value." It defines the "normal value" of a good as the comparable price, in the ordinary course of trade, for the same or a similar product "when destined for consumption in the exporting country." Thus, in evaluating whether an export price constitutes dumping, the best baseline for comparison is the domestic sales price of comparable goods in the exporting country (i.e., the home country).

However, such comparable sales may not be available, either because comparable products are not sold domestically, or because the usual retail transaction there is not comparable (e.g., leasing rather than a sale). In that situation, the Antidumping Agreement provides a hierarchy of alternative computation methods to achieve an approximate valuation. Among these alternatives, the preferred one uses the price for the same or a similar product in the ordinary course of trade for export to a third country. The next alternative is to calculate the cost of production of the exported goods in the country of origin, plus a reasonable amount for profits and for administrative, selling and any general costs, and then compare that to the price of the product when sold for export to the foreign country.

The WTO Antidumping Agreement, adapted from the earlier Tokyo Round GATT "Antidumping Code," focuses upon dumping determinations (particularly criteria for allocating costs) and material injury determinations (particularly causation). The Agreement also has a few special rules that are worthy of emphasis. First, it forbids duties for *de minimis* dumping, defined as less than two percent of the product's export price, and in such cases member states must terminate any AD investigations immediately. Second, it permits "cumulation" of imports—i.e., imports of the same goods from more than one country—if the dumping from each is more than *de minimis* and this is otherwise appropriate under the circumstances.

Third, it recognizes, but does not expressly allow or disallow, AD petitions by employees and their union representatives. Fourth, member states must notify the WTO of any changes to their domestic antidumping laws as well as any related administrative actions. More generally, a special WTO "Committee on Anti-Dumping Practices" oversees implementation of the Agreement by member states. Finally, when another member state challenges the imposition of ADs before the WTO, the DSB panel may rely on the facts developed in the domestic administrative proceedings and must accept those facts if the domestic evaluation "was unbiased and objective, even if the panel might have reached a different conclusion."

ORIGINS OF U.S. ANTIDUMPING LAW

Controversies over dumping of goods in the United States go back as far as complaints by Secretary of the Treasury Alexander Hamilton in 1791. The subject continues to excite interest and even passion. In general, U.S. antidumping statutes have long compared the price at which articles are imported or sold in the United States with the actual market value or wholesale price of such articles in the principal markets of the country of their production. This approach was established by the Antidumping Act of 1916, a rarely used criminal statute. Considered a form of unfair competition law, the Act provided for criminal prosecution and treble damages for certain types of dumping.

The European Union, Japan, and other states successfully challenged these aspects of the 1916 Act in WTO dispute settlement proceedings as inconsistent with the Antidumping Agreement. The pressure of the adverse rulings by the WTO's DSB ultimately led the United States to repeal the 1916 Act in 2004.

U.S. PROCEDURES RELATING TO THE IMPOSITION OF TRADE REMEDIES

AD and CVD Duties

The procedures and rules for the imposition of antidumping duties (AD) or countervailing duties (CVD) under U.S. law broadly correspond to their WTO Codes. They involve a complicated interaction between two administrative agencies: The International Trade Administration (ITA), and the United States International Trade Commission (ITC). See Chapter 3. Such trade remedy cases may be initiated either by the Department of Commerce or by a group or association of aggrieved domestic interests. The ITA's function is to assess claims of a substantive unfair trade practice—i.e., to determine whether there has been a countervailable subsidy or a sale at less than fair value ("dumping"). The ITC has a separate responsibility to assess causation and injury issues—i.e., to determine whether a practice has substantially caused or threatens to cause material injury to a domestic industry.

In general, AD and CVD trade remedy procedures involve the ITA first making a determination that a petition adequately alleges the relevant statutory requirements. Before initiating an investigation, the ITA also must find that a sufficient percentage of the affected domestic industry supports the petition. This normally requires that the industry or workers who support the petition account for (a) at least 25 percent of the total industry, and (b) at least 50 percent of those that have actually expressed an opinion for or against the petition.

After an initial investigation, the ITA then makes a "preliminary determination"—based on the "best information available at the time"—on whether there is "a reasonable basis to believe" that dumping or a countervailable subsidy exists. Use of the "best information available" approach has been upheld by the WTO Appellate Body. This approach has the effect of incentivizing foreign party participation in U.S. antidumping and countervailing duty proceedings lest their absence increase the likelihood of AD or CVD duties being imposed on their exports.

The ITC conducts its proceedings in parallel with those of the ITA. The ITC also makes a preliminary determination "based on the best information available" as to whether there is "a reasonable indication" that the challenged practice presents a real or threatened material injury to the affected domestic industry. An affirmative preliminary determination by the ITC is required *before* the ITA may proceed to make its own preliminary determination.

If both the ITC and the ITA make affirmative preliminary determinations, then each conducts a further investigation and ultimately makes a "final determination" in its respective area of responsibility. The ITA has final authority over the appropriate extra AD or CVD duty to offset any proven unfair trade practice. AD and CVD duties are treated as statutory remedies, meaning they are *not* formally subject to Presidential review and authority.

Thus the U.S. chain of decision-making in antidumping proceedings (and also most countervailing duty proceedings) runs as follows:

ITC Preliminary Injury Determination

ITA Preliminary Dumping Determination

ITA Final Dumping Determination

ITC Final Injury Determination

Congress has repeatedly amended U.S. antidumping law so as to accelerate the rate at which these determinations are made and tighten the administrative rules used in them. For example, the so-called Level Playing Field Act of 2015 notably did so. At this point, it is common for the proceeding to be completed within one year. U.S. antidumping duties are then and in the future assessed retrospectively for each importation, the amount payable varying for each importer and transaction.

Trade Safeguards

Only the ITC is involved in Safeguard (escape clause) proceedings. Upon the filing of a petition by a representative of an affected industry the Trade Act of 1974 requires the ITC to conduct an investigation into whether the statutory standard is satisfied. If it makes an affirmative determination on substantial causation and serious injury standards, the ITC submits its findings and any recommendation for relief to the President.

The Trade Act then grants the President broad discretion in determining the appropriate temporary safeguard measures to protect the affected domestic industry. These may range from increased tariffs to import quotas to "trade adjustment assistance" for workers. President Trump exercised this discretion in imposing global import safeguard tariffs on solar panels and clothes washers in 2018. See Chapter 8.

National Security Import Controls

The ITA and the ITC are not involved in national security trade remedy determinations. The decision to "adjust imports" in the name of national security is made by the President after a report with recommendations from the Secretary of Commerce. President Nixon mandated a 10% tariff surcharge as part of his successful efforts to get Germany and Japan to revalue their currencies against the U.S. dollar and reduce their trade surpluses. President Trump exercised this discretion in imposing global import national security tariffs on steel and aluminum. See Chapter 8.

The Importance of the ITA Preliminary AD and CVD Determinations

As a practical matter, the ITA's *preliminary* determination that dumping or a countervailable subsidy has occurred will place significant, often overwhelming, pressure on the importers of the relevant goods. This is because at that point any covered goods become subject to the CVD or AD duties that are ultimately determined to apply once the ITA and ITC complete their investigations.

Hence the preliminary ITA determination tends to discourage or even cut off the imports. At that point importers generally must post cash or bonds to cover any AD or CVD duties preliminarily determined by the ITA. At a minimum, importers likely will have to raise their prices—unless and until either the ITA or the ITC makes a contrary final determination once the agencies have completed their administrative proceedings.

Once an antidumping petition is filed, importers will not know what their liabilities for duties are going to be, and may be required to post an expensive bond in the meantime to gain entry. Foreign exporters frequently raise their "United States prices" to the level of home market prices soon after such a preliminary determination. If they do, antidumping law will have accomplished its essential purpose. However, the U.S. Tariff Act disfavors termination of the proceeding on the basis of voluntary undertakings of compliance.

United States antidumping proceedings may be settled by the ITA if the respondents formally agree to cease exporting to the United States within six months or agree to revise their prices so as to eliminate the margin of the dumping. Because price revision agreements are hard to monitor, they are disfavored by the ITA. But an agreement to cease exports also cancels any outstanding suspension of liquidation. The total time secured in this manner may allow foreigners a window of opportunity to establish market presence prior to shifting production to the United States.

If requested, the ITA and ITC may proceed to their final determinations after a settlement is agreed. If the respondents prevail, normal trading will resume; but if the petitioners prevail, the settlement agreement will remain in effect. The ITA monitors all settlement agreements and may assess civil penalties (in addition to antidumping duties) in the event of a breach.

A party to an administrative proceeding on an AD or CVD matter may appeal an adverse final determination of the ITA or ITC to the U.S. Court of International Trade (CIT). The CIT also hears appeals from ITC determinations in escape clause proceedings, but in these cases review is limited to procedural irregularities or clear statutory misconstructions.

International Tribunals

International institutions also play an increasingly significant role in the resolution of trade disputes. The most important of these is the WTO's Dispute Settlement Body ("DSB"). Dissatisfied parties in domestic administrative proceedings may convince their government to challenge an adverse CVD, AD, Safeguard or national security decision before the DSB based on alleged violations of a WTO Agreement. A large number of such complaints have been filed against the United States. As Chapter 2 examines in detail, proceedings before the DSB are governed by a separate WTO Agreement, the Dispute Settlement Understanding (DSU).

Separately, a unique international institution exists for trade remedy disputes involving the three member states—the U.S., Canada, and Mexico—of the North American Free Trade Agreement (NAFTA 1994). NAFTA 1994 provides for resolution of antidumping and countervailing duty disputes through "binational panels." Such panels apply the domestic law of the *importing* country, and provide a substitute for judicial review of the decisions of administrative agencies of the importing country. Indeed, the initiation of a review under NAFTA 1994 divests the CIT of jurisdiction over the same dispute. Retention of the NAFTA binational panels has been a contentious issue in NAFTA 1994's re-negotiation.

Although the decisions of NAFTA 1994 binational panels are not formally binding in U.S. law, the ITA or ITC may decide to and usually does review any administrative action to conform to an adverse panel decision, including through a revocation or reduction of CVDs or ADs.

U.S. LAW ON ANTIDUMPING DUTIES

The modern U.S. rules and procedures governing antidumping duties are set forth in a statute that is still known as the Tariff Act of 1930. But, significantly, the U.S. amended this Act in 1994 to implement the WTO Antidumping Agreement. In conformance with that Agreement, the fundamental determination under U.S. law is whether a sale is at "less than fair value" (LTFV). This in turn requires a comparison of the U.S. price of imported goods with their "normal value."

ITA Dumping Determinations

"Normal value" is usually determined by the price charged for the goods in the exporter's *domestic* market (the home market) in the ordinary course of business. If the ITA determines that the home market is not "viable" (i.e., is not sufficiently large or otherwise inappropriate), it may use the price in sales in a comparable third country. Finally, if neither of those measures is appropriate, the ITA may use a "constructed value" based on the cost (properly adjusted) to produce the goods (not the price).

The ITA then compares this price with the price of the goods for export to the United States. Generally, for this measure the ITA uses the "export price," which means the price at which the goods are first sold *outside* of the United States to an unaffiliated person *for exportation to* the United States. If, however, the foreign exporter first sells the goods to an affiliated person outside the United States—such that this "export" price is not a reliable one—then the ITA may use the "constructed export price," which means the price at which the goods are first sold to an unaffiliated person *in* the United States.

Ultimately, the ITA compares the appropriate "normal value" (again, generally the home country price) with the U.S. price (again, generally the export price for goods destined for the U.S.) to determine whether there has been a sale at "less than fair value" (i.e., "dumping").

ITC Injury Determinations

The ITC separately makes determinations on causation and injury in AD proceedings. In order to impose ADs, the statute requires an affirmative determination by the ITC that a challenged practice presents an actual or threatened "material injury" to a domestic industry or that the practice has "materially retarded" the establishment of such an industry. Much, therefore, depends upon a workable definition of "material injury."

The statute defines the term as "harm which is not inconsequential, immaterial, or unimportant." It further provides that, in making a determination of "material injury," the ITC "shall" consider the volume of imports involved, the effect of the imports on U.S. prices for "like products," and the impact of the imports on U.S. producers of "like products," but only in relation to production operations in the United States. The ITC is directed to evaluate both the actual and potential declines not only in production, sales and profits, but also in the market share and productivity of the domestic industry. It is also directed to evaluate actual and potential negative effects on employment and growth, and on the ability to raise capital and investment.

All effects are to be measured on an industry-wide basis, and not in relation to an individual company. But a threat to a "major portion" of a national industry is sufficient. In order to assess "material injury," the ITC also must identify the relevant domestic industry affected by an alleged dumping practice. It does so by, first, defining the relevant "the domestic like product" that competes with the imported goods. From this, it then defines the relevant "domestic industry" as those domestic producers, "as a whole," of a "domestic like product" or as those producers "whose collective output of a domestic like product constitutes a major proportion" of the total domestic production.

Antidumping Duties

If the sales of imported goods both are at LTFV and cause or threaten "material injury" to a domestic industry, or retard the development of a domestic industry, then the statute provides that an antidumping duty "shall" be imposed. In other words, AD are statutory remedies which neither the President nor others may deter.

The antidumping duty levied is in addition to the usual tariffs charged on such products. But because the duties are not imposed to support any specific domestic price, they may not exceed the "margin of dumping"—i.e., the amount of the difference between the normal price and the price at which the goods are sold for export to the United States. The antidumping duty is to remain in force only as long as the dumping occurs.

U.S. Antidumping Rules and Nonmarket Economies

Congress has enacted special rules to govern antidumping duty analysis of imports from nonmarket economy countries (NMEs). The Department of Commerce gets to decide which countries have NMEs. Russia was "graduated" from this status in 2002. China, under its WTO accession protocol, appears to have been promised graduation late in 2016. Amendments to U.S. antidumping law vest considerable discretion in the DOC "in particular market situations" to apply NME rules in AD proceedings where the producer's costs do not accurately reflect ordinary trade costs. These amendments were apparently adopted with China's potential antidumping graduation in mind. At this writing, the United States and the EU have refused to grant China market economy status, and China has filed a WTO complaint challenging those refusals.

The NME rules are based on the assumption that "normal value" cannot be determined by NME prices, which are bureaucratically determined and therefore not sufficiently subject to the forces of competition to form an accurate standard for comparison. Whether that assumption is accurate for all NMEs, notably China, is a matter of some debate.

When applicable, the ITA will "construct" a NME "normal value" by determining the factors of production (labor, materials, energy, capital, etc.) actually used by the NME to produce the goods destined for export to the United States. The ITA then assigns a value for each of those factors using prices prevailing in a suitable market economy, a "surrogate" country. In one proceeding, for example, Paraguay served as a surrogate for China. Finally, the ITA adds appropriate amounts from values in the surrogate market economy country for factory overhead, sales expenses, general and administrative expenses, packing, and profit.

The result is a "constructed value" for goods from the exporting NME. Although the statutory definition refers to a "nonmarket economy country," which implies use of a single standard for a whole political unit, the ITA has differentiated between imports from specific NME countries based on whether particular factors of production in specific fields are considered to be market driven or not.

Needless to say, these calculations typically result in findings of dumping at healthy margins, which NME would strongly prefer to avoid.

Other Provisions of U.S. Law Designed to Conform to the WTO Antidumping Agreement

When it accepted the substantial changes to the WTO system in 1994, the U.S. also made a variety of more specific changes to domestic law to conform to the WTO Antidumping Agreement. First, the U.S. amended the Tariff Act of 1930 to provide for an exclusion of *de minimis* dumping margins. Specifically, the ITA, in making its preliminary dumping determinations, must disregard any weighted average dumping margin that is less than two percent *ad valorem* or the equivalent specific rate for the subject merchandise. The ITA likewise must disregard any weighted average dumping margin that is *de minimis* when making final determinations.

Other changes to the Tariff Act have reduced the discretion previously available by imposing strict statutory time limits. In the case of an antidumping petition, the ITA must make an initial determination on whether the petition alleges the required statutory elements within twenty days after the petition is filed. This time limit may, in exceptional circumstances, be extended to forty days if it becomes necessary to poll or otherwise determine support for the petition in the affected domestic industry. The statute also imposes a 45-day deadline from the filing of the petition for the ITC to make a preliminary determination on injury and a 140-day deadline for the ITA to make a preliminary determination on whether the challenged sales are at less than fair value.

Further WTO-derived amendments authorize an adjustment to sales-below-cost calculations for start-up costs, thought to be particularly beneficial to high-tech products. The 1994 amendments also included a controversial "captive production" section intended to remove intra-enterprise sales from ITC injury determinations. The United States, however, failed to implement fully the average-to-average or transaction-to-transaction dumping calculations mandated by the Antidumping Agreement.

The 1994 amendments permit the use of weighted average approaches in the investigatory phase, but the traditional U.S. practice of comparing individual U.S. sales to average home (or third country) sales will continue in subsequent administrative reviews. Adjustments for profits from further manufacturing, selling, and distribution of products in the U.S. are authorized. And the amendments strengthened existing U.S. anti-circumvention provisions despite their absence from the WTO Antidumping Agreement.

Still more WTO-driven changes require the ITC to provide all parties to the proceeding with an opportunity to comment, prior to the Commission's vote, on all information collected in its investigations. In addition, a 1994 amendment requires that an antidumping investigation cease if the volume of dumped imports from a single country is negligible— that is, less than three percent of total imports of a product in the most recent 12-month period preceding the filing of the petition.

Separately, the ITC is ordinarily required to consider "cumulation" of imports from two or more countries if the imports are subject to investigations as a result of petitions filed on the same day. It may continue an investigation, notwithstanding the rule on negligible dumping, if the volume of imports of a product from several countries, each accounting for less than three percent of the imports, together account for more than seven percent of total imports. The Commission must make any cumulative analysis on the basis of the same record, even if the simultaneously filed investigations end up with differing final deadlines.

The ITC also must consider the magnitude of the dumping margin in making material injury determinations. Lastly, the Commission must conduct a review no later than five years after an antidumping or countervailing duty order is issued to determine whether revoking the order would likely lead to continuation or recurrence of dumping or subsidies and material injury. Known as the "sunset" provision, this WTO rule requires a review of all existing antidumping and countervailing duty orders at regular intervals.

U.S. Anti-Circumvention Rules

In 1988, Congress enacted important amendments to Tariff Act to address the "circumvention" of antidumping and countervailing duties. These "anti-circumvention" rules entered into force while the subject was under discussion in the GATT Uruguay Round negotiations. Ultimately, the WTO Antidumping Agreement included no substantive rules on anti-circumvention, but also did not forbid the practice.

The Tariff Act addresses circumvention in a variety of ways. First, it allows the ITA to ignore fictitious markets in the source country when calculating the foreign market "normal value." Moreover, the ITA may include within the scope of an antidumping order merchandise "completed or assembled" in the United States if such merchandise includes "parts or components produced in the foreign country" that is the original subject of the order. The principal requirements are that the process of completion or assembly in the United States is "minor or insignificant" and the value of the components themselves is a "significant portion of the total value of the merchandise.

Similarly, when the exporter ships the components to a third country for assembly and subsequent exportation to the United States, such circumvention efforts can be defeated by extending an antidumping order to those goods as well. Again, such an action is appropriate if the assembly in the third country is "minor or insignificant" and the components themselves represent the principal value of the merchandise. The Trump Administration has accused China and various Asia countries of willfully engaging in circumvention of U.S. tariff rules. See Chapter 8.

U.S. ANTIDUMPING PROCEEDINGS REVIEWED BY THE WTO

The WTO Appellate Body has taken a restrictive view of what constitutes permissible antidumping duties.

Zeroing

In a series of decisions, the WTO's Appellate Body ruled against "zeroing," a methodology used in dumping margin calculations by the United States and other countries. This practice involved disregarding any sales in the home market that were below the export price. The Appellate Body has reasoned, however, that a proper understanding of the home market price should involve a weighing of both positive and negative numbers in calculating weighted average dumping margins.

Notwithstanding these decisions, the Federal Circuit repeatedly upheld the zeroing methodology as a reasonable interpretation of the actual language in the Tariff Act and described the analysis of the Appellate Body as not "sufficiently persuasive." See, e.g., *Corus Staal BV v. Department of Commerce*, 395 F.3d 1343 (Fed.Cir.2005). In response to the repeated adverse rulings by the WTO, however, the Commerce Department has adjusted its approach to discontinue zeroing in antidumping investigations, but maintain the practice in antidumping duty reviews.

Material Injury Issues

More generally, the Appellate Body (AB) has rejected cursory material injury determinations and stressed that member state governments must consider all relevant economic factors in making such decisions. Thus, in the *United States-Hot-Rolled Steel from Japan* dispute, the AB found bias in the determination of normal value when low-priced sales from a respondent to an exporter were automatically excluded. The AB also indicated that injury determinations must include an analysis of captive production markets in addition to merchant markets. Causation in such determinations must be rigorously scrutinized.

A WTO panel also ruled that the Commerce Department's refusal to revoke an antidumping order against South Korean DRAMS was inconsistent with Article 11.2 of the Antidumping Agreement. Hence, U.S. regulations regarding the likelihood of continued dumping after a three-year hiatus are suspect under the Antidumping Agreement. The Court of International Trade, on the other hand, found the U.S. regulations in question consistent with the WTO Antidumping Agreement. The Court took the position that the WTO panel ruling was not binding precedent, merely persuasive.

The Byrd Amendment

The WTO Appellate Body also repeatedly ruled against the U.S. with respect to the Continued Dumping and Subsidy Offset Act of 2000 (CDSOA, the so-called "Byrd Amendment"). The controversial aspect of that Act was a mechanism under which the U.S. government funneled the antidumping duties that it collected back to the members of the affected domestic industry. In this way, millions of dollars were collected by the U.S. government and distributed to U.S. companies in, among others, the steel, bearings, candy, candle, cement, computer chip, and lumber industries.

Other countries promptly filed challenges against the Act with the WTO's DSB, and the Appellate Body ultimately determined that the CDSOA was inconsistent with the Antidumping Agreement (as well as various provisions of other WTO Agreements). When the U.S. failed to comply with this decision, the WTO authorized the claimant countries to retaliate in their domestic trade laws as permitted under the WTO's Dispute Settlement Understanding. On this basis, the European Union, Canada, Japan and others imposed WTO-authorized retaliatory trade sanctions on U.S. exports to their markets. Ultimately, Congress bowed to the pressure created by the WTO decisions and repealed the CDSOA in a late 2005 budget bill.

SUBSIDIES AND COUNTERVAILING DUTIES

A WTO member state may impose an increased tariff payable on an imported item beyond the regular tariff schedule as a "countervailing duty." Such duties are based not on a foreign exporter selling goods as less than fair value, but rather on a foreign government providing "subsidies" that support production for exportation and thus permit the exporter to sell at lower prices in exports to other countries. Subsidies come in many forms, including, among others, tax reductions or rebates; tax credits; loan guarantees; subsidized financing; equity infusions; and outright grants.

In theory, a countervailing duty offsets exactly the unfair subsidy. Proponents of countervailing duties argue that they are necessary to keep imports from being unfairly competitive based on foreign government support. Opponents of countervailing duties argue that there is no coherent standard of "fairness" vs. "unfairness" to justify a rational assessment of such duties. Such opponents argue that it is often difficult to identify precisely when a subsidy exists as compared with general governmental actions to support beneficial commercial activity. Still others argue that if a government is stupid enough to subsidize products, consumers should take the money and run.

Rapidly developing countries also routinely offer to give some form of subsidy for initial foreign investments designed to produce exports. But subsidies are not only a phenomenon for developing countries. In the United States, for example the Export-Import Bank (EXIMBANK) has routinely offered low cost loans to overseas buyers of Boeing and GE products exported from the United States. Other developed countries have similar programs. In all cases, the critical legal issue is which subsidies may be "countervailed" by CVD duties under the rules of the WTO Agreement on Subsidies and Countervailing Measures (SCM).

WTO AGREEMENT ON SUBSIDIES AND COUNTERVAILING MEASURES

International concern with unfair subsidies and countervailing duties is reflected in Articles VI, XVI, and XXIII of the GATT 1994 and in the 1994 WTO "Agreement on Subsidies and Countervailing Measures" (SCM Agreement). A WTO member state may impose an increased tariff on an imported item beyond the regular tariff schedule as a "countervailing duty." Such duties are an authorized response to a foreign government providing a "prohibited" or "actionable" subsidy that permits their exporters to sell at lower prices in other countries. In all cases, the critical legal issue is which subsidies may be countervailed by CVD duties under the rules of the WTO SCM Agreement.

Under the SCM Agreement, the authorities of the importing member state may impose a countervailing duty (CVD) in the amount of the subsidy for as long as the subsidy continues. The SCM Agreement also provides substantive rules governing when, and under what circumstances, a member state may impose CVDs to offset a claimed governmental or "public body" subsidy. State-owned-enterprises (SOEs) are not generally treated as public bodies unless performing governmental functions.

The CVD may only be imposed after an investigation, begun on the request of an affected industry, has demonstrated the existence of a prohibited or actionable "specific" subsidy that has adverse trade effects, such as injury to a domestic industry or "serious prejudice" to the interests of the importing state. Finally, there must be a causal link between the subsidy and the alleged injury.

The SCM Agreement attempts to shift the focus of subsidy rules from a national forum, as was the exclusive case under GATT, to the multinational forum provided by the WTO. As a result, disputes over subsidies may occur either in the national forum or before the WTO's DSB (or both). In addition, a special WTO "Committee on Subsidies and Countervailing Measures" supervises the implementation of the SCM Agreement by the member states.

Countervailable Subsidies

The SCM Agreement established three classes of subsidies: (1) prohibited subsidies (also known as "red light" subsidies); (2) actionable subsidies, i.e., those that are permissible unless they cause adverse trade effects ("yellow light"); and (3) non-actionable and non-countervailable subsidies ("green light").

Under the terms of the SCM Agreement, however, the "green light" category expired in 2000. The SCM Agreement also granted special exemptions for developing countries that permitted them to phase out their export subsidies and local content rules on a gradual basis. These exemptions were to have expired by 2003, but as of 2018, a few countries— principally in the Caribbean and Central America— continue to operate under an extension of this deadline granted by the WTO's Committee on Subsidies and Countervailing Measures.

SCM Dispute Procedures

The SCM Agreement also prescribes procedural rules for the investigation and imposition of CVDs by domestic authorities. It addresses, among other things, the initiation of CVD proceedings, the conduct of investigations, the calculation of the amount of subsidy, and the right of all interested parties to present information. The Agreement also has special rules relating to subsidies that cause a "serious prejudice" to the interests of another member state (although some of these rules have lapsed). The SCM also has rules on the gathering of evidence in CVD proceedings, on the imposition and collection of CVDs, on provisional measures, and on the permitted length of any allowed CVDs (typically five years).

As noted above, an aggrieved country may challenge another member state's CVD laws or actions before the WTO's DSB, but the SCM also has special dispute settlement procedures regarding such actions. Those procedures first provide for consultations between the complaining member state and the subsidizing member state. If these do not resolve the dispute within 30 days for a "prohibited subsidy" (red light) or 60 days for an "actionable subsidy" (yellow light) either party may request that the DSB establish a panel to investigate the dispute and issue a written report.

The DSB panel will have 90 days (red light) or 120 days (yellow light) to investigate and prepare its report. The panel report is appealable on issues of law to the Appellate Body. The Appellate Body has 30 days (red light) or 60 days (yellow light) to decide the appeal. Panel and Appellate Body decisions are adopted without modification by the DSB unless rejected by an "inverted consensus." See Chapter 2 for more detail on DSB procedures.

If a prohibited or actionable subsidy is found to exist, the subsidizing state is obligated under WTO to withdraw the subsidy. If the subsidy is not withdrawn within a six-month period, the WTO may authorize the complaining member state to take countermeasures. Such countermeasures may not be countervailing duties, but may instead comprise increased tariffs by the complaining member on exports from the subsidizing state.

Boeing v. Airbus

A classic, longstanding pair of subsidy disputes concerning Boeing and Airbus aircraft have been decided by the WTO Appellate Body. In 2011, the European Union and various member states were found by a WTO Panel to have illegally subsidized Airbus, mainly through "launch aid", by $22 billion. In 2012, the Appellate Body determined that the U.S. and various state governments had subsidized Boeing by about $4.3 billion under procurement contracts and tax loopholes.

At this writing, neither side seems inclined to comply with these rulings. No settlement is in sight and hence mutual trade retaliation could occur. See Chapter 2 on WTO remedies.

Furthermore, in a notable ITC decision of 2018, the agency, sitting with four Obama-era members, unanimously refused to find material injury asserted by Boeing in an antidumping suit against Bombardier of Canada. Bombardier had secured a Delta airlines mid-size plane order that Boeing did not even bid upon. Bombardier's precarious financial position and this proceeding caused it to partner with Airbus to build the planes in Alabama, thus providing Boeing's chief competitor with a major market entry opportunity. President Trump quickly appointed three additional members to the ITC, no doubt more in line with his America First agenda.

U.S. COUNTERVAILING DUTY LAW

United States law has long considered the grant of a subsidy by a foreign government to aid its exporters to be an unfair trade practice. Laws granting a right to impose countervailing duties to counter unfair subsidies have existed since 1897, long before the creation of the GATT. The origin of U.S. laws against export "bounties" or "grants" can be traced to Section 5 of the Tariff Act of 1897.

For many years, this law vested almost complete discretion in the Treasury Department to levy CVDs as it saw fit. Several early CVD tariffs targeted tax subsidies on sugar exports. The U.S. Supreme Court essentially gave the Treasury Department *carte blanche* to impose CVDs whenever foreign government regulations favored exports reaching the United States.

Prior to the Trade Act of 1974, U.S. law on CVDs was largely administered as a branch of U.S. foreign policy, not as a private international trade remedy. Indeed, it was not until 1974 that negative bounty or grant determinations by the Treasury Department became subject to judicial review. The Trade Act of 1974 also gave private parties a number of procedural rights, notably time limits for Treasury decisions on their petitions for CVD relief and mandatory publication of Treasury rulings. It is from this point, therefore, that a systematic body of case law interpreting and applying U.S. bounty, grant, and CVD provisions began to develop.

The next major development in the U.S. statutes governing this field arrived in the Trade Agreements Act of 1979. This Act, *inter alia,* codified the rules on the use of CVDs to counteract unfair "export subsidies" as agreed in the Tokyo Round GATT Subsidies Code. In addition, the 1979 Act authorized limited use of CVDs against foreign *domestic* subsidies, a subject the GATT Subsidies Code did not address. Furthermore, the 1979 Act adopted the GATT requirement of proof of an actual injury to a domestic industry.

The Uruguay Round Agreements Act of 1994 implemented the numerous changes of the WTO SCM Agreement into U.S. law. Most important, the URAA amended the Tariff Act of 1930 to reflect a rough arrangement similar to the "red light," "yellow light," and "green light" (now lapsed) categories of the SCM Agreement. The requirements of the Tokyo Round Subsidies Code relating to material injury continued in substantially the same form.

Two U.S. Statutory Tests

The United States currently has two statutory structures on countervailing duties: Section 1671 of the Tariff Act of 1930 provides a test for products imported from countries that participate in the WTO SCM Agreement (or its equivalent), as compared to products imported from other countries.

The most important difference between the two is that for imports from a "Subsidies Agreement Country," CVDs may be imposed only upon an affirmative determination that a U.S. industry is "materially" injured, or threatened with such injury, or its development is materially retarded. For the relatively few other countries, CVDs may be imposed *without* any finding of injury to a domestic industry.

In most other significant respects, the two tests are the same. Nonetheless, with the continuing growth in the membership of the WTO (roughly now 160 member states), the possibility of imposing CVDs without a showing of material injury is rapidly decreasing in significance.

The Tariff Act of 1930 contains the U.S. statutory provisions on countervailing duties for products imported from WTO member states. Those provisions permit the imposition of duties if the ITA and the ITC find that a product is subsidized, and that as a result a U.S. industry is materially injured or threatened with such injury or its development is materially retarded.

The U.S. amended its rules on countervailing duties in 1994 to conform to the SCM Agreement. The amendments changed many concepts under U.S. law. Although mostly consistent in substance, however, the U.S. rules follow a slightly different structure as compared to the SCM Agreement.

In general, the U.S. rules state that "there shall be imposed. . .a countervailing duty" if the ITA determines that an exporting country is providing, "directly or indirectly," a disallowed subsidy, and the ITC makes an affirmative injury determination. Thus, U.S. law defines essentially three elements for the imposition of a CVD: (1) a "countervailable subsidy," (2) that is "specific," and (3) that causes or threatens a material injury to a domestic industry.

Once again, as in antidumping proceedings, the ITA's preliminary determination that a countervailable subsidy exists has important practical consequences for importers and exporters. See the discussion of these consequences above in the coverage of U.S. antidumping law.

The Subsidy Requirement

A "subsidy" is defined in U.S. law as a "financial contribution" by a governmental entity that confers a "benefit" on the exporter of the subsidized product. It includes governmental grants, loans, equity infusions and loan guarantees, as well as tax credits and the failure to collect taxes. It can also include the governmental purchase or providing of goods or services on advantageous terms.

Further, direct governmental action is not required: A subsidy may also arise if a government provides any of the above through a private body. A financial contribution provides a "benefit" if it grants an exporter a better deal than would be available through normal market mechanisms.

The Specificity Requirement

In addition to a financial contribution and a benefit, under U.S. law a subsidy must be "specific" to a particular industry or enterprise. This is where U.S. law uses a slightly different structure, or at least different terminology, as compared to the structure of the SCM Agreement (although the latter also refers to specificity).

U.S. law employs the notion of "export subsidies" to correspond to the "prohibited" (red light) subsidies under the SCM Agreement. These are deemed to be specific as a matter of law. Similarly, U.S. law employs the notion of "domestic subsidies" to correspond to "actionable" (yellow light) subsidies under the SCM Agreement. These may be subject to CVDs if they cause "adverse trade effects" based on a variety of further factual considerations.

Export Subsidies

U.S. CVD law provides that a subsidy is an "export subsidy," and thus is specific as a matter of law, if "in law or in fact" it is "contingent upon export performance," even where that condition is only one of several. The same applies for a subsidy that is "conditioned upon the use of domestic goods over imported goods" ("import substitution subsidy"). As noted, these rules correspond to the "prohibited" (red light) subsidies under the SCM Agreement. (Annex I to the SCM Agreement also provides an "Illustrative List of Export Subsidies.")

A footnote to the SCM Agreement explains that a subsidy also is contingent on exports if it is "in fact tied to actual or anticipated exportation or export earnings." A 2011 WTO Appellate Body decision in the long-running dispute between the E.U. and the U.S. over aircraft subsidies explained that this concept applies "[w]here the evidence shows, all other things being equal, that the granting of the subsidy provides an incentive to skew anticipated sales towards exports." Although U.S. law does not expressly incorporate the language of the SCM Agreement footnote, a fair interpretation of the definition of an "export subsidy" would seem to capture it as well.

Domestic Subsidies

U.S. CVD law covers the category of "actionable" (yellow light) subsidies under the concept of a "domestic subsidy." Such a subsidy exists if as a matter of law or fact it is provided to a specific enterprise or industry, even if not linked to export performance.

The law lists four "guidelines" for determining whether a subsidy so qualifies as a domestic subsidy:

(1) If the subsidizing country "expressly limits access" to the subsidy to an enterprise or industry, then it is "specific as a matter of law."

(2) If the subsidy is in fact automatically granted to all enterprises or industries that meet written and objective criteria or conditions, it is "not specific as a matter of law."

(3) A subsidy may be "specific as a matter of fact" where the actual recipients are limited in number; one enterprise or industry is the predominant user or receives a "disproportionately large amount" of the subsidy; or the manner in which the granting authority exercises its discretion indicates that one enterprise or industry is favored over others.

(4) Finally, a subsidy is specific if it is limited to an enterprise or industry in a "designated geographic region" and is granted by the governmental authority of that region.

Two other categories originally recognized under the SCM Agreement, and incorporated into U.S., have lapsed. A so-called "dark amber" subsidy was one that exceeded five percent of the cost basis of the product, or provided debt forgiveness, or covered the operating losses of a specific enterprise industry more than once. The dark amber provisions lapsed in 2000. As noted above, the "green light" category of allowed subsidies—for industrial research and development, regional development, and adaptation of existing facilities to new environmental standards—also lapsed after five years and was not renewed.

The Injury Requirement

In parallel with the rules for antidumping duties, the ITA and ITC have separate responsibilities for making determinations on countervailing duties. The ITA makes determinations on whether a "countervailable subsidy" exists and whether it is "specific." The ITC's separate responsibility is to determine whether such a subsidy meets the statutory requirements for causation and injury.

As with ADs, the ITC must determine whether "by reason of" the sale of subsidized goods, (a) a domestic industry producing like products "is materially injured," (b) such an industry "is threatened with material injury," or (c) "the establishment of an industry is materially retarded." The definition of the relevant "domestic industry" likewise parallels that for AD proceedings (see above).

U.S. CVD Enforcement Procedures

The procedures for investigating and imposing CVDs generally are the same as those for ADs. In general, the ITA first makes a determination that a petition adequately alleges the statutory requirements. After an initial investigation, the ITA then makes a "preliminary determination" on whether there is a "reasonable basis to believe" that the statutory definition of a countervailable subsidy is met. At the same time, the ITC conducts its own investigation and then makes a preliminary determination on whether there is "a reasonable indication" that a subsidy presents a real or threatened material injury to the affected domestic industry.

If both make affirmative preliminary determinations, the goods are immediately subject to any countervailing duties imposed later; as noted above, this usually has the effect of reducing imports of such goods. Following more detailed investigations, the ITA and ITC then proceed to final determinations in their respective areas of responsibility and, if both determinations are affirmative, the ITA determines and imposes an appropriate CVD. Final determinations may be appealed to the CIT, then to the Federal Circuit, and ultimately to the Supreme Court.

Subsidies, CVDs and Nonmarket Economies

The subject of subsidies is particularly difficult with respect to nonmarket economies (NMEs). The longstanding view was that such duties were not appropriate because the NME government in effect is responsible for the entire economy. In accordance with this view, the Federal Circuit Court of Appeals ruled in 1986 that economic incentives given to encourage exportation by the government of an NME cannot create a countervailable "subsidy." *Georgetown Steel Corp. v. United States*, 801 F.2d 1308 (Fed.Cir.1986).

The court's rationale was that, even though an NME government provides export oriented benefits, the NME can direct sales to be at any set price, so the benefits themselves do not distort competition. The court also suggested that imports from NMEs with unreasonably low prices should be analyzed under the rules for antidumping duties.

Beginning in the early part of this century, the Commerce Department pushed against this view. In 2008 and 2010, it thus imposed CVDs against imports of certain products from China and Vietnam respectively. In 2011, the Federal Circuit rejected this effort based on its reading of congressional intent in the substantial amendments of CVD law in 1994. See *GPX Intern. Tire Corp. v. United States*, 666 F.3d 732, 745 (Fed.Cir.2011).

In 2012, however, Congress annulled that decision by special legislation, with the result that countervailing duties also may be imposed on goods from non-market economies such as China and Vietnam. China's challenge of this legislation in WTO proceedings failed.

Softwood Lumber Dispute

The Trump Administration has emphasized at length its opposition to Chinese subsidization of goods. But it has not forgotten alleged Canadian subsidization of softwood lumber, imposing in 2017 a 20% CVD tariff as a sequel to a decades long subsidy dispute with the United States dating back to the Canada-U.S. FTA (CUSFTA 1989), which created binational panels (instead of national courts) to hear AD and CVD appeals from national administrative proceedings. Retention of these panels has been intensely advocated by Canada in NAFTA's re-negotiation.

Binational panel dispute settlement under CUSFTA 1989 in the five years prior to NAFTA 1994 was voluminous. With a few exceptions, most analyses of these decisions suggest an objective and not terribly politicized process. But the ability of binational panels to expertly rule under Canadian and United States law was hotly contested. A prominent U.S. judge involved as a panelist in the infamous *Softwood Lumber* dispute regarding Canadian "stumpage fees" for timbering on public lands wrote a blistering dissent. See ECC-94-1904-01-USA (Wilkey, J.). Some administrative determinations had to be repeatedly reviewed by CUSFTA panels before compliance was achieved.

Appeals to CUSFTA Extraordinary Challenge Committees demonstrated limited opportunities for relief. The bitterly disputed binational panel decisions on U.S. countervailing duty actions against Canadian exports of softwood lumber did not conclude with the *third* Extraordinary Challenge Committee proceeding in 1994 from which Judge Wilkey so vigorously dissented. Trade tensions and negotiations continued. Canada, the victor before the Challenge Committee, appeared to realize that it might lose the next time around if changes in U.S. countervailing duty law were recognized. Indeed, these changes were undertaken specifically for that purpose. In 1996, a "settlement" was reached.

The 1996 Softwood Lumber Agreement applied to Alberta, British Columbia, Ontario and Quebec. It committed Quebec, for example, to raising its "stumpage" (timbering) fees. British Columbia (the largest exporter) promised to impose taxes on shipments of lumber to the U.S. above designated levels starting at 9 billion board feet. In addition, the Canadian federal government promised to impose taxes if exports exceed 14.7 billion board feet. The U.S. government and forest industry, in turn, pledged not to commence a countervailing duty action for 5 years so long as the agreement was followed.

In 2001, the 1996 Agreement lapsed and U.S. countervailing duties on Canadian lumber were renewed, followed by Canadian challenges under NAFTA and within the WTO. Billions of dollars in U.S. antidumping and countervailing duties on

Canadian lumber were collected. In 2006, a second Softwood Lumber Agreement was achieved. Canada, then with about 34 percent of the U.S. softwood lumber market, agreed to impose rising export taxes if prices fall below specified trigger levels. About 80 percent of the duties previously collected were returned to Canadian producers. The Second Agreement was to be "dispute-free" for a minimum of three years. Nevertheless, the U.S. commenced arbitration proceedings before the London Court of Arbitration (LCIA) in 2007 and 2009 challenging the adequacy of Canadian implementation of the Agreement. Several LCIA rulings subsequently found Canada in breach of the 2006 Agreement. The 2006 Agreement was extended to October 2015.

To this day, softwood lumber disputes continue. Indeed, the Trump Administration levied 20% countervailing duties on Canadian lumber prior to commencing re-negotiation of NAFTA 1994 in 2017. Canada promised compensation to its exporters, also filing yet another dispute under NAFTA and before the WTO.

SAFEGUARD (ESCAPE CLAUSE) MEASURES

GATT Article XIX permits—even in absence of an unfair trade practice in the form of a subsidy or dumping—temporary suspension of agreed tariff concessions if increased quantities of imports cause or threaten to cause *serious* injury to a domestic industry. A member state may only undertake such an "emergency action" after consultation with the affected WTO exporting country. Similar to ADs and

CVDs, a special WTO "Agreement on Safeguards" concluded during the Uruguay Round of negotiations governs the imposition of safeguard measures.

On this authority, the United States has authorized suspension of tariff concessions through "escape clause proceedings" (also known as Section 201 proceedings) under the Trade Act of 1974. Similar to all other WTO Covered Agreements, Congress amended this Act to implement the Safeguards Agreement in December of 1994 as part of the Uruguay Round Agreements Act.

The rationale for such "escape clause" measures is that the reduction of trade barriers under the WTO/ GATT system may cause serious dislocations for certain industries and workers. If sudden increases in imports thus cause or threaten to cause a "serious injury" to a domestic industry, protective duties are allowed on a *temporary* basis to permit the industry to adjust to the unexpected international competition.

In addition, "market disruption proceedings" can also provide temporary relief from import competition. Market disruption proceedings concern imports from "communist" nations and are authorized by Section 406 of the 1974 Trade Act. They are similar but not identical to escape clause proceedings. Either may result in the imposition of U.S. import restraints.

Import injury relief available under the Trade Act of 1974 is basically of two kinds: (1) Presidential relief designed to temporarily protect domestic producers of like or directly competitive products; and (2) governmental assistance to workers and firms economically displaced by import competition. This assistance is intended to enhance job opportunities and competitiveness.

Protective relief tends to be awarded when the President believes that U.S. industry needs time to adjust. Governmental assistance is seen as a means to accommodate the injury caused by import competition. In either case, adjustment to import competition is the longer term goal, hopefully resulting in more competitive U.S. industries and markets. President Trump chose to impose notable import tariffs on solar panels and clothes washers in 2018. See Chapter 8.

WTO AGREEMENT ON SAFEGUARDS

The WTO's Safeguards Agreement defines the substantive and procedural requirements for the imposition of protective relief by a member state in response to increased import competition. Most important, the Agreement states as a fundamental rule that such measures are only allowed for a "serious" injury or a threat of a "serious" injury. In addition, it permits safeguard measures "only to the extent necessary" to prevent or remedy such an injury and to "facilitate adjustment."

Such measures are allowed for a maximum of four years, and on a progressively decreasing basis (although, upon a further investigation, a member state may extend the measures, but not beyond a total period of eight years). The exporting countries whose goods are covered by allowed safeguard measures also may not generally retaliate for the first three years. However, if there was no absolute increase in imports (a "surge"), the exporting nations may immediately employ countermeasures of substantially equivalent value, often referred to as "rebalancing tariffs". A number of major U.S. trade partners have instituted rebalancing tariffs against the Trump Administration's steel and aluminum "national security" tariffs. See Chapter 8.

Special rules limit the use of safeguard measures against imports from developing countries and allow such countries to impose safeguard measures to protect domestic industries for up to ten years.

Perhaps the most important provision of the Safeguards Agreement is that it expressly prohibits a member state from seeking, undertaking, or maintaining voluntary export or import restraint agreements (VERs or OMAs). These were quite common, especially by developed countries to protect against unwanted imports, prior to the adoption of the Safeguards Agreement in 1994. President Reagan, for example, negotiated VERs with Japan limiting auto sales to the United States. The WTO provision barring VERs raises questions concerning the legality export quotas on steel and aluminum secured by the Trump administration from various countries. See Chapter 8.

U.S. SAFEGUARD LAW

As noted above, the United States has implemented the authority for safeguard measures granted by GATT Article XIX and the Safeguards Agreement through "escape clause proceedings" in Section 201 of the Trade Act of 1974. Decisions about such import adjustments are made by the President upon the recommendation of the International Trade Commission (ITC).

Any entity that is "representative of an industry," including a "trade association, firm, certified or recognized union, or group of workers," may file a petition requesting such import relief. The petition must state the "specific purposes" for any requested action "which may include facilitating the orderly transfer of resources to more productive pursuits, enhancing competitiveness, or other means of adjustment to new conditions of competition." The petitioner industry or worker group may—and is well advised to—submit its own specific plan "to facilitate positive adjustment to import competition" during the term of any protective relief.

The ITC also must initiate an escape clause proceeding at the request of the President, the United States Trade Representative, and certain congressional committees, and may do so "on its own motion." The ITC then investigates to determine whether the import competition meets the statutory standard for temporary escape clause relief.

The Statutory Standard

The ITC traditionally has divided the statutory standard into three separate criteria. In order to make an affirmative determination on an escape clause petition, the ITC must find, as it stated in the famous (or infamous) *Steel Safeguards* case, that:

"(1) imports of the subject article are in *increased quantities* . . . ;

(2) the domestic industry producing an article that is like or directly competitive with the imported article is *seriously injured or threatened with serious injury*; and

(3) the article is being imported in such increased quantities as to be a *substantial cause* of serious injury or threat of serious injury to the domestic industry."

The 1974 Trade Act also provides more detail on these elements.

(a) On the requirement of *increased quantities of imports*, the Act provides that the increase may be "either actual or relative to domestic production," and in consideration of imports from all sources.

(b) In determining whether *serious injury* exists, the ITC may consider "all economic factors which it considers relevant," including a significant idling of productive facilities in the domestic industry, an inability of a significant number of firms to carry out domestic production operations at a reasonable level of profit, and significant unemployment or underemployment within the domestic industry.

(c) In determining whether a *threat of serious injury* exists, the ITC may consider a decline in sales or market share; higher and growing inventories; a downward trend in production, profits, wages, or employment (or increasing underemployment); the extent to which affected domestic firms are able to generate adequate capital to modernize and to maintain current levels of research and development; and the extent to which the U.S. "is the focal point for diversion of exports" because of export requirements in the home country or import restraints in another country.

(d) The *substantial cause* element is among the most controversial in application to actual cases. The Trade Act defines the term as "a cause which is important and not less than any other cause." As a result, increased imports must be both "an important cause" and one that is "equal to or greater than any other cause."

The Act directs the ITC to consider all relevant economic factors, including "an increase in imports (either actual or relative to domestic production) and a decline in the proportion of the domestic market supplied by domestic producers." The difficulty with the "substantial cause" element comes in determining whether increased imports are "equal to or greater than" the myriad of other competing factors that may cause harm to an industry, including inept management, negative general economic or market trends, and technological innovations.

As a foundation for all of these analyses, the ITC must identify the specific domestic "industry" that is affected by the increased imports. The Act identifies the relevant industry as "the domestic industry producing an article that is like or directly competitive with the imported article." In turn, the Act defines a "domestic industry" as the "the producers as a whole" of the competitive goods or those producers "whose collective production. . . constitutes a major proportion" of total production of the competitive goods.

Protective Relief, Compensation

The statute requires the ITC to report its findings to the President within four months after the petition is filed. If the ITC finds that imports have increased, and that this increase has been a "substantial cause" of actual or threatened serious injury to the industry, it will make recommendations to the President on appropriate protective relief. In doing so, the Trade Act requires the ITC to consider what relief measures would prevent or remedy the injury; any "adjustment plans" submitted by the petitioner as well as any "individual commitment" it has made; available information concerning domestic and global competition; and whether international negotiations may address the domestic injury or facilitate adjustment by the industry.

The Act authorizes the President to grant escape clause relief only if the ITC has made an affirmative finding that the increased imports have caused or threaten to cause serious injury. But if the ITC makes an affirmative finding, the President "shall" take all appropriate and feasible action to facilitate efforts by the industry to make "a positive adjustment to import competition."

The President need not, however, follow the ITC's relief recommendations. Thus, even though the word "shall" is used, the Act leaves substantial discretion to the President in defining the appropriate protective action. In other words, unlike antidumping and countervailing duty proceedings, the President has effective control over both whether any relief will be given in a Section 201 proceeding, and what form of relief will be granted. The Act generally sets a four-year limit on any such relief.

One reason why protective escape clause relief is difficult to obtain is that the Safeguards Agreement entitles most trading partners to seek *compensation* for the adverse effects of any relief granted by another member state. Formal retaliation through a return suspension of concessions on exports generally is prohibited for three years.

Because escape clause proceedings do not concern any unfair trade practice, protective relief measures typically are a source of substantial friction in world trade. This perspective helps explain why the President frequently decides that it is not in the economic interest of the United States to impose escape clause relief or, if granted, decides to terminate the relief before three years have expired.

If nonetheless granted by the President, escape clause measures for an affected industry and its workers may be in the form of either protective relief or trade adjustment assistance (see below). The former is directed toward the imported goods and can include increased tariffs, tariff rate quotas (tariffs which increase after reaching a certain quota), import quotas, or—at least according to the statute's text—orderly marketing agreements (OMAs).

In the past, the threat of such protective relief prompted some countries to agree to such OMAs "voluntarily" and thus to limit the volume of their exports or otherwise limit competition. Prominent examples included the agreements by Japan in the 1980s to restrain auto exports to the United States and Europe. These restraints caused Japanese automakers to invest in the USA and Europe. As explained above, however, the 1994 Safeguards Agreement now expressly prohibits such agreements.

Special Safeguard Rules for Chinese Imports

In addition to the general rule in Section 201, U.S. law has a special provision—which arose in connection with China's accession to the WTO in 2000—for safeguard measures relating to imports from China. Because of worries over a flood of inexpensive Chinese imports, these "Section 421" safeguard measures require only that increased imports be a "significant cause" of a "material" injury to a domestic industry. These standards are significantly lower than for regular safeguard measures, which (as noted above) require a cause that is "equal to or greater than any other cause" and a real or threatened "serious" injury to a domestic industry.

The special Section 421 safeguards rule played a much more significant role than the traditional Section 201 rule (above). Between 2003 and 2012, the ITC initiated six investigations under Section 421, but none under Section 201. A prominent example was President Obama's imposition in June 2009 of protective tariffs of 35% on vehicle tires from China. Rather than safeguarding U.S. tire makers, low cost tires from other countries largely filled the gap in Chinese exports, a good example of "country-hopping" to avoid trade remedy tariffs. China, for its part, levied retaliatory tariffs on U.S. exports of apples, oats chicken feet and other goods.

The special Safeguard rules for Chinese imports expired in 2013.

U.S. SAFEGUARD ACTIONS REVIEWED BY THE WTO

The rulings of the WTO's Appellate Body concerning the Safeguards Agreement have strictly limited the use of escape clause remedies. Indeed, the United States has lost a number of related disputes before the WTO, including in complaints brought by Australia and New Zealand on lamb; by the European Union on wheat gluten; by India and Pakistan on wool shirts and blouses; by South Korea on line pipe; and by Japan and numerous others on steel.

In 2001 alone, the Appellate Body (AB) ruled against the United States in three separate safeguard cases. In *U.S.-Wheat Gluten from the EC*, the AB emphasized the critical issue of causation. The AB found that the ITC's causation analysis lacked clarity and inadequately addressed factors other than imports that may have caused domestic industry injury. It also criticized the U.S. for a failure to give timely notice and to allow for a "meaningful exchange" in the required consultations.

In *U.S.-Lamb Meat from New Zealand*, the AB reiterated that all causation factors must be isolated and examined. Further, it rejected the "domestic industry" definition adopted by the ITC because growers were included. Both of these decisions also emphasized the need for the ITC to find "unforeseen developments" in its injury determinations. The third 2001 AB ruling against U.S. safeguard measures concerned cotton yarn from India and Pakistan. In this decision, the AB rejected an exclusion of vertically integrated yarn producers from the definition of "domestic industry."

In its 2002 decision on U.S. safeguards on line pipe from Korea, the WTO similarly criticized the ITC for a "mere assertion" that challenged imports were "an important cause of serious injury and. . .not less than any other cause." More generally, the AB has repeatedly emphasized that the U.S. may not exclude consideration of imports from NAFTA countries (Canada and Mexico) in making safeguard determinations (the concept of parallelism).

The Bush Administration U.S. Steel Safeguards Dispute

Perhaps the most controversial recent escape clause action by the United States was the imposition of tariffs on steel by President George W. Bush in 2002. The ITC found, following an extensive investigation and numerous hearings, that certain categories of steel imports caused, or threatened to cause, serious injury to the domestic steel industry. President Bush then imposed tariffs of up to 30 percent on imported steel for three years. This escape clause relief was tempered by exclusions for selected steel from selected countries. Most Australian and Japanese steel products, for example, were not subject to the extra U.S. tariffs. About half of all EU steel imports were exempt. Canada and Mexico, as members of NAFTA 1994, were fully exempt.

Numerous WTO member states promptly challenged the imposition of this safeguard relief before the WTO's Dispute Settlement Body (as well as in U.S. federal court). In 2003, the Appellate Body (AB) ultimately ruled that the special U.S. tariffs on steel were illegal under the WTO Safeguards Agreement.

The AB held that the U.S. erred in utilizing the protective tariffs some four years after the surge of steel imports during the Asian economic meltdown, and in excluding NAFTA partners Canada and Mexico. It also found that the ITC failed properly to address the requirement of "unforeseen developments." Although the AB acknowledged that the term does not appear in the Safeguards Agreement, it reiterated its earlier holdings that the Agreement must be understood against the backdrop of GATT Article XIX, which conspicuously includes such a requirement.

The European Union then threatened over $2 billion annually in retaliatory tariffs on U.S. exports of clothing, citrus, and boats, products thought to be politically damaging to the Bush Administration. But before the WTO could authorize such sanctions, President Bush rescinded the duties, which are thought to have generated a substantial net loss of jobs in the United States because of their impact on steel users versus producers, in December 2003 pursuant to corresponding authority in the Trade Act.

Interestingly, during the Bush steel safeguard tariff period, domestic interests separately petitioned the ITA and ITC to impose CVDs or ADs on many of the same products. Reasoning that the temporary safeguard measures effectively mitigated the damaging effects of imports, the ITC concluded that there was no material injury to justify responsive duties on either basis. See *Nucor Corp. v. U.S.*, 414 F.3d 1331 (Fed.Cir.2005).

U.S. TRADE ADJUSTMENT ASSISTANCE

Escape clause proceedings often lead to separate "trade adjustment assistance" for affected workers (and sometimes firms). This assistance is designed to provide financial relief for the effects of the increased imports, not to prevent, reduce, or restrict the imports. Escape clause relief is always considered temporary, but adversely affected workers may be provided with "adjustment assistance" payments and other displacement benefits for a longer period. For example, automobile workers have received such assistance because foreign automobile manufacturers enjoyed great marketing success in the United States.

Trade adjustment assistance decisions for workers are made by the U.S. Department of Labor, for firms by the Department of Commerce. Such assistance does not require an affirmative determination by the ITC on import injuries (as is required for protective relief, see above). *Adjustment assistance is also available to workers whose plants relocate to U.S. free trade partners, or GSP, CBI, Andean or African trade preference countries. Since 2015, workers affected by trade with any country, say China or India, are eligible.* During the past 40 years, trade adjustment assistance has benefitted over 2 million U.S. workers.

U.S. law permits petitions for trade adjustment assistance by a "group of workers," union, or "employers of such workers." Generally, three groups of workers may be eligible for adjustment assistance: (1) those who have lost their jobs because increased imports caused significant harm to production by their former employer; (2) those who lost their jobs because increased imports caused their former employer to shift production to a foreign country; and (3) "adversely affected secondary workers"—those who lost their jobs with a supplier of a primary firm harmed by increased imports.

Congress expanded the trade adjustment assistance (TAA) programs significantly in 2002, 2009, 2011 and 2015. Among the variety of benefits and services available for eligible workers are employment counseling and job referrals; job search allowances for travel and related costs; "relocation allowances" to cover moving expenses; retraining assistance; and, perhaps most important, income support after state unemployment benefits have run out.

Recent expansions of the TAA programs also now allow financial assistance for health insurance as well as special wage subsidies for workers over fifty. Congress also has authorized a separate, but more limited, program of Trade Adjustment Assistance for Firms (TAAF) which is administered by the Department of Commerce.

Such expansions and extensions of trade adjustment assistance often are closely connected with the granting of Trade Promotion Authority ("fast track") by Congress to the President for free trade agreements, as well as to actual congressional approval of such agreements once concluded by the President. An example is the extension of the enhanced TAA programs in 2011 in connection with the approval of the free trade agreements with South Korea, Colombia, and Panama. The 2015 expansion was coordinated with the President's revived fast track trade promotion authority, which terminates June 30, 2018.

PROTECTION FROM PIRATED AND IP INFRINGING IMPORTS

Remedies Against Counterfeiting and IP Infringement

Theft of intellectual property and use of counterfeit goods are rapidly increasing in developing and developed countries. Such theft is not limited to consumer goods (Pierre Cardin clothing, Rolex watches). Industrial products and parts (e.g., automotive brake pads) are now being counterfeited. Some developing countries see illegal technology transfers as part of their economic development. They encourage piracy or choose not to oppose it. Since unlicensed producers pay no royalties, they often have lower production costs than the original source.

This practice fuels the fires of intellectual property piracy. Unlicensed low cost reproduction of entire copyrighted books (may it not happen to this book) is said to be rampant in such diverse areas as Nigeria, Saudi Arabia, and China. Apple computers have been inexpensively counterfeited in Hong Kong. General Motors estimates that about 40 percent of its auto parts are counterfeited in the Middle East. Recordings and software are duplicated almost everywhere without license or fee. And the list goes on.

Mandatory IP infringement and anti-counterfeiting remedies are included in the TRIPS, for both domestic and international trade protection. There are specific provisions governing injunctions, damages, judicial and customs seizures, and discovery of evidence. Willful trademark counterfeiting and copyright piracy on a commercial scale must be criminalized. Counterfeit goods may not be re-exported by customs authorities in an unaltered state.

U.S. law distinguishes between counterfeiting intended to deceptively duplicate branded goods, and "merely" infringing imports likely to cause public confusion. Counterfeit goods must be seized and, absent written consent, forfeited. Merely infringing goods *may* be seized and forfeited. U.S. Customs will allow merely infringing goods to enter if the objectionable mark is obliterated. See 19 C.F.R. Section 133.21(a), (c)(4).

U.S. Section 337 Proceedings

Legal protection against intellectual property theft and counterfeit goods is not very effective. In the United States, trademark and copyright holders may register with the Customs Service and seek the blockade of pirated items made abroad. Such exclusions are authorized in the Lanham Trademark Act of 1946 and the Copyright Act of 1976. Patent piracy is most often challenged in proceedings against unfair import practices under Section 337 of the Tariff Act of 1930.

Section 337 proceedings traditionally involve some rather complicated provisions in Section 1337 of the Tariff Act of 1930. Prior to 1988, the basic prohibition was against: (1) unfair methods of competition and unfair acts in the importation of goods, (2) the effect or tendency of which is to destroy or substantially injure (3) an industry efficiently and economically operated in the United States Such importation was also prohibited when it prevented the establishment of an industry, or restrained or monopolized trade and commerce in the United States.

The Omnibus Trade and Competitiveness Act of 1988 revised Section 337. The requirement that the U.S. industry be efficiently and economically operated was dropped. The importation of articles infringing U.S. patents, copyrights, trademarks or semiconductor chip mask works is specifically prohibited provided a U.S. industry relating to such articles exists or is in the process of being established. Proof of injury to a domestic industry is not required in intellectual property infringement cases. Such an industry exists if there is significant plant and equipment investment, significant employment of labor or capital, or substantial investment in exploitation (including research and development or licensing).

Determination of violations and the recommendation of remedies to the President under Section 337 is the exclusive province of the International Trade Commission (ITC). Most of the case law under Section 337 concerns the infringement of patents. While not quite a per se rule, it is nearly axiomatic that any infringement, even after lawful entry as a result of how imported goods are used, of U.S. patent rights amounts to an unfair import practice for purposes of Section 337.

Patents and General Exclusion Orders

Section 337 proceedings result in general exclusion orders permitting seizure of patent counterfeits at any U.S. point of entry. However, the Customs Service finds it extremely difficult when inspecting invoices and occasionally opening boxes to ascertain which goods are counterfeit or infringing. Many counterfeits do look like "the real thing."

For most seizure remedies to work, the holder must notify the customs service of an incoming shipment of offending goods. Use of private detectives can help and is increasing, but such advance notice is hard to obtain. Nevertheless, the Customs Service seizes millions of counterfeit goods each year. In 2009, U.S. officials seized about $260 million in counterfeit goods. Chinese gangs accounted for the bulk of these goods, which were most often footwear, consumer electronics, luxury goods and pharmaceuticals. U.S. military and civilian procurement agencies have begun actively targeting counterfeit suppliers.

Patent-based Section 337 proceedings are multiplying. For example, in a major 2007 decision, the ITC excluded the importation of cell phones containing Qualcomm microchips found to infringe Broadcom patents. In 2012, Samsung succeeded before the ITC in alleging patent infringement by imported Apple cellphones, but the President denied a general exclusion order because the patents in question were part of an industry standard and thus he determined it was against the public interest to exclude the imports on the basis of such patent infringement.

This was the first denial of ITC-recommended Section 337 relief since President Reagan. Apple's subsequent attempt to bar Samsung cellphones on patent infringement grounds were upheld by the ITC. Absent involvement of industry standards, no Presidential veto was forthcoming.

ITC decisions take about 12 to 15 months, versus three to five years for federal court lawsuits. General exclusion orders are typically sought. Hearings are held before one of four administrative law judges specializing in patent law, with final decisions taken by the ITC. Infringing products are excluded from importation during the appeals process. About one-fourth of all 337 proceedings find infringements. An increasing number of foreign owners of U.S. patents are invoking 337 procedures. About half of all such complaints are settled, often using cross-licensing among the parties.

Section 337 proceedings can result in general exclusion orders permitting seizure of patent counterfeits at any U.S. point of entry. Apple Computer, for example, was able to get such an order against computers sold under the label "Orange" that contained infringing programs and color display circuits. However, as previously noted, the Customs Service finds it extremely difficult when inspecting invoices and occasionally opening boxes to ascertain which goods are counterfeit or infringing. Many counterfeits do look like "the real thing." For most seizure remedies to work, the holder must notify the Customs Service of an incoming shipment of patent offending goods. Such advance notice is hard to obtain.

Other U.S. Trade Remedies Against Counterfeit and IP Infringing Imports

Infringement and treble damages actions may be commenced in U.S. courts against importers and distributors of counterfeit goods, but service of process and jurisdictional barriers often preclude effective relief against foreign pirates. Even if such relief is obtained, counterfeiters and the sellers of counterfeit goods have proven adept at the "shell game," moving across the road or to another country to resume operations. Moreover, the mobility and economic incentives of counterfeiters have rendered the criminal sanctions of the Trademark Counterfeiting Act of 1984 largely a Pyrrhic victory.

Ex parte seizure orders are also available under the 1984 Act and the Lanham Trademark Act when counterfeit goods can be located in the United States. Goods so seized can be destroyed upon court order.

International solutions have been no less elusive. The WTO agreement on TRIPS addresses these problems by mandating certain national remedies, but their effectiveness remains to be tested. Various U.S. statutes authorize the President to withhold trade benefits from or apply trade sanctions to nations inadequately protecting the intellectual property rights of U.S. citizens. This is true of the Caribbean Basin Economic Recovery Act of 1983, the Generalized System of Preferences Renewal Act of 1984, the Trade and Tariff Act of 1984 (amending Section 301 of the 1974 Trade Act), and Title IV of the 1974 Trade Act as it applies to most favored nation tariffs.

Slowly this carrot and stick approach has borne fruit. Under these pressures for example, Singapore drafted a new copyright law, South Korea new patent and copyright laws, and Taiwan a new copyright, patent, fair trade and an amended trademark law. Brazil introduced legislation intended to allow copyrights on computer programs. Though these changes have been made, there is some doubt as to the rigor with which the new laws will be enforced when local jobs and national revenues are lost.

France and Italy have made it illegal to knowingly purchase counterfeit goods. For example, if a student buys a "Louis Vuitton" bag for $15 in a Paris or Florence flea market, he or she may be arrested, fined and imprisoned. France has gone a step further. A new agency monitors Internet piracy. French offenders are subject to a "three strikes" rule: Two warnings are issued before Net accesses can be terminated and fines imposed by court order. South Korea and Taiwan also employ warnings and penalties against illegal downloading.

TRADE IN GRAY MARKET GOODS

One of the most controversial areas of customs law concerns "gray market goods," goods produced abroad *with authorization* and payment but which are imported into *unauthorized* markets. Trade in gray market goods has dramatically increased in recent years, in part because fluctuating currency exchange rates create opportunities to import and sell such goods at a discount from local price levels. Licensors and their distributors suddenly find themselves competing in their home or other "reserved" markets with products made abroad by their own licensees. Or, in the reverse, startled licensees find their licensor's products intruding on their local market shares.

In either case, third party importers and exporters are often the immediate source of the gray market goods, and they have little respect for who agreed to what in the licensing agreement. When pressed, such third parties will undoubtedly argue that any attempt through licensing at allocating markets or customers is an antitrust or competition law violation.

In the early part of the century, gray market litigation provoked a U.S. Supreme Court decision, *A. Bourjois & Co. v. Katzel*, 260 U.S. 689 (1923), blocking French cosmetics from entering the United States. A U.S. firm was assigned the U.S. trademark rights for French cosmetics as part of the sale of the American business interests of the French producer. The assignee successfully obtained infringement relief against Katzel, an importer of the French product benefitting from exchange rate fluctuations. The Supreme Court reversed a Second Circuit holding which followed a line of cases allowing "genuine goods" to enter the American market in competition with established sources. The Supreme Court emphasized the trademark ownership (not license) and independent public good will of the assignee as reasons for its reversal.

U.S. Genuine Goods Exclusion Act

Congress, before the Supreme Court reversal, passed the Genuine Goods Exclusion Act, now appearing as Section 526 of the Tariff Act of 1930. This Act bars *unauthorized importation* of goods bearing trademarks of U.S. citizens. Registration of such marks with the Customs Service can result in the seizure of unauthorized imports. Persons dealing in such imports may be enjoined, required to export the goods, destroy them or obliterate the offending mark, as well as pay damages.

The Act has had a checkered history in the courts and Customs Service. The Customs Service view (influenced by antitrust policy) was that genuine (gray market) goods may be excluded only when the foreign and U.S. trademark rights are not under common ownership, or those rights have been used without authorization. The practical effect of this position was to admit most gray market goods into the United States, thereby providing substantial price competition, but uncertain coverage under manufacturers' warranty, service and rebate programs. Some firms excel at gray market importing and may provide independent warranty and repair service contracts. Since 1986, New York and California require disclosure by sellers of gray market goods that manufacturers' programs may not apply.

A split in the federal courts of appeal as to the legitimacy in light of the Genuine Goods Exclusion Act of the Customs Service position on gray market imports resulted in a U.S. Supreme Court ruling. In an extremely technical, not very policy oriented decision, the Supreme Court in *K Mart Corp. v. Cartier, Inc.*, 486 U.S. 281 (1988) arrived at a compromise. The Customs Service can continue to permit entry of genuine goods when common ownership of the trademarks exists. The Service must seize such goods only when they were authorized (licensed), but the marks are not subject to common ownership. Many believe that the bulk of U.S. imports of gray market goods have continued under this ruling.

Other U.S. Gray Market Import Barriers

An attempt in 1985 by Duracell to exclude gray market batteries under Section 337 of the Tariff Act of 1930 as an unfair import practice was upheld by the U.S. International Trade Commission, but denied relief by President Reagan in deference to the Customs Service position.

Injunctive relief under trademark or copyright law is sometimes available against gray market importers and distributors. When available, injunctive relief applies only to the parties and does not prohibit gray market imports or sales by others. This remedy is thus useful, but normally insufficient. In *Lever Bros. v. United States*, 877 F.2d 101 (D.C.Cir.1989), the D.C. Circuit allowed Trademark Act injunctive relief against materially different gray market goods where those differences had not been disclosed in labeling.

In *Quality King Distributors, Inc. v. L'anza Research Intern., Inc.*, 523 U.S. 135 (1998), however, the U.S. Supreme Court held that the "first sale doctrine" bars injunctive relief under the Copyright Act against gray market re-importation of U.S. exports. More recently, the Supreme Court went further and denied copyright injunctive relief against foreign-made gray market goods in *Kirtsaeng v. John Wiley & Sons*, 200 U.S. 324 (2013). This decision allowed an entrepreneurial student to import gray market textbooks from Asia.

Gray Market Trading Outside the USA

An excellent, though dated, review of the treatment of gray market goods in other jurisdictions is presented in an article by Takamatsu at 57 Wash. L. Rev. 433 (1982). This review is of particular interest to U.S. *exporters* of gray market goods. For the most part, his review indicates that other jurisdictions permit gray market goods to enter. This is true of the *Parker Pen* cases under Japanese law, the *Maja* case under German law and the *Agfa-Gevaert* case in Austria, all of which are reviewed by Takamatsu. Canadian Supreme Court law strongly supports free trade in gray market goods. See *Consumers Distributing Co., Ltd. v. Seiko Time Canada Ltd.*, 1 Can. Sup. Ct. 583 (1984).

The legal analysis contained in these opinions has been very influential in European Union law. EU law basically posits that once goods subject to intellectual property rights of common origin have been sold on the market with authorization, the holders can no longer block importation of those goods ("parallel imports") through the use of national property rights. Such use is not thought to have been intended as part of the original grant of rights and is said to have been "exhausted" upon sale.

An extensive body of EU law permits parallel imports (even of qualitatively different goods) as part of the promotion of the Common Market and rejects attempts to divide the market territorially along the lines of national property rights. Product labeling as to source and contents is thought sufficient notice to consumers that qualitatively different goods are involved.

In a major decision, the European Court of Justice ruled that trademark rights can be used to block gray market imports into the Common Market. These rights are not exhausted once the goods are voluntarily put into the stream of international commerce. An Austrian maker of high-quality sunglasses was therefore entitled to bar imports from Bulgaria prior to its EU membership. See *Silhouette International v. Hartlauer,* 1998 Eur. Comm. Rep. I-4799. In other words, the exhaustion doctrine does not apply externally. Levi Strauss, for example, seized upon this distinction to actively pursue EU importers of its blue jeans from non-EU sources. The jeans were being sold cheaply at a British supermarket.

China allows gray market auto imports into its Shanghai and other free trade zones, subject to the same warranty and recall policies of the manufacturer.

CHAPTER 5
EXPORTS

U.S. Export Controls	**U.S. Boycotts**
U.S. Anti-Boycotts	**Foreign Corrupt Practices**

A merchant in the United States wishing to export goods must consider all limitations imposed by the *importing* nation which affect the proposed transaction. Foreign import controls may or may not be comparable to the U.S. import controls discussed in Chapter 3. For nations which are members of the WTO, the import controls are likely to be relatively similar.

A merchant in the United States must also consider that the U.S. may have *export* controls which affect goods or technology. Additionally, if there are any third party nation components in the goods to be exported, the export controls of that third nation must also be reviewed. For example, if a U.S. manufacturer of shirts made of materials from India wishes to export the finished shirts to Pakistan, it must consider whether India prohibits or regulates that trade.

Control of the re-export (including trans-shipment or diversion) of goods from a foreign nation is difficult to police and creates ill feeling on the part of the re-exporting nation. Assume that India is engaged in a trade embargo of Pakistan and attempts to halt the export of the shirts mentioned above from the United

States, Sri Lanka or Bangladesh. All three governments might ignore the Indian demand. Canada and Argentina, for example, ignored demands by the United States to halt shipping to Cuba automobiles made in GM and Ford subsidiary plants in Canada and Argentina, respectively.

Why does a nation control exports? Exports earn revenue and create jobs. This suggests that export controls are imposed more for political or foreign policy reasons than for economic reasons. But sometimes the controls have a mixture of these goals. For example, exports may be limited to protect national security (military weapons and technology, regulated in the U.S. by the Arms Export Control Act of 1976), to limit the spread of nuclear components (partly controlled by the Nuclear Nonproliferation Act), to preserve natural resources (endangered species, subject to an international convention— CITES), to reserve resources for domestic use (certain hardwoods for making furniture), or to hold resources for sale at expected higher prices in the future (oil).

Apart from the law of export subsidies and countervailing duties and to a degree the law of export quotas, the WTO package of agreements marginally touches upon export issues. See Chapter 2. Why does the World Trade Organization fail to have extensive legal disciplines regarding exports?

The answer is less than clear. National export controls have certainly been less numerous, and therefore less on the international trade radar screen. Restricting exports is often counterintuitive to trade policy. Exports represent local production, employment and earnings, whereas imports may disrupt domestic companies, jobs and economic growth. Governments are therefore inclined to promote exports, not inhibit them. In the developing world, for example, there has been a major policy shift away from import substitution in favor of export enhancement.

In the absence of WTO rules on export controls, member states have pursued different policies. The United States, one of the world's top exporters, shipping trillions of dollars of goods, services and technology each year, has nevertheless maintained an extensive system of export controls. The U.S. system is the focus of this Chapter.

U.S. EXPORT POLICY

To understand the U.S. regulation of imports, one must understand a complex matrix of trade acts and agreements. See Chapter 3. To understand the regulation of exports as opposed to imports, the path is somewhat less cluttered. There is no comparable extensive matrix of laws regulating U.S. exports. There is one major U.S. export law which is especially important to those engaging in international trade. It is the Export Administration Act of 1979 (EAA).

This Act makes a number of Congressional policy statements that suggest an intent to restrict export controls only to the extent necessary to achieve certain political goals. It outlines the licensing procedure for exports, requiring a license only in a limited number of specific export situations. It includes the concept of "foreign availability", that export controls should not be placed on goods which are readily available from other sources. Additionally, it is within the EAA that Congress has placed the foreign anti-boycott provisions prohibiting U.S. persons from taking part in boycotts against countries friendly to the United States.

U.S. export policy primarily involves questions of *what* goods may be exported, and to *which* countries they may not be exported. There is usually less immediacy about controlling the nature of the goods as opposed to their destination. Restrictions are often introduced to punish nations for actions so distasteful that limits on U.S. exports to that country are thought justified, despite economic losses caused by the diminished exports.

The President is thought to be in a better position than Congress to respond quickly to foreign acts which may justify immediate export controls. For example, President Reagan took action after the Soviets imposed martial law in Poland, prohibiting the export of component parts for the Siberian oil pipeline. The President's decision generated substantial adverse reaction from several European nations which were the location of U.S. owned subsidiaries affected by the order.

The provisions of the EAA, as in the case of several trade laws, are followed-up by extensive administrative regulations. Finally, the EAA contains very severe penalties for violating U.S. export controls, including loss of all export rights.

This leads to preventative lawyering under ongoing, proactive compliance programs.

U.S. EXPORT GOVERNANCE

United States export controls involve three primary laws and government agencies:

1. The U.S. Dept. of Commerce, Bureau of Industry and Security (BIS), administers the Export Administration Act Regulations (EAR, 22 C.F.R. Parts 730–774), and the U.S. anti-boycott laws.

2. The U.S. Dept. of the Treasury, Office of Foreign Asset Controls (OFAC), administers U.S. boycott laws.

3. The U.S. Dept. of State administers the International Traffic in Arms Regulations (ITAR, 22 C.F.R. Parts 120–130).

The United States also supports various non-proliferation treaties, and U.N. Security Council Resolution 1540 calling on all nations to enforce effective laws against non-state actors' possession and use of weapons of mass destruction, particularly for terrorist purposes.

The United States enacted the Enhanced Proliferation Control Initiative (EPCI), motivated by the Iraq conflict. This enactment seeks to establish greater control where commodities or technical data are destined for a prohibited nuclear, chemical or biological weapons or missile development use or end user. Considerable emphasis is placed on making the exporter aware of the nature of the buyer and where the items are going.

The EPIC consists of Sections 744.1–744.6 of the C.F.R. EPIC addresses how technology and goods are used rather than by their description. They include essentially the "design, development, production, stockpiling, or use" of nuclear explosive devices, missiles, or chemical or biological weapons. The end result is that a license is required where otherwise it might not be. Exporters are thus given the responsibility to know more about their dual-use goods. The use of the EPCI in the control of weapons of mass destruction, especially after September 11, 2001, is clear.

Exports are thus subject to a mix of regulations *by* different persons or agencies, *of* different products, *for* different purposes, and *to* different places.

EXPORT ADMINISTRATION ACT (EAA)

U.S. exports are principally regulated by the Export Administration Act (EAA), and several hundred pages of associated regulations. Congress' power to regulate exports as expressed in these laws originates in the *foreign commerce* clause. It is the same provision establishing Congressional authority to regulate imports. This power often conflicts with the President's conception of *foreign affairs* powers, and can lead to disagreements with the executive branch over the extent to which Congress may restrict Presidential discretion in limiting exports to achieve foreign policy goals.

The Export Administration Act is of limited duration. The last one was enacted in 1979 and amended (extended) in 1985. It expired in 1994. Since that time the executive and legislative branches have not been able to agree on the substance of a new act. President George H. P. Bush vetoed one attempt in 1990 to adopt a new EAA because he believed that his powers were unduly restricted by Congress. In order to continue controls over exports, every President since 1994 has extended the duration of the EAA by declaring a state of emergency under the International Emergency Economic Powers Act (IEEPA).

The policy of the United States toward export controls is set forth in Section 3 of the Export Administration Act of 1979, which provides:

> It is the policy of the United States to use export controls only after full consideration of the impact on the economy of the United States and only to the extent necessary—
>
> (A) to restrict the export of goods and technology which would make a significant contribution to the military potential of any other country or combination of countries which would prove detrimental to the national security of the United States;
>
> (B) to restrict the export of goods and technology where necessary to further significantly the foreign policy of the United States or to fulfill its declared international obligations; and

(C) to restrict the export of goods where necessary to protect the domestic economy from the excessive drain of scarce materials and to reduce the serious inflationary impact of foreign demand . . .

* * *

It is the policy of the United States. . . to oppose restrictive trade practices or boycotts fostered or imposed by foreign countries against other countries friendly to the United States or against any United States person.

No EAA Judicial Review

Reliance on the IEEPA to maintain U.S. export controls has an important consequence: There are no appeals from EAA decisions. In other words, there is no judicial review of EAA rules and enforcement. See *Micei International v. Dept. of Commerce*, 613 F.3d 1147 (D.C. Cir. 2010).

EAA REGULATIONS

The EAA does not contain many substantive provisions regulating exports. They are contained in the Export Administration Regulations (EAR). These regulations constitute an extensive set of provisions detailing the governance of U.S. exports, *and re-exports*. Following the "nationality of the goods", the EAR are primarily focused on the "end-use" or "end-user" of U.S. exports, including technology. The EAR rely heavily on "know your customer" determinations by exporters.

Important questions to which the exporter must give thought include:

What is the item?

Where is it going?

Who will actually receive and use it?

What will the item be used for?

Answers to these questions will help the exporter determine whether the EAR are applicable. The BIS maintains a list of "Red Flags" to assist with compliance and signal the need for further inquiries by exporter.

The EAR covers: (1) items subject to the exclusive jurisdiction of another federal agency; (2) publicly available technology and software; (3) re-export of U.S. origin items; (4) foreign made items incorporating less than a *de minimis* level of U.S. parts, components and materials; (5) foreign made items incorporating more than a *de minimis* level of U.S. parts, components and materials, and (6) foreign made items produced with certain U.S. technology for export to specified destination.

Control of U.S. exports and re-exports is principally done by The Department of Commerce's Bureau of Industry and Security (BIS). But other departments also have some regulatory authority, especially the Department of State where the goods are "dual-use" items, meaning that they have both commercial and military application. Application for a license may be done electronically under the Simplified Network Application Process Redesign

(SNAP-R), but only if the exporter has a BIS Company Identification Number (CIN).

A party who wishes to know whether a license is required may obtain an Advisory Opinion from the BIS. Receipt of an opinion does not mean the subsequent application will be granted, opinions are not binding. But the BIS is likely to help the applicant in the preparation of an application which will meet the Advisory Opinion's requirements. Certainly, obtaining an unfavorable opinion and then exporting without a license creates a rather clear case of intent to disregard the law. But the Advisory Opinion is a good route to follow. If an unfavorable opinion is received, the BIS may explain what is required to obtain permission, unless the case is a clear one where no exports are permitted.

The BIS processes tens of thousands of export licenses annually, affecting hundreds of billions of dollars of U.S. exports. In recent years, for example, high-tech goods involving encryption software and advance semiconductor chips with military applications have been a focus of these licenses.

Deemed Exports

Note particularly that under the EAR disclosure of controlled technology or technical data to a foreign national located *in the United States* constitutes a "*deemed export*". Virtually any exchange of information—including telephone conversations, fax communications, the sharing of computer data bases, briefings, training sessions, and even question and answer exchanges—can involve an export of technical data. Visits to U.S. plants by foreign nationals raise export control issues because plant tours may visually convey technical data, such as manufacturing know-how, even without the exchange of written information.

In addition, exports of technical data can occur through licensing or joint venture arrangements, technical assistance or training, or a U.S. person's use of his or her own technical expertise abroad if the information was acquired in the United States. This means, for example, universities must be careful about deemed exports to foreign students. Transfers to foreign affiliates or subsidiaries within a corporate family are also treated as exports, as are electronic transmissions, donations and hand-carried items.

THE PROCESS OF LICENSING U.S. EXPORTS

U.S. merchants contemplating exports of their products or technology must understand the licensing regulations. Prior to 1996 essentially *all* commercial exports had to be licensed. But that was deceptive. Most exports required only a *general* license (i.e., one which did not require individual application and approval), which the exporter acquired by use of the Department of Commerce form "Shipper's Export Declaration." The exporter actually issued its own general license.

But in some cases the exporter needed to obtain a *validated* license (i.e., one authorizing a specific export, issued after approval of an application). Time and changing attitudes generated many variations of licenses, such as a general license GLV allowing shipments of limited value which otherwise would have required a validated license, or a validated license authorizing multiple exports to approved distributors or users in non-controlled countries, or sales to foreign subsidiaries, or sales to an entire activity or project, or sales of replacement or spare parts for goods previously sold.

The current regulations eliminate the terms "general license" and "validated license". "License" refers to an authorization to export granted by the Department of Commerce. The change is to some degree a matter of semantics. General licenses, which were in a sense "self-granted", are abolished in favor of referring to such exports as exports permitted without any license. The new export "license" replaces the old "validated license."

Much more was accomplished in the 1996 rearrangement of the EAA regulations. The myriad of "special" licenses has been redone. There are now ten general prohibitions making up Part 736 of the C.F.R., rather than the previous scattering of the prohibitions throughout the regulations. These prohibitions indicate the circumstances where a license must be obtained.

Although delay is attendant to many export applications, there is a timetable which governs processing license applications. Within 10 days after proper submission, the Secretary of Commerce must acknowledge receipt of the application and provide advice about any other applicable procedures. Unless referral to another government department is necessary, the license should be granted formally or denied within 90 days. Even if referral is necessary, the statutory timetable requires issuance or denial within 180 days of the application. If the exports are to certain countries designated terrorist supporting nations, Congress may have to be advised and the approval period is further extended.

The statutory timetable of the EAA is not always met, despite Congressional attempts to mandate administrative conduct. Delay has been used by the government, especially by the Department of Defense, as a means of discouraging exports which might be permissible, but to which the Department objects. The *Daedalus Enterprises, Inc. v. Baldrige,* 563 F. Supp. 1345 (D.D.C. 1983) case is an example. Twenty-nine months after the filing of an application, the Department of Commerce had not reached a decision. The company had to seek a court order that the Secretary comply with the statutory timetable.

When delay occurs, there is little a company can do. It may not export the goods when the time period has expired if no response has been made by the government. It must go to court at each stage when the government fails to comply with the statute. Fortunately, the *Daedalus* case is an exception, and this kind of delay has been much diminished. The filing process is considerably improved.

Product and Country Control Lists

Whether or not a license is required depends primarily on two issues; the type of goods or technology to be exported, and the destination

country. The Bureau of Industry and Security (BIS)
maintains the Commerce Control List (CCL). This
includes all items subject to export controls, except
for those under the control of another branch of the
government, such as the control of defense articles
and services by the Department of State. The
transfer by Executive Order of control over
encryption devices from State to Commerce in 1996
was particularly contentious.

The CCL is divided into ten general categories
(e.g., "Category 3—Electronics"). Within each
category are five different groups of products,
identified by letters A through E (e.g., "Group C—
Material"). Three further numbers identify the
reasons for control (001 for national security, for
example). Together this makes a four digit and one
letter Export Control Classification Number (ECCN,
i.e., 3C001).

The Commerce Control List Supplement No. 1
includes the many variations of ECCNs. For each
ECCN, this Supplement includes the License
Requirements, the License Exceptions, and the List
of Items Controlled. Gradually this list has been
relaxed, notably to allow exports of high performance
computers in 2002. The 1996 revisions provide a
fairly easily understood path through the maze of
regulations by means of a 29 step process to
determine whether a license is needed, and if needed
whether there are applicable exceptions.

Use of the process involves reference to the
Commerce Country Chart, which helps identify
countries subject to controls for such reasons as

national security, missile technology, U.N. or U.S. embargo, etc. For example, Country Group A includes several dozen nations with which the U.S. generally has good political and trade relations. Country Group E, contrastingly, includes the few nations currently subject to either a U.N. or U.S. trade embargo, such as North Korea.

Licensed Exports and Re-Exports

When a license is required, a critical decision usually made by counsel to the exporter, application is made to the BIS in the Department of Commerce. The application must be approved and the license issued before the goods or technology may be exported or re-exported. In many cases, a license will only be issued upon certain conditions, such as limiting the capability of the export product, restricting it to civilian use and prohibiting its use for any military or intelligence gathering purposes, or prohibiting resale to another controlled country.

There is often a considerable negotiating process between the exporter and the BIS. When a license is issued, the exporter is responsible for the performance of all terms and conditions of the license, both by the foreign licensee and by foreign buyers or subsequent buyers. It is important for the exporter to know what conditions might be imposed on the license at the time the original contract is signed, so that such conditions may also be imposed in the contract on the foreign parties.

Speed may be important in processing an application for a license. But the administration of the EAA often has been characterized by delay, uncertainty and lack of accountability, as conflicts arise between national defense and export promotion policies. Many sensitive items have nevertheless evaded export controls, demonstrated in the 1980s sale to the USSR by Toshiba of Japan and Kongsberg of Norway of propeller milling machines and numerical controllers, respectively, which allowed the manufacture of submarine propellers which would function as quietly as U.S. submarines. The companies were subjected to sanctions prohibiting some trade to the United States.

COCOM and Wassenar Export Controls

Before its demise, a multilateral review by COCOM might extend the review period to 240 days. COCOM was the Coordinating Committee of the Consultative Group on Export Controls. It was an informal multilateral organization of the U.S. and its military allies (NATO countries less Iceland, plus Japan) established to regulate certain strategic materials exports to communist countries. The U.S. rules were often more restrictive than were those of COCOM, and COCOM review was sometimes used as leverage to grant rather than to deny an application.

COCOM members continually tried to convince the United States to relax some of its export rules. But the United States often acted alone in regulating sensitive exports, as it did in 1990, when President George H. P. Bush announced the "Enhanced Proliferation Control Initiative," which expanded controls on items used in chemical and biological weapons. Following changes in Eastern Europe and the breakup of the USSR, COCOM was abolished in 1994, with promises by many of its members to create a new organization for multilateral export review.

The successor organization, established in 1995 and composed of about 28 nations, is the Wassenaar Arrangement on Export Controls for Conventional Arms and Dual-Use Goods and Technologies. Its purpose is similar to that of COCOM.

Sanctions for EAA Violations, Non-U.S. Entities Included

Violation of laws and regulations governing U.S. exports brings into play both the basic law and the regulations. The EAA contains provisions governing violations of both the EAA and EAR. The Export Administrative Regulations contain supplementary provisions, applying strict liability standards. The general sanction for violations of the export laws, where the conduct was entered into *knowingly,* is a fine of the higher of $250,000 or twice the value of the exports. This can obviously be *very* substantial. In 2017, for example, Exxon was fined $2 million for "reckless disregard" of U.S. export sanctions against Russia, imposed after its annexation of Crimea.

Willful violations, with knowledge that the commodities or technology will be used to benefit, or are destined for, a controlled country, may result in a fine for business entities of the higher of $1 million per violation. For individuals who engage in such willful violations the fine is $1,000,000 and/or 20 years imprisonment. A number of non-U.S. nationals have been jailed for violations of U.S. export control law. For example, Christopher Tappin of Britain was sentenced to 33-months imprisonment in January 2013 after being found in violation of U.S. export controls against Iran.

Cases involving violations of the licensing requirements tend to be quite complex. If the party exported to a controlled country commodities or technology under a license with knowledge that the commodities or technology were being used for military or intelligence gathering purposes, and willfully fails to report this use, the business entity fine is the same as above, the higher of $1 million or five times the value of the exports, but for the individual the imprisonment drops to five years, with the fine remaining the same, $250,000. Even possession of goods or technology either with the intent to export in violation of the law, or knowing that the goods might be so exported, can result in a fine.

Civil violations of the EAR, which do not require any showing of intent or knowledge, are punished by penalties of up to US$250,000 per violation or twice the value of the transaction. The US Department of Commerce encourages voluntary self-disclosures, which is considered a great weight mitigating factor.

In certain circumstances, disclosure is required when an item that has been exported/re-exported in violation of the EAR needs to be sold, transferred, re-exported, removed, stored, used, loaned, disposed of, transported, forwarded, or otherwise serviced. In 2005, for example, the South African company

ProChem (Proprietary) Ltd paid administrative penalties totaling $1.54 million to settle allegations that a predecessor company Protea Chemicals (Proprietary) Ltd. violated the EAR by reselling sensitive U.S.-origin chemicals (cyanide and potassium cyanide) to end users in South Africa when the conditions of the U.S. export license did not authorize resales.

The EAR repeat and expand upon these statutory sanctions. They further add provisions dealing with actions including "causing, aiding, or abetting" a violation, and "solicitation and attempt", and "conspiracy." More details are provided addressing misrepresentation and concealment of facts, or evasion, failing to comply with reporting and record keeping requirements', alterations of documents, and acting contrary to the terms of a denial order.

The high profile nature of export controls is emphasized by judicial refusal to agree to a settlement negotiated between a company accused of violations of the export laws and the Justice Department. In one instance a bargained $1 million fine was rejected by the court, which imposed a $3 million fine.

Debarment

Furthermore, the DOC may *suspend or revoke the authority to export select or ALL products and technology to select or ALL parties.* This "debarment" (denial order) sanction is used in extreme cases. It was used in the Toshiba dispute, where Toshiba (Japan) and Königsberg (Norway) enterprises sold to the Soviet Union technology allegedly useful for developing submarine propellers which would be sufficiently silent to avoid detection.

DOC Denied Persons Register Lists can effectively "blacklist" foreign violators, barring U.S. firms from dealing with named parties, such as Dresser France in the Reagan-era Russian pipeline dispute. Temporary Denial Orders can also be employed against "related parties", as they were against Delft Instruments concerning the illegal export of munitions and night-vision devices. At one point, the Denial Order was extended to all 47 Delft companies located in 13 countries!

Subsequently, the Multilateral Export Control Enhancements Act in 1988 amended the EAA stipulating trade prohibition sanctions for two to five years. These sanctions are applied whether or not other nations take action against their companies.

Non-U.S. entities may be prosecuted for violations of U.S. export controls. For example, Dubai-incorporated Super Net Computers LLC was placed on the Denied Persons Register for its role in the receipt of computer equipment from a U.S. company and a subsequent trans-shipment to Iran without an export license. The U.S. exporter was also prosecuted, resulting in denial of its export privileges for five years, and large criminal and civil fines. In 2007, the British corporation Proclad International Pipelines Ltd admitted violations of US laws and was fined and denied export privileges for seven years following attempts to export nickel alloyed pipes to Iran through the UK and the UAE.

In 2017, the Chinese smartphone firm of ZTE Corp. paid $892 million after pleading guilty to violating the U.S. boycott of Iran and North Korea, and obstructing a federal investigation into its activities. ZTE, perceived by China as a national champion, was particularly concerned with the threat that the U.S. would prohibit the export of processors, software and other goods to it. In 2018, it was announced that U.S. exports to ZTE would be *completely* banned for seven years after it emerged that ZTE had given bonuses to staff who secured these sales, a violation of the 2017 sanction order. U.S. chip exporters like Qualcomm stood to take a major hit and ZTE production ground to a halt.

President Trump, apparently at the request of President Xi and after expressing his sympathy for jobs lost in China, negotiated a new sanctions settlement of $1 billion, a change in management and inclusion of a U.S. monitor inside ZTE. Qualcomm stock rose the next day.

INTERNATIONAL TRAFFIC IN ARMS REGULATIONS (ITAR)

In 1976 Congress enacted the Arms Export Control Act (AECA) (22 U.S.C. § 2778) "[i]n furtherance of world peace and the security and foreign policy of the United States." The AECA provides the President with authority to control the export of defense articles and services. Executive Order 11958, as amended, delegated the President's statutory authority to the Secretary of State. The Secretary of State promulgated regulations, the International

Traffic in Arms Regulations (ITAR) (22 C.F.R. §§ 120–130), to implement the AECA via its Directorate of Defense Trade Controls.

ITAR controls the export of defense-related articles and services by requiring approval for the exportation and temporary importation of items it designates as defense articles or services. In general, ITAR prohibits sharing or disclosing any defense related articles or technology with anyone who is not a U.S. citizen or permanent resident without authorization from the Secretary of State.

ITAR Part 121 contains the United States Munitions List ("Munitions List") and related provisions. The Munitions List is a categorized list containing in-depth descriptions of items, services, and related technical data ITAR defines as "defense articles" and "defense services" within the meaning of the AECA.

U.S. BOYCOTTS

Boycotts affect both exports and imports. Most nations, including the United States, use trade boycotts as a means to achieve political goals, although there is considerable debate regarding their effectiveness. A boycott by many nations, such as that imposed under U.N. auspices against South Africa in the 1970s and 1980s, was only questionably effective, and certainly caused a loss of jobs for those it was intended to benefit. But formal apartheid ended and the boycott deserves partial credit.

When a boycott is by only one nation against another, contrastingly, such as the U.S. boycott of trade with Cuba, the likelihood of success in achieving a political goal is considerably diminished. The intention of the Cuban boycott has been to remove the Castro brothers from leadership. Some sixty years later Raul Castro continues in office, frequently invoking the U.S. boycott as justification for harsh domestic Cuban policies.

Such invocations were tempered by improving "normalized" Cuba-U.S. relations in the final years of the Obama administration, reinstituted in part by President Trump. There is less freedom for Americans to travel independently under self-certifications to Cuba, and no business may be done with Cuba's military and intelligence affiliated companies. The latter restriction bans American use of numerous Cuban hotels, resorts and retail chains affiliated with the Cuban military. At this writing, a milder version the U.S. boycott continues.

U.S. boycotts tend to be the subject of specific legislation directed towards identified countries, for example North Korea, Syria, Sudan, Cuba and Iran. Enforcement is shifted from the Department of Commerce to the Department of the Treasury. The Office of Foreign Assets Control (OFAC) within Treasury is the responsible agency for controlling these specific boycotts.

The pattern of governance is a broad assets control law with additional laws directed to specific countries, such as the Cuban Assets Control Regulations. The various country specific regulations prohibit specific transactions and transfers. By controlling the flow of currency, whether to pay for imports or be paid for exports, trade is thereby restricted. Terminating the flow of currency is intended to terminate trade. It works, but not completely, because considerable trade may take place through third nations. Many U.S. goods are sold in Cuba, transferred first to middle-men in such nations as Mexico or Panama. Unilateral boycotts which are unpopular in other nations are difficult to enforce.

U.S. boycott policy, as expressed in such laws as the Cuban Democracy Act of 1992, the Iran and Libya Sanctions Act of 1996, the Cuban Liberty and Democratic Solidarity (Libertad) Act of 1996 ("Helms-Burton"), and the Burmese Freedom and Democracy Act of 2003, may attempt to reach the conduct of third party nations toward the boycotted country. Such devices seek to exert extraterritorial power over entities located in third nations. The United States thus attempts to draw these third nations into the boycott. It is not surprising that third nations have often responded with extremely strong criticism about interference with their sovereignty by the United States.

Iran, for example, protested long and hard against U.S. boycott sanctions commenced in 1995. These sanctions embraced arms, missiles, nuclear technology, oil and gas, banking, insurance, shipping, goods (save food and medicines) as well as the freezing of Iranian assets, coverage of elite Revolutionary Guard Corps military officials and companies, and blockage of international bank transfers (payments). The EU and to a lesser extent the UN joined the United States in this boycott effort. The combined impact of these sanctions was powerful, sufficient to drive Iran into a 2015 nuclear accord in return for their gradual removal.

The sanction of "designating" foreign nationals merits separate consideration because it is so potentially restrictive. The Office of Foreign Assets Control (OFAC) in the Department of the Treasury may designate individuals and companies owned or controlled by, or acting for or on behalf of, targeted companies. They become so-called "specially designated nationals" or "SDNs." Their assets are blocked and U.S. persons are for the most part prohibited from dealing with them or their businesses.

Additionally, *non-U.S.* persons can face secondary sanctions for engaging with or "causing" U.S. parties to deal with SDNs. The list of such designated nationals exceeds 550 pages. It can be a devastating designation and effectively end trade with the United States, an outcome not lost on the U.S. when it "blacklisted" 271 workers at Syrian agencies involved with chemical weapons.

EAA, ITAR AND BOYCOTT SANCTIONS

A range of sanctions may apply to violations of the EAA, ITAR and U.S. boycott rules. Some sanctions may derive from the United Nations (e.g., North Korea) or be undertaken with others (e.g., U.S.-EU sanctions on Russia). Individual and/or business sanctions may be imposed, and may apply extraterritorially to persons, activities and businesses located outside the United States. For example, though not rejected elsewhere, Huawei, a global Chinese telecommunications giant making wireless gear, towers, routers and switches is basically banned out of fear of espionage or cyberattacks in the USA.

Individual sanctions typically result in U.S. visa denials, the seizure of U.S.-based individual assets, and/or prohibitions against U.S firms doing business with the sanctioned individuals. In 2018, prominent individual sanctions were outstanding against foreign leaders Kim Jong Un of North Korea, Robert Mugabe of Zimbabwe, Bashar al-Assad of Syria and Nicolas Maduro of Venezuela. High ranking officials in Russia, Iran, Venezuela, Syria and North Korea were also named in the U.S. sanctions lists.

Business sanctions can involve U.S. asset seizures, denial of U.S. financing, credit lines and bank or other financial services, imposition of internal control systems, prohibitions against doing business with sanctioned entities or individuals, and/or extension of sanctions to third parties not directly named on sanctions lists. For example, U.S. sanctions have been applied to: (1) Revolutionary Guard businesses in Iran; (2) Russian oil, gas, defense, bank, and intelligence companies and oligarchs; (3) Chinese firms said to be enabling North Korean missile and nuclear efforts, (4) Cuban resorts and hotels owned by its military forces; and (5) any company assisting Venezuelan debt financing or financing owed to Venezuela.

The blacklist designation in 2017 of Rosneft, the state-owned Russian oil company, made it unlikely that Rosneft could obtain via a loan collateral agreement control of Citgo, a U.S. subsidiary of Venezuela's state-owned oil company PdVSA which owns refineries, pipelines and storage tanks in the USA. The blacklisting in 2017 of various Venezuelan officials caused a number of global bond traders to halt buying or selling secondary market bonds of PdVSA, even though U.S. export sanctions covered only new Venezuelan bonds.

Some of the Russian sanctions adopted in the Countering America's Adversaries through Sanctions Act (2017) (CAATSA) were particularly notable because they barred repeal by Executive Order of the President. In 2018, President Trump stringently blacklisted dozens of Russian firms, private and state-owned, and senior officials and prominent oligarchs. He cited Russian meddling in U.S. elections, cyberattacks, Ukraine and Crimea invasions, and military support of Syria as reasons for these sanctions.

Blacklist designations extend to all who "knowingly facilitate significant financial transactions" on behalf of the blacklisted parties. This essentially *removes the listed Russians from access to the U.S. dollar economy*, a powerful sanction previously executed against Iranians with considerable impact. A prominent Russian oligarch agreed to sell his stake in Rusal, a major aluminum company, in order to escape U.S. sanctions.

Since payments and collections for much of the world's trade is conducted in U.S. dollars via U.S.-based financial institutions (including foreign banks), this gives the United States jurisdiction and a broad power to sanction objectionable transactions and parties. It can do so regardless of whether trade transactions actually involve U.S. persons, goods or services. The two big U.S. payments systems, Fedwire and CHIPS, handle trillions of payments daily. As one commentator observed: "The global financial system is like a sewer and [nearly] all of the pipes run through New York".

In May of 2018, President Trump withdrew the United States from the multi-nation pact on Iranian nuclear development. With few exceptions, all export and financial sanctions that were in place before January 2016 will be re-imposed by November 2018, including secondary sanctions that penalize non-U.S. persons who do business with Iran. Non-U.S. subsidiaries of U.S. companies will not be permitted to do business in Iran. This will likely pose significant risk for European and Asian traders and investors, who may be subject to extraterritorial "secondary" U.S. export sanctions.

U.S. ANTI-BOYCOTT PROVISIONS

Curiously, and perhaps hypocritically, the United States attempts in its export control laws to expressly reject boycotts of other nations. U.S. anti-boycott laws most notably concern the Arab boycott of Israel.

While boycotts are governed as outlined above by regulations enforced by the Department of the Treasury, the Export Administration Act addresses a special problem relating to exports—anti-boycotts. The provisions are a direct consequence of the Arab League economic boycott against Israel commenced initially in 1954, and erratically enforced since then.

When the Arab boycott was extended beyond the primary level (no trading with Israel), to the secondary level (no trading with any nation's enterprise which trades with Israel), and to the tertiary level (no trading with any third party nation's enterprise trading with Israel if it obtained components from a nation trading with Israel), Congress began to debate whether U.S. companies ought to be allowed to assist the boycott of a nation friendly to the United States.

After several years of debate and the failure of voluntary controls to have any effect, the EAA was amended in 1977. The purpose of the anti-boycott provisions is to prohibit any U.S. person "from taking or knowingly agreeing to take [certain actions] with intent to comply with, further, or support any boycott" against a country friendly to the United States. It specifically exempts boycotts pursuant to U.S. law. The requirement of intent is essential, but what constitutes intent may seem marginal.

In *United States v. Meyer,* 864 F.2d 214 (1st Cir.1988), the defendant Meyer was held to have knowledge that a form required by Saudi Arabia to have a trademark registered in that country was not used to obtain information needed for the

registration, but to further the boycott of Israel.
Meyer claimed that his actions were inadvertent and
not intentional. But Meyer's knowledge and
intention were rather clearly illustrated by his
receipt of information from the Department of State
that it could not notarize the form because of the
boycott, and his subsequent acquisition of a
notarization through the U.S.-Arab Chamber of
Commerce. The *Meyer* decision involves a clear
attempt to find a way past the law. It is thus not very
helpful for a case where the intent is based on less
apparent criteria.

Focus on the Arab Boycott of Israel

The U.S. anti-boycott rules are intended to achieve
a political end, to assist Israel, although the language
of the law never refers to any country by name.
Nevertheless, of 376 boycott requests notified to the
Office of Anti-Boycott Compliance in 2011, 369
involved an Arab League member.

The EAA provisions include broad language which
directs the President to issue regulations prohibiting
any U.S. person from doing business in a boycotting
country; refusing to hire or discriminating against
any U.S. person; furnishing a broad range of
information; or paying, honoring or confirming
letters of credit, where such action would comply
with, further or support the boycott of a country
friendly to the United States.

Refusals to Deal

The first prohibition in the EAA is against directly refusing to do business with or in the boycotted country (i.e., Israel), or with a national or resident of that country. Also prohibited is any refusal to do business with the boycotted country by agreement with or response to requests from any other person. This means a U.S. company may not refuse to do business with Israel at the request of the central boycott office of the Arab nations in Damascus. Intent to refuse to do business is not established by the absence of any business relationship with the boycotted country.

Discrimination

The second statutorily prohibited conduct is refusing to employ or otherwise discriminating against any U.S. person on the basis of race, religion, sex or national origin, where such conduct is intentional and in furtherance of an unlawful boycott.

This section addresses the Arab nations' attempts to injure Jewish people wherever they may live, rather than to harm Israel as a nation. Thus, a company may not refuse to employ Jewish persons so that it may gain favor with Arab clients. In one of the few court decisions involving the anti-boycott provisions, Baylor College of Medicine was found to have persistently appointed non-Jewish persons for a project with Saudi Arabia. See *Abrams v. Baylor College of Medicine,* 581 F. Supp. 1570 (S.D.Tex.1984), *aff'd,* 805 F.2d 528 (5th Cir.1986).

The antidiscrimination section of the EAA includes both refusals to employ and *other discrimination*. For example, a requirement that a U.S. company not use a six-pointed star on its packaging of products to be sent to the Arab nation would be a violation because it is part of the enforcement effort of the boycott. But it is not a violation if the demand is that no symbol of Israel be included on the packaging. The former is a religious symbol generally, the latter an acceptable request which does not include reference to any person's religion.

This example can be found in the EAA anti-boycott regulations. It illustrates a general attempt to acknowledge that the boycotting nations are entitled to have *some* control over what comes into their nation. They are entitled to say no imports may be stamped "Products of Israel", but they may not attack the Jewish religion more broadly by requiring certification that no religious symbols appear on any packages. The United States is attempting to say that Arab nations may have a right to engage in a primary boycott against Israel, but they may not draw U.S. persons into supporting that boycott.

Furnishing Information

The third specific prohibition relates to the refusal to hire for reasons of race, religion, sex or national origin, discussed immediately above. This provision prohibits furnishing information with respect to race, religion, sex or national origin. It is supplemented by regulations that make it applicable whether the information is specifically requested or offered voluntarily and whether stated in the affirmative or negative. Furthermore, prohibited information includes place of birth or nationality of the parents, and information in code words or symbols that would identify a person's race, religion, sex or national origin. The regulations also reaffirm the element of intent.

The examples in the regulations illustrate the difficulty of clearly defining "prohibited information". If the boycotting nation requests a U.S. company to give all employees who will work in the boycotting nation visa forms, and these visa forms request otherwise prohibited information, the company is not in violation for giving the forms to its employees or for sending the forms back to the boycotting country party. This is considered a ministerial function and not support of the boycott. But the company may not itself provide the information on race, religion, sex or nationality of its employees, if it meets the intent requirement. The company might certify that none of its employees to be sent to the boycotting nation are women, where the laws of the boycotting country prohibit women from working. The reason for the submission has nothing to do with the boycott.

Blacklists

The fourth prohibition is one that is often at issue. It involves the use of blacklists. The Arab nations maintain a blacklist of persons and companies with whom they will not do business. Arab nations often ask a prospective commercial agreement party to certify that none of the goods will include components obtained from any companies on the blacklist.

Persons are prohibited from furnishing information about an extensive list of business activities ("including a relationship by way of sale, purchase, legal or commercial representation, shipping or other transport, insurance, investment, or supply"), with an equally extensive list of business relationships ("with or in the boycotted country, with any business concern organized under the laws of the boycotted country, with any national or resident of the boycotted country, or with any other person which is known or believed to be restricted from having any business relationship with or in the boycotting country"). At the end is a statement that the section does not prohibit furnishing "normal business information in a commercial context as defined by the Secretary." Thus, U.S. businesses are very extensively governed with regard to the flow of information between the company and the boycotting country.

The most publicized blacklist case involved Baxter International Inc., a large U.S. medical supply company. As a result of an informant's disclosure, Baxter was investigated and charged with violating the EAA because of the way in which it attempted to have its name removed from the Arab blacklist. Commerce was prepared to charge Baxter and a senior officer with providing over 300 items of prohibited information to Syrian authorities and a Saudi Arabian firm. The company and the officer admitted civil and criminal violations and were assessed total civil penalties of $6,060,600—the highest at the time. The case would not have succeeded without the informant providing substantial documentation of the violations.

Anti-Boycott Sanctions, Private Claims

Since the 1977 amendments to the EAA which introduced the anti-boycott provisions, relatively few cases have reached the courts. There have been many challenges by the Department of Commerce's Office of Anti-Boycott Compliance, but most have ended in a consent decree. The same severe sanctions as outlined above for violations of the U.S. export laws apply to violations of the anti-boycott provisions, but consent decrees often have resulted in negotiating the minimum fines under the EAA, substantially less than the costs and adverse publicity of litigation.

For example, in 1995 U.S. subsidiaries (and a corporation counsel) of the French L'Oréal S.A. agreed to pay fines of $1.4 million for allegedly furnishing or agreeing to furnish information by the subsidiaries to the French parent about business relationships with Israel. The penalties were among the highest negotiated under the laws.

There is no clear indication whether the EAA includes a private right of action. A Texas federal district court, in *Abrams v. Baylor College of Medicine,* 581 F. Supp. 1570 (S.D.Tex.1984), *aff'd* 805 F.2d 528 (5th Cir.1986) addressed a claim by two Jewish medical students that Baylor University denied them opportunities when it excluded Jews from medical teams it sent to Saudi Arabia.

But in *Bulk Oil (ZUG) A.G. v. Sun Co.,* 583 F. Supp. 1134 (S.D.N.Y.1983), *aff'd* 742 F.2d 1431 (2d Cir.1984), the Second Circuit rejected the existence of a private right of action, affirming a New York federal district court decision involving an accusation of violation of the anti-boycott provisions by failing to deliver oil to Israel. The Seventh Circuit has also rejected private causes of action under U.S. anti-boycott law (*Israel Aircraft Ind. v. Sanwa Business Credit Corp.,* 583 F. Supp. 1134 (S.D.N.Y.1983), *aff'd* 742 F.2d 1431 (2d Cir.1984)).

U.S. FOREIGN CORRUPT PRACTICES ACT

One further export and foreign investment issue involves the practice of U.S. companies making payments to foreign government officials or agents to encourage purchasing the company's products or services (or accept or extend its direct foreign investment). During the Watergate investigations of payments to U.S. political candidates, it was discovered that many U.S. companies had been making payments to foreign officials, notably to obtain sales of Lockheed airplanes to Japan and The Netherlands. The response was swift.

The Foreign Corrupt Practices Act was passed in 1977. The original law included three substantive sections, one establishing stringent accounting and disclosure standards requiring that a bribe must be labeled a bribe. Two sections govern "corruptly" made payments or gifts of value to foreign officials or *state instrumentalities* to obtain, retain or influence business, and payments to "other" persons (think well-connected consultants), where those persons "knew or had reason to know" payments would be passed on to a foreign official.

Payments made to state-owned or state-controlled companies have been deemed to fall within the scope of the FCPA. You might ponder whether extorted payments or gifts involve acting "corruptly." The law included no definitions and only a brief exclusion for payments which were "ministerial" in nature, such as minor "grease" payments often necessary to pass goods through customs.

The law was ambiguous, and from the beginning U.S. businesses requested that the Department of Justice issue guidelines. None were forthcoming until 2012. Like the anti-boycott laws discussed above, few cases reach the courts, most being settled with consent decrees and fines, thus avoiding the label "corrupt payor".

1988 Amendments

Business interests continued to press for changes, which were finally forthcoming in the 1988 trade law. The most significant change was replacing the "reason to know" language with a requirement that any payment to a third person be made "knowing that" it would be passed on to a foreign official. But new definition provisions state that "knowing" may well include reason to know. Having "a firm belief" or being "aware of a high probability" is sufficient to constitute "knowing."

Another important amendment was the further clarification of permissible "grease" payments. Payments are allowed for a "routine government action," which includes obtaining permits to do business, processing papers, providing certain routine services such as police protection or telephone or power, and "actions of a similar nature." But it specifically does not include any decision by a foreign official regarding new business or retaining old business, decisions which are more than merely routine government actions.

The 1988 amendments law also included an affirmative defense section which stipulates several payments which are not prohibited. They include payments permissible under the *written* laws of the other nation, and reasonable and bona fide expenditures such as travel and lodging if related to the promotion or performance of contracts. Other changes to the FCPA in 1988 include some clarification of the accounting provisions.

One difficulty with the FCPA is defining what constitutes a wrongful payment. Because the payment is made to a foreign official, cultural standards of that official's nation may affect the payment. Conflicts of interest by government officials may be governed by very different notions. While apparently no foreign country has written laws permitting foreign officials to accept bribes to influence their conduct, the "operational code" or unwritten law of many countries makes such conduct reasonably commonplace.

A final change in 1988 removed what was known as the Eckhardt provision, which prohibited bringing a suit directly against an employee without first having received a judgment finding the employer in violation of the Act. With the removal of the Eckhardt provision, corporate officers may find themselves scapegoats, and required to defend charges while the company remains free of any litigation.

1998 Amendments

The FCPA was amended in 1998 to comply with U.S. obligations under the 1997 OECD Convention on Combating Bribery of Foreign Officials in International Business Transactions, discussed below. The Convention included language, added to the FCPA, making it unlawful to make payments directly or indirectly to gain "any improper advantage". The OECD concept of improper advantages is broad. For example, procurement contracts, tax benefits and customs preferences, and foreign investment privileges fall within its scope.

The FCPA was further amended to expand its scope to cover prohibited acts by "any person." Domestic concerns other than issuers and "other" persons are now covered. This makes the FCPA cover all *foreign* natural and legal persons who commit acts, however minor, while in the United States.

The amendments also reach extraterritorial payments by business entities and persons taking place wholly outside the United States, and payments to officials of international agencies as well as political parties. In 2015, for example, Hitachi of

Japan agreed to pay $19 million to settle FCPA charges concerning payments made to South Africa's ruling party regarding power station construction contracts.

Finally, penalties for non-U.S. citizen employees and agents of U.S. employers and principals, previously limited to civil sanctions, now include the same criminal sanctions as for U.S. citizen employees and agents.

FCPA Sanctions

FCPA violations for making illegal payments are governed by two different provisions, for issuers and domestic concerns, respectively, and their officers, directors, agents and shareholders acting on behalf of the entity. Each section leads to the same levels of penalties.

The entities are subject to fines of not more than $2 million or double the intended benefit. The officers, directors, employees, agents, and shareholders acting on behalf of the concerns are subject to fines up to $250,000, or five years' imprisonment, or both, if the violation was willful. Only willful violations are subject to criminal penalties. See *Trane Co. v. O'Connor Securities*, 718 F.2d 26 (2d Cir.1983). Any criminal fine imposed on a person under the FCPA may not be paid or indemnified by the company directly or indirectly.

Individual and corporate civil penalties may also be assessed, along with disgorgement of corruptly obtained proceeds. These penalties illustrate that the

U.S. government is serious about violations of the FCPA. For example, two units of Litton Industries pleaded guilty in 1999 to fraud and conspiracy in making payments to obtain defense business in Greece and Taiwan. Litton agreed to pay $18.5 million to settle the matter (including an amount to reimburse the Department of Justice for the costs of the investigation).

Violations of the record-keeping and internal accounting-control FCPA standards, may lead, where there is a willful violation, or a willful and knowing making of a false or misleading statement in filed applications, statements or reports, to a criminal penalty for individuals of not more than $5,000,000 and not more than 20 years of imprisonment, or both. Corporate criminal violations can result in up to $25 million fines or double the intended benefit. Individual and corporate civil penalties may also be assessed, along with disgorgement of corruptly obtained proceeds.

Other "sanctions" are less formal, but potentially no less severe. Reputational damage, procurement exclusion, shareholder lawsuits and higher capital costs may follow. FCPA settlements typically also impose ongoing compliance costs. For example, in 2015 a small Florida company (IAP) paid over $7 million to settle criminal charges regarding procurement payments to Kuwaiti officials made via a consultant. In addition, IAP promised high-level commitment against corruption, a clear corporate policy against corruption and regular corruption risk reviews, assignment of compliance responsibilities to a senior executive reporting to independent monitoring bodies, extensive training, reporting and investigation systems, disciplinary procedures, and corruption due diligence in mergers and acquisitions.

Enforcement of the FCPA

Particularly in the last decade, the FCPA has been strongly enforced. Some 150 U.S. investigations are pending at this writing, encouraged by Dodd-Frank whistleblower rewards. While the FCPA has mostly concerned foreign investment practices, it has also been applied where corrupt practices favor U.S. exports. Anyone dealing with the FCPA should read the 2012 Department of Justice Resource Guide to the U.S. Foreign Corrupt Practices Act.

The severity of penalties for violations of the FCPA mandates close consideration of its provisions by all persons doing business abroad. Subsidiaries owned or controlled by U.S. companies fall within its jurisdictional scope. Violations of the FCPA are dealt with principally by the SEC (which monitors the record keeping) and the Department of Justice (which enforces the anti-bribery provisions). Over 400 companies have been investigated since 1977, with at least 50 firms charged with FCPA violations in numerous countries around the world, most notably of late China.

It is not only the largest corporations which have been the subject of FCPA actions. One action, for example, involved an individual who owned a postage stamp concession for a Caribbean island and who paid for flights for citizens to return to the island to vote for the reelection of the president, allegedly to influence the government to renew the concession.

Investigations are often reported in the news. For example, some allegations involved IBM and Mexico in 1993, during the sensitive negotiations for the North American Free Trade Agreement. An Iranian-born British businessman was retained by IBM to be its agent in a tender bid for a new air-control system in Mexico City. The agent alleged that soon after a meeting with several Mexican officials at which they tried to obtain a $1 million bribe, IBM's bid was rejected and the contract given to the French Thomson Company.

The agents' subsequent public disclosure and numerous newspaper articles led nowhere, but caused a sensation in Mexico. The Minister of Communications was ousted in a cabinet reorganization. The agent alleged that the Mexican government later tried to buy him off. IBM did not support the agent in his claims, and settled with the agent out of court.

The whole episode illustrates many problems. The U.S. government showed no inclination to become involved or investigate the matter. There were foreign policy problems, NAFTA priorities, perhaps a sense that the story was not implausible, but a realization that this is how things work. Aliases or no names, secret meetings, finger pointing, and leaks to the press were all part of the game. No one seems to have asked how the French Thomson Company got the bid so quickly after IBM was rejected.

IBM was subsequently again in the news regarding an investigation of bribes in Argentina to obtain a $250 million contract to modernize the computer system for the Banco de la Nación. IBM allegedly paid bribes to CCR, a computer systems company, in connection with obtaining a contract with Nación, money which soon found its way into Swiss accounts.

Comparatively few actions brought by the Department of Justice have reached the appellate courts. One example, involving the International Harvester Company, alleged participation in a series of charges relating to dealings with officials of Petroleos Mexicanos (PEMEX), the national oil company. The company pleaded guilty to conspiracy to violate the FCPA. See *McLean v. International Harvester Co.*, 902 F.2d 372 (5th Cir.1990).

Nearly all FCPA enforcement proceedings are settled, often under deferred prosecution agreements. This explains the relative absence of case law, and reinforces the power of the SEC and DOJ to interpret the FCPA as they see fit. In 2010, the DOJ and SEC collected over $1.8 billion in FCPA fines and penalties. Other significant recent prosecutions and settlements include Lucent Technologies, involving payments to Chinese officials and resulting in penalties of $137 million. KBR/ Halliburton settled for $579 million in 2009, BAE for $400 million in 2010, Daimler for $185 million also in 2010, and Johnson & Johnson for $70 million in 2011.

The FCPA can apply to extraterritorial activities of foreign as well as U.S. firms. For example, Siemens

AG of Germany paid bribes in numerous countries and an agreed to fine of $800 million in 2008. The Siemens' FCPA settlement remains the largest to date, though a 2015 settlement with the French firm, Alstom, came close at $772 million. German and 20 other anti-bribery law enforcement authorities also pursued Siemans, which is reported to have spent over $1 billion in legal and accounting fees. The Siemens cases involved the Oil-for-Food program, which resulted in four other settlements against Akzo Nobel of the Netherlands for $3 million in penalties, against Flowserve Corporation for $10.55 million, against AB Volvo for $12.6 million, and against Fiat for $17.8 million in civil and criminal penalties.

The Rise in FCPA Enforcement

FCPA prosecutions rose dramatically under the George W. Bush and Barack Obama presidencies. Most FCPA investigations are settled under deferred or non-prosecution agreements. This explains the relative absence of FCPA case law and reinforces the wide discretion to the SEC and DOJ to interpret the Act as they see fit. For example, the DOJ asserted J. P. Morgan's hiring of relatives of influential Chinese officials was covered by the FCPA. The firm maintained spread sheets showing the cost of "Sons and Daughters" hires and their value in terms of increased business. In 2016, J.P. Morgan settled the investigation for roughly $264 million.

Here are some additional FCPA settlement examples: Siemens AG paid bribes in numerous countries and an agreed in 2008 to an FCPA fine of $800 million. The Siemens' FCPA settlement remains the largest to date. German and 20 other anti-bribery law enforcement authorities also pursued Siemens, which is reported to have spent over $1 billion in legal and accounting fees. The Siemens cases involved the Oil-for-Food program, which resulted in four other settlements against Akzo Nobel of the Netherlands for $3 million in penalties, against Flowserve Corporation for $10.55 million of criminal and civil penalties, against AB Volvo resulting in $12.6 million in penalties, and against Fiat for $17.8 million civil and criminal penalties.

The French engineering giant, Alstom, pleaded guilty in 2014 and agreed to pay $772 million in record FCPA criminal fines. Alstom failed to disclose its misconduct or cooperate with U.S. authorities concerning its corrupt payments via consultants in Indonesia, Egypt, Saudi Arabia and the Bahamas. The total fines amounted to over 2.5 times Alstom's profits from its corrupt activities and delayed GE's due diligence leading to acquisition of Alstom for several years pending settlement. Alstom also faces criminal charges before Britain's Serious Fraud Office.

In 2016, Teva Pharmaceutical paid $519 million, the hedge fund, Och-Ziff settled for over $400 million, VimpelCom $398 million (notably in part for payments to a charity affiliated with an Uzbek official). Odebrecht/Braskem of Brazil paid $632 million in FCPA fines along with additional sums to

Switzerland and Brazil in the "Car Wash" investigation focusing on Petrobras and corrupt practices throughout Latin America involving construction work order addenda. The Presidents of Brazil and Peru fell from office as a consequence.

In 2015, Hitachi of Japan agreed to pay $19 million to settle FCPA charges concerning payments made to South Africa's ruling political party regarding power station construction contracts. In prior years, Lucent Technologies paid settlement penalties of $137 million, KBR/Halliburton settled for $579 million, BAE for $400 million, Johnson & Johnson for $70 million, and Daimler for $185 million. Avon voluntarily reported itself concerning illegal payments in China leading to a "moderate" FCPA settlement of $135 million in 2014, along with the placement of an independent FCPA "monitor" inside the company.

The list of corporate FCPA settlements goes on: Embraer, Novartis, Nordion, AB InBev, SciClone Pharmaceuticals, Bilfinger, Parker Drilling, Diebold, Pfizer, Eli Lilly, Alcoa, Total, Stryker, Hewlett-Packard, Philips, Weatherford, and Ralph Lauren.

A New York Times feature article in December 2012 described bribes allegedly made by Wal-Mart in Mexico. The payments led to a Department of Justice investigation that is still ongoing, an expensive global in-house review of payments' practices by Wal-Mart (reportedly costing over a million dollars a day!), and a dramatic drop in the value of Wal-Mart stock. Wal-Mart is said to be afraid of a settlement ban on participation in the Food Stamp SNAP program, treated as a U.S. procurement contract. Wal-Mart's SNAP sales run close to $13 billion a year. Wal-Mart has already instituted extensive FCPA compliance programs.

Individual and STING Prosecutions

There have also been individual prosecutions, often following corporate settlements, assuming personal jurisdiction can be had. Individual prosecutions have for example, included some high profile persons. Albert Stanley, CEO of KBR, a subsidiary of Halliburton, agreed to serve seven years in prison and pay $10.8 million in restitution. In 2010, the FBI conducted its first FCPA sting operation ("Shot Show"), resulting in the arrest of 22 executives from military and law enforcement products companies. The government has also seized personal assets (pensions, cars and homes) of "willful" violators as forfeited proceeds of bribery.

Voluntary Disclosures

Towards the end of the Obama administration, the DOJ commenced a pilot program (ending, unless renewed, April 2018) reducing corporate fines if companies voluntarily disclosed violations *and* the names of individuals, fully cooperated, and demonstrated remediation in exchange for approximately 20 to 50% reductions in financial penalties under the U.S. Sentencing Guidelines. The SEC has followed similar policies, continuing to focus on China and misconduct generally in the pharmaceutical and financial services industries.

During 2016, roughly $2.5 billion in FCPA fines were collected, the highest in the history of the statute.

FCPA Compliance Programs

The severity of FCPA sanctions and dramatic increase in FCPA proceedings during recent years, combined with minimal jurisdictional requirements and major reputational and corrective action costs (not to mention share price declines), have caused widespread adoption of company compliance policies and programs. Online and in person training of all employees who might have contact with foreign officials has become routine. Such training is repeated regularly, and recorded in personnel files. Such records may at a later date support "rogue employee" assertions by corporations.

Vendors, customs brokers, transport carriers, construction and other service providers of U.S. corporations engaged are being required to undergo FCPA training. Such third parties must also complete FCPA audits, and sign contract clauses and affidavits as to compliance and awareness of FCPA risks. Some firms decline absolutely to make any grease payments.

Dealing with agents and consultants creates special problems. They should be asked for details about the existence of any relatives or business associates who are in the government. The company should contact various persons in the U.S. government, Chambers of Commerce, local counsel, and the like to check on their reputation, and conduct a Google search. All this "due diligence" might help to later establish that the company did not act "while knowing" (the FCPA standard) that payments to third parties would end up going corruptly to officials. Finally, the agreement with the agent or consultant should contain a clause that none of the funds paid to the agent will be used in any manner which might violate the FCPA.

Corporate policies and compliance programs cannot assure that illegal payments will not be made. But even if illegal payments are later found to have been made, a written policy, acknowledged by employees' signatures, will to establish the company's good intentions and should help in minimizing penalties. Morgan Stanley is thought to have avoided penalties completely when one of their Chinese employees "went rogue" despite major repeated training and compliance efforts.

FCPA due diligence in connection with international mergers and acquisitions has become the norm. The resulting business assumes FCPA liabilities, though it may seek indemnification. Record keeping and internal control compliance programs are critical to adhering to the strict FCPA accounting and disclosure rules, which require a bribe to be labeled a bribe.

OECD AND U.N. ANTI-CORRUPTION CODES

The FCPA imposed a U.S. ethic on conduct in the United States and abroad by U.S. persons, and to conduct within the United States by foreign persons. For 20 years, the United States stood almost alone in the global community on foreign corrupt practices law.

A few nations attempted to prohibit payments by their nations' entities, but some encouraged such payments by allowing them to constitute deductions against taxes as ordinary business expenses. Attempts within the United Nations to govern payments to foreign officials on the international level initially failed. The U.S. Trade Representative began an intense effort in 1996 to gain agreement by other nations to prohibit such deductions.

The influential NGO organization, Transparency International, urged adoption of laws prohibiting such payments, and has published annually maps of the world reflecting levels of perceived official corruption. Every country is rated from very clean (e.g., Denmark) to highly corrupt (e.g., Somalia). Perhaps the most difficult "corruption" to address is that which is culturally ingrained, for example "ttokkap" (rice cake expenses) in Korea.

Finally, efforts of the Organization for Economic Cooperation and Development (OECD) led to the 1997 OECD Convention on Combating Bribery of Foreign Officials, which obligates signatories to criminalize bribery of foreign officials and sanction inaccurate accounts. Some 35 major nations participate, including China, Russia, Nigeria, Brazil, France, Britain, Germany, India and Japan. Particularly because the OECD Convention contains an extraterritorial element, multinational enterprises can simultaneously be exposed to criminal bribery sanctions in multiple jurisdictions.

In 2004, the United Nations promulgated a widely ratified Convention against Corruption. The United States ratified this Convention in 2006, which did not require amendments to the FCPA. Some 170 nations have subscribed to the U.N. Convention. It notably includes cooperative provisions facilitating the recovery of corrupt payment "assets" hidden abroad by officials.

British Bribery Act

The British Bribery Act of 2010 (BBA) may have been late in arriving, but is now widely perceived to be one of the most rigorous. It extends not just to payments to foreign officials, but also to *private parties*. The Act applies to *solicitation* as well as *receipt* of bribes, and appears to have no statute of limitations. Its coverage is broad in scope (for example, "grease payments" are not exempted) and its criminal and civil liability is *strict* with no need to prove corrupt intent. It is also a crime under the BBA to fail to prevent bribery. A violator can be disbarred from competing for public contracts.

Formal criminal charges were commenced for the first time by the Serious Fraud Office in 2013 against individuals associated with a bio fuel investment fund, and the first criminal corporate conviction secured in 2016.

Administered by Britain Serious Fraud Office (SFO), the BBA governs the activities of firms around the world. Alstom of France, already having paid the DOJ $772 million for FCPA violations, stands charged under the BBA for making $75 million in payments to secure $4 billion in Egyptian, Saudi Arabian, Bahamian and Indonesian projects. The SFO need not take into account the FCPA fines Alstom has already paid.

Deferred prosecution agreements (DPA) with corporate offenders have been authorized and undertaken with cooperating parties since 2014. A record fine of nearly 500 Pounds Sterling was paid by Rolls Royce under a DPA in 2017, and the company also paid considerable FCPA fines. The BBA extends to essentially all firms doing business in the U.K. Hypothetically, therefore, the BBA reaches U.S. firms with U.K. stock listings or sales offices, and perhaps those processing illegal payments via British banks. The BBA governs the activities of firms around the world, say bribes in India.

The Act is tempered by an undefined "adequate procedures" compliance defense not found in the FCPA. A serious, effective anti-bribery compliance system may constitute "adequate procedures". In the Skansen Interiors prosecution of 2018, a jury found inadequate procedures in a corporate criminal prosecution because the self-reporting defendant did not have a specific policy against Bribery Act violations, nor a dedicated compliance officer, nor BBA training for staff, who were not asked to agree to comply with the Act.

In sum, neither the OECD or U.N. Convention, nor the British Bribery Act, is a clone of the FCPA, but the lonely U.S. position on foreign corrupt practices law now has allies.

CHAPTER 6
TECHNOLOGY TRANSFERS

Tech Transfers: EU, China   U.S. Section 301

TRIPS Basics and Disputes   Made in China 2025

A U.S.-China Tech War?

Apart from technology and intellectual property theft and counterfeiting (see Chapter 4), there are many variations of lawful technology transfer agreements. But they all in some way address the transfer of intellectual property across borders. The agreement may be exclusively for that purpose, or the transfer may be part of a larger agreement, such as the creation of a joint venture or a franchise agreement. What is included within the definition of intellectual property or technology transfers tends to be quite broad. The transfer may involve property which is granted protection under laws protecting and regulating patents, copyrights and trademarks, or the transfer may involve property which is not granted such protection, but where some protection is maintained by controlling who obtains trade secrets or knowhow.

A comparatively new form of transferring technology is by way of a strategic alliance. It is a kind of joint venture where two firms (or more) from different nations agree to jointly exploit technology. The participants often make different contributions to the alliance. One may contribute technology, another capital, or a distribution network, or service facilities, etc. Perhaps the most important part of a strategic alliance is the technology license agreement. It is not always clear whether the alliance structure also transfers enforcement or improvement rights to the licensee of the technology.

The process of transferring technology involves an agreement which outlines the relationship between the transferor and the recipient. The extent to which the agreement is detailed may depend upon the character of the transferee. Even when the technology is transferred to a wholly owned subsidiary in a foreign nation, there is almost always some agreement, at the very least for tax purposes. The corporate structure using a parent and a foreign subsidiary demands that the separate nature of the two entities be maintained. If not, the parent may be held responsible for the debts of the subsidiary under veil piercing theory.

Consequently, the transfer of technology from a parent to a subsidiary should be at arms-length to avoid transfer pricing allegations and represented by a written agreement. But if the parent is convinced that there is little likelihood that the subsidiary's management will adversely affect the value of the technology, or produce poor quality goods using the technology, there are likely to be fewer provisions in the agreement than where the transferee is an independent entity, unrelated to the transferor.

When the agreement is to transfer technology to an entity which is not part of the transferor's corporate structure, there will be a sense that more detail ought to appear in the technology agreement. For example, disputes will not be settled "within" the company, as they may when the transfer of technology is to a subsidiary, but by judicial or arbitral tribunals. A transfer within a corporate structure is usually easily worked out, but a transfer to an independent recipient may involve considerable negotiation of many details.

One foundational question for TT across borders is whether specific intellectual property rights are recognized and how they treated in the jurisdictions involved. Fortunately, the Trade-Related Intellectual Property Rights Agreement (TRIPS), part of the WTO package of agreements adopted by WTO members, creates some baseline IP rules.

Computer Software, Management and Knowhow Contracts

The laws of some nations may recognize computer software as protectable property by copyright, patent or as a trade secret. Even when there is legal recognition of computer software as protectable property, it may be best not to transfer it if the risk of loss is high. Where the computer technology is contained in the end product, such as the bar coding process for retail products, the software technology may be protected by retaining it in the home country and only transferring the end use product. De-compilation rules, like those of the EU software directive, may allow relatively easy de-coding of software which with a few tweaks may allow registration of new copyrights by locals. See generally R. Folsom, *European Union Law including BREXIT in a Nutshell.*

Many enterprises, especially in the hotel industry, function by means of management contracts. The transfer usually involves knowhow, the knowledge of how to operate a facility. Often the most important aspect of the transfer is the experience of the manager of the management company. That experience is reflected in the manager's day to day decisions. It is an experience which has proven that it has value. For example, many Cuban government organizations attempted to manage hotels to develop tourism beginning in the mid-1980s. But the hotels were inefficiently managed until foreign management was obtained. The management contract may include training of host nation persons in hotel management. Even if the management contract is not also a training contract, there will be a certain amount of transfer of training involved, simply by the other employees viewing how a well-managed unit functions.

Knowledge of how to undertake a particular function or functions has value. That knowledge may be transferred as licensed knowhow. Except under EU law, knowhow is not commonly recognized as protectable IP. Like trade secrets, knowhow is a high risk area of technology. Once released (say on the Net by a disgruntled employee or retiree) knowhow is almost impossible to secure against use by others.

THE BASICS OF TRIPS

The 1995 WTO package of trade accords include an agreement on trade-related intellectual property rights (TRIPS). This agreement is binding upon the roughly 165 nations that are members of the World Trade Organization. In the United States, the TRIPS agreement has been ratified and implemented by Congress under the Uruguay Round Agreements Act. There is a general requirement of national and most-favored-nation treatment among the parties.

Many developed nations had been trying unsuccessfully to promote expanded intellectual property rights through the U.N.-created World Intellectual Property Rights Organization (WIPO). WIPO agreements are not mandatory, and much of the developing world had declined to opt into their terms. Much to the benefit of private parties in the developed world, the TRIPS Code covers the gamut of intellectual property. It has *de facto* become a near-global IP Code.

On copyrights, there is TRIPS protection for computer programs and databases, rental authorization controls for owners of computer software and sound recordings, a 50-year motion picture and sound recording copyright term, and a general obligation to comply with the Berne Convention (1971 version), except for its provisions on moral rights.

On patents, the Paris Convention (1967 version) prevails, 20-year product and process patents are available "in all fields of technology", including pharmaceuticals and agricultural chemicals. However, patents can be denied when necessary to protect public morals or order, to protect human, animal or plant life or health, and to avoid serious environmental prejudice. The TRIPS provisions did not stop the Indian Supreme Court in 2013 from denying Novartis a patent on its cancer drug, Gleevac. The court took the view that Novartis was engaged in "evergreening", i.e., making small, inconsequential changes to existing patents and that Indian law could require proof of "improved therapeutic efficacy" before a patent grant.

Article 31 of the TRIPS permits compulsory licensing of patents in national emergencies or other circumstances of extreme urgency, subject to a duty to reasonably compensate the patent owner. Thailand, for example, has issued compulsory licenses on a range of cancer, heart disease and AIDS drugs. There is considerable controversy over pharmaceutical patents based on traditional medicines of indigenous peoples, which some see as bio-piracy. Proposals have been made to amend TRIPS to require disclosure of the origins of bio-patents, obtain informed consent from the indigenous communities involved, and share the benefits of such patents.

For trademarks, the Paris Convention controls, service marks become registrable, internationally prominent marks receive enhanced protection, the linking of local marks with foreign trademarks is prohibited, and compulsory trademark licensing is banned. Protection for industrial designs is provided.

Certain geographical indicators of origin (Feta cheese, Canadian Whiskey, Parma ham) are protected unless they have become generic terms (California champagne anyone? Perhaps with a U.S. parmesan on ciabatta?).

Note that by incorporating the Berne and Paris conventions, TRIPS and the WTO DSU become an enforcement mechanism for those longstanding treaties. See Chapter 2. Gray market trading and its related IP issues (see Chapter 4) are explicitly not covered by TRIPS, allowing each WTO member state to differ on such law. There is no coverage in TRIPS of knowhow TT (below).

Special 301—Prioritization of U.S. Intellectual Property Rights Disputes

The Special 301 procedures established by the 1988 Omnibus Trade and Competitiveness Act are permanent features of United States trade legislation. See generally U.S. Section 301 Proceedings below. These procedures are located in Section 182 of the Trade Act of 1974. Under these procedures the United States Trade Representative is required to identify foreign countries that deny adequate and effective protection of intellectual property rights, or deny fair and equitable access to United States persons that rely upon intellectual property protection.

The USTR is given discretion to determine whether to designate certain of these countries to be "priority countries." If so designated, a mandatory Section 301 investigation must follow in the absence of a determination that this would be detrimental to U.S. economic interests or a negotiated settlement of the intellectual property dispute. Once designated, Special 301 investigations and retaliations against priority countries must ordinarily be decided within 6 months by the USTR. Whether to retaliate or not is discretionary with the USTR, but retaliation is not authorized if the country in question enters into good faith negotiations or makes "significant progress" in bilateral or multilateral negotiations towards increased protection for intellectual property rights.

Many commentators have observed that unilateral use of Section 301 prior to creation of the WTO helped push the U.S. agenda in the TRIPS negotiations. Since 1994, if the dispute is covered by the WTO TRIPS agreement, the United States must avoid using unilateral Section 301 trade sanctions and pursue WTO dispute settlement. See Chapter 2. In identifying priority foreign countries in the intellectual property field, Section 182 indicates that the USTR is to prioritize only those countries that have the most "onerous or egregious" practices, whose practices have the greatest adverse impact on United States products, and are not entering into good faith negotiations bilaterally or multilaterally to provide adequate and effective protection of intellectual property rights.

For these purposes, the term "persons that rely on intellectual protection" covers those involved in copyrighted works of authorship or those involved in the manufacture of products that are patented or subject to process patents. Interestingly, this definition does not include those who rely on United States trademarks. However, the relevant definitions include trademarks in connection with the denial by foreign countries of adequate and effective protection of intellectual property rights. The definition of practices that deny fair and equitable market access in connection with intellectual property rights appear to be limited to copyrights and patents. This denial must constitute a violation of provisions of international law or international agreements to which both the United States and that country are parties or otherwise constitute a discriminatory nontariff trade barrier. Regular reports to Congress are required of the USTR by Section 182.

The USTR has chiefly placed foreign country intellectual property practices on watch lists rather than formally designating priority countries. These watch lists are divided as between "priority watch lists" and "secondary watch lists." Many nations have been listed by the USTR since 1989 in this fashion. This has the practical effect of placing pressure on those nations to enter negotiations with the United States that will improve their protection of intellectual property rights. The use of these lists gives the USTR more room to negotiate settlements with the countries concerned. For example, the USTR formally named China, India and Thailand as the first "priority countries" for Special 301 purposes.

The formal process of negotiation backed up by a mandatory Section 301 investigation and potential sanctions was begun. Thailand was cited for its failure to enforce copyrights and for the absence of patent protection for pharmaceuticals. India was named because its patent laws are deficient from the U.S. perspective, particularly on compulsory licensing and the absence of pharmaceutical protection. Extensive book, video, sound recording and computer software piracy in India was also cited. United States Special 301 investigations and watch lists, now including "Out-of-Cycle Reviews of Notorious Markets", have continued relentlessly in spite of the WTO TRIPS agreement.

The USTR has filed numerous TRIPS complaints with the WTO (below). Filings have been made, for example, against Denmark, Sweden, Ireland, Ecuador, Greece, Portugal, India, Russia, Pakistan, Turkey and, not surprisingly, China.

TRIPS Disputes

Dozens of TRIPS complaints have been initiated under WTO dispute settlement procedures. Most have been settled, but a few have resulted in WTO Panel and Appellate Body Reports. Here is a sampling of those disputes:

1. India—Patent Protection for Pharmaceutical and Agricultural Chemical Products, WT/DS50/AB/R (1998) ("mailbox rule" patent applications for subjects not patentable in India until 2005 inadequate, denial of exclusive marketing rights in breach of TRIPS Article 70.9).

2. Canada—Term of Patent Protection, WT/DS170/AB/R (2000) (pre-TRIPS Canadian patents must receive 20-year term).

3. U.S.—Section 110 (5) Copyright Act, WT/DS160/R (2000) (copyright exemption for "home-style" dramatic musical works consistent with Berne Convention, "business use" exemption inconsistent with Berne and therefore in breach of TRIPS) (settled by payment).

4. Canada—Pharmaceutical Patents, WT/DS114/R (2000) (Canadian generic pharmaceutical regulatory review and stockpiling patent rights' exceptions not sufficiently "limited").

5. U.S.—Section 211 Appropriations Act, WT/DS176/AB/R (2002) (prohibition against registering marks confiscated by Cuban government, e.g., HAVANA CLUB rum, without original owner's consent violates Paris Convention and TRIPS, trade names covered by TRIPS).

6. EC—Trademarks and Geographical Indications WT/DS 174,290/R (2005) (EC regulation violates national treatment and most-favored treatment obligations to non-EC nationals, procedural violations also found).

7. China—Measures Affecting the Protection and Enforcement of Intellectual Property Rights, WT/DS362/R (2009) (China's implementation of TRIPS upheld as to criminal law thresholds and disposal of confiscated,

infringing goods by customs authorities, rejected as to denial of copyright protection for works not authorized for release in China).

8. China—Measures Affecting Trading Rights and Distribution Services for Certain Publications and Audiovisuals Entertainment Products, WT/DS363/AB/R (2009) (China's ADV restrictions limited to state-owned or approved channels violate WTO Accession Protocol, GATT 1994 and GATS; Restraints not necessary to protect public morals).

9. European Communities—Information Technology Tariffs, WT/DS375–377 (2010) (EU tariffs on cable converter boxes with Net capacity, flat panel computer screens and printers that also scan, fax or copy violated 1996 Information Technology Agreement zero tariff rules).

Trump Administration TRIPS Complaint

The Trump Administration notably filed a WTO complaint, joined by Japan and the European Union, against alleged patent violations of Articles 3 and 28 of TRIPS. These allegations assert that foreign patent holders are unable to stop Chinese licensees from continuing to use patented technology after licenses expire. They also assert Chinese discrimination against and less favorable mandatory adverse contract terms for imported foreign technology.

The U.S. specifically cited four Chinese laws as the source of these TRIPS violations: The PRC Foreign Trade Law, Contract Law, Chinese-Foreign Equity Joint Venture Law, and the PRC Regulations on the Administration of the Import and Export of Technologies. See Chapter 8.

DEVELOPING WORLD TECHNOLOGY TRANSFER CONTROLS

When transfer of technology rules do not exist in the recipient country, the technology transfer (TT) agreement is the conclusion of the bargaining of the two parties. The agreement will not be public; it will not be registered. But in some nations, especially developing nations and nonmarket economy nations, the government may be involved in the determination and regulation of the technology transfer agreement.

Typically, without approval from a technology transfer commission, the TT agreement is void and unenforceable. In such jurisdictions, the parties end up negotiating terms for their agreement that are acceptable to the TT Commission. During the 1970s a number of developing nations enacted transfer of technology laws. In Latin America, Decision No. 24 of the ANCOM group pioneered the use of regulatory TT Commissions.

The ANCOM approach spread like wildfire throughout Latin America. The laws were adopted both as part of the general attempt to control foreign investment and technology transfers, but also to preserve scarce hard currency at a time of severe balance of payment problems. The developing nations viewed technology transfer agreements as an area where there were serious abuses, and believed that their laws would adequately address these issues. The principal abuses were thought to include the following:

- Transfer of obsolete technology;

- Excessive price paid for the technology;

- Limitations on use of new developments by the transferee by grant back provisions;

- Little research performed by the transferee;

- Too much intervention by the transferor in transferee activities;

- Limitations on where the transferee may market the product;

- Requirements for components be purchased from the transferor which are available locally or could be obtained from other foreign sources more cheaply;

- Inadequate training of transferee's personnel to do jobs performed by personnel of the transferor;

- Transfer of technology which has adequate domestic substitutes and is therefore not needed;

- Too long a duration of the agreement; and

- Application of foreign law and use of foreign tribunals for dispute resolution.

Some nations had different reasons for wishing to more closely govern technology transfers. But these reasons provide an outline of what areas transfer of technology laws in the 1970s attempted to govern. The result of these restrictive laws was the transfer of less technology, and of technology less valuable to the source. It was often older technology over which the company was willing to relinquish some control.

The bureaucracies established to register and approve or disapprove the agreements were often staffed with persons who knew little about technology, less about international business, but who possessed all of the inefficiency and incompetence of many government agencies. The laws did not bring in more technology, but less. The consequence was that they did not serve the purpose of helping the balance of payments.

Furthermore, the nations which adopted strict rules regulating the transfer of technology often did not have laws which protected intellectual property. In the 1980s and 1990s, some of these restrictive laws were dismantled, whether by formal repeal or replacement by more transfer encouraging and intellectual property protecting laws, or by a relaxed interpretation of the laws and a general automatic approval of what the transferor and transferee agreed upon. Mexico, for example, eliminated its Technology Transfer Commission in 1991.

Ironically, some technology agreements which were used in the 1960s before the enactment of the strict laws, and which became unusable after such enactments, are now once again being used in the developing world. That said, a substantial number of "technology transfer" control laws remain in force in Latin America, China (below) and in the decidedly developed European Union.

EU TECHNOLOGY TRANSFER REGULATION

The European Union, as befits a major technology center, has a strong intellectual property regime. The EU adheres to the TRIPS agreement (see Chapter 4), and has created regional EU Trademarks and EU Unitary Patents, in addition to traditional national IP rights of the member states. See my *European Union Law including BREXIT in a Nutshell.*

Subsequent to major decisions of the European Court of Justice, the EU adopted separate patent licensing and knowhow licensing regulations in 1984 and 1989, which were later merged into the Transfer of Technology Regulations (TT) outlined immediately below. These regulations are called "group exemptions" under EU business competition law, encouraging parties and their lawyers to draft patent and knowhow license agreements that conform to their contents. Failure to do so, can result in Commission prosecutions, fines and penalties, as well as voiding of the agreement or parts thereof.

Transfer of Technology Regulation 240/96

In 1996 the European Commission enacted Regulation 240/96 on the application of Article 101(3) of the Treaty on the Functioning of the European Union (TFEU) to transfer technology agreements. The intention of this Regulation was to combine existing patent and knowhow business competition law exemptions into a single regulation covering technology transfer agreements, and to simplify and harmonize the rules for patent and knowhow licensing. It contained detailed lists of permitted, permissible and prohibited clauses.

Regulation 240/96 stated that Article 101(1) of the Treaty did not apply to "pure patent and knowhow licensing agreements" as well as to agreements with ancillary provisions relating to intellectual property other than patents, when only two undertakings were parties and when one or more of eight listed obligations were included. These were obligations of limitation, such as not to license other undertakings to exploit the technology, and fell under Article 1 of the Regulation. There were time limits (5 years patents/10 years knowhow) for the exemption of these eight obligations in certain situations.

Article 2 of Regulation 240/96, the Permissible List, allowed technology transfers even when certain clauses existed (17 were listed). These clauses were considered generally not restrictive of competition. There were various obligations on the licensee, such as not divulging knowhow communicated by the licensor.

Article 3 of Regulation 240/96, known as the Black List, indicated that Articles 1 and 2 did not apply when any one of seven obligations were present, such as restricting a party in the determination of prices, competition restrictions, limitations on production quantity, licensee improvement grant-back requirements, etc.

Article 4 carried the scope of the exemption provided for in Articles 1 and 2 to certain other restrictive agreements which were notified to the Commission and received no Commission opposition. Article 4 was known as the Gray List. Regulation 240/96, according to Article 5, did not apply to four classes of agreements, such as most agreements within a joint venture. But under Article 5 it did apply to three forms of agreements, including where the licensor is itself a licensee of the technology and was authorized to grant sub-licenses.

The Commission retained power to withdraw benefits of the Regulation 240/96 if in a specific case the exempted agreement was incompatible with the conditions of Treaty Article 101(3). Final articles provided some definitions, a list of what were deemed patents, preservation of confidentiality of information, and the repeal of the two regulations combined in this regulation.

Transfer of Technology Regulation 772/2004

The detailed regulation of technology transfer agreement clauses contained in Regulation 240/96 was replaced by Regulation 772/2004, which generally applied to patent, knowhow, production trademark and software copyright licensing. This Regulation distinguished between agreements of "competing" and "noncompeting" parties, the latter being treated less strictly than the former. Parties were deemed "competing" if they compete (without infringing each other's IP rights) in either the relevant technology or product market, determined in each instance by what buyers regard as substitutes.

If the competing parties had a combined market share of 20 percent or less, their licensing agreements were covered by group exemption under Regulation 772/2004. Noncompeting parties, on the other hand, benefited from the group exemption so long as their individual market shares do not exceed 30 percent. Agreements initially covered by Regulation 772/2004 that subsequently exceeded the "safe harbor" thresholds noted above lost their exemption subject to a two-year grace period. Outside these exemptions, a "rule of reason" approach applied.

Inclusion of certain "hardcore restraints" caused license agreement to lose their group exemption. For competing parties, such restraints included price fixing, output limitations on both parties, limits on the licensee's ability to exploit its own technology, and allocation of markets or competitors (subject to exceptions). Specifically, restraints on active and passive selling by the licensee in a territory reserved for the licensor were allowed, as were active (but not passive) selling restraints by licensees in territories of other licensees.

Licensing agreements between noncompeting parties could not contain the "hardcore" restraint of maximum price fixing. Active selling restrictions on licensees could be utilized, along with passive selling restraints in territories reserved to the licensor or (for two years) another licensee. For these purposes, the competitive status of the parties was decided at the outset of the agreement.

Other license terms deemed "excluded restrictions" also caused a loss of exemption. Such clauses included: (1) mandatory grant-backs or assignments of severable improvements by licensees, excepting nonexclusive license-backs; (2) no-challenges by the licensee of the licensor's intellectual property rights, subject to the licensor's right to terminate upon challenge; and (3) for noncompeting parties, restraints on the licensee's ability to exploit its own technology or either party's ability to carry out research and development (unless indispensable to prevent disclosure of the licensed knowhow).

Transfer of Technology Regulation 316/2014

Regulation 316/2014 replaced Regulation 772/2004, with a one-year transition period to adapt existing TT agreements. Regulation 316/2014 is valid until 2026, and clarifies that it applies to technology transfers only if other EU regulations concerning research and development (Regulation 2659/2000) and/or specialization agreements (Regulation 2658/2000) are inapplicable. The distinction between competing and noncompeting parties under Regulation 772/2004 is retained, as are their market share thresholds.

Restrictive changes were made in 2014 to the TT group exemption regulation as follows:

(1) All exclusive grant-back licensee obligations require individual assessment, as do

termination clauses triggered by licensee challenges to the validity of the technology. Such clauses are no longer covered by the group exemption.

(2)   Purchase requirements from licensors of raw material or equipment are group exempt only if directly related to the production or sale of products made with the licensed technology.

(3)   No passive sales restrictions on licensees are group exempt unless objectively necessary for the licensee to penetrate a new market.

(4)   Settlement agreements which lead to delayed or limited ability for licensee launch of the product in any market ("pay-for-delay" or "reverse payment" agreements) may be prohibited under certain conditions, as may no challenge clauses in settlement agreements, particularly if the patent was granted on the basis of incorrect or misleading information.

(5)   Technology licensing pools now enjoy a comprehensive, detailed group exemption provided they adhere to Regulation 316/2014. In all cases, exemption under Regulation 772/2004 or Regulation 316/2014 may be withdrawn where in any particular case an agreement has effects that are incompatible with Treaty Article 101(3).

TECHNOLOGY TRANSFERS AND THE PRC

Major changes have been undertaken in the licensing and intellectual property law of the People's Republic of China since the Cultural Revolution. These changes reflect China's desire to create a modern economy by importing technology and by fostering its development. According to a report issued by central authorities in Beijing, the importation of technology augments China's modernization program in four ways:

1)   By decreasing the gap on product quality and standards between China and the developed world;

2)   By helping to promote the technological upgrading of Chinese enterprises;

3)   By enhancing the ability of Chinese enterprises to independently develop their own new products and technology; and

4)   By improving enterprise management. China's desire to modernize its economy through technological imports is most evident in PRC patent and licensing law.

A host of technology import regulations authorizing license agreements with foreign sources has been enacted. These regulations are not a blank check permitting technology importation at any cost. Rather, they are carefully constructed rules intended to promote technology transfers to China under acceptable terms and conditions.

China IP Law

China's legal framework for the protection of intellectual property is comprehensive, but the challenge is for China to enforce the legislation effectively and transparently. The complaints from foreign investors in this area are universal and ongoing. China is a member of the WTO and consequently a party to all major intellectual property conventions of the organization, as well as others, including the Paris Convention, Patent Cooperation Treaty, Berne Convention, Universal Copyright Convention, Geneva Convention and Madrid Agreement on International Registration of Marks.

PRC Patents

The Patent Law of the People's Republic of China (the "Patent Law") was amended on December 27, 2008. The revision came into effect on October 1, 2009 and was supplemented in 2010 with revised Implementing Regulations (the "Implementing Regulations"). The Implementing Regulations were published on December 30, 2009 and came into effect on February 1, 2010 and there have been subsequent judicial interpretations.

There are three types of patents: Patents for inventions of 20 years duration from the application filing date; patents for utility models of 10 years duration; and design patents of 10 years duration. The system is compliant with the WTO Agreement on Trade-related Aspects of Intellectual Property Rights (TRIPS, above). China has adopted a "first-to-file" rather than "first-to-invent" system and foreign applicants are required to submit patent applications in China through an officially designated patent agent.

PRC Trademarks

The Trademark Law of the People's Republic of China (the "Trademark Law") was amended for the third time with effect on May 1, 2014. The revisions to the Implementing Regulations of the Trademark Law (the "Implementing Regulations") were published on April 29, 2014 and also came into effect on May 1, 2014. A trademark registration is valid for 10 years from the final date of approval (i.e., upon expiration of the three-month opposition period or, for international trademark registrations extended to the PRC under the Madrid Agreement or the Madrid Protocol, the date of filing), with further 10-year renewal terms available.

The law imposes a strict first-to-file rule for obtaining trademark rights, whereby the first party to file for registration of a mark pre-empts later applicants. Prior use of an unregistered mark is generally irrelevant for trademark registration purposes, unless the prior mark in question is a well-known mark, or the later filing is a bad-faith pre-emption of the prior mark that has achieved a certain degree of fame through use.

PRC Copyrights

The Copyright Law of the People's Republic of China (the "Copyright Law") was amended with effect from October 27, 2001, and its Implementing Regulations (the "Implementing Regulations") were amended with effect from September 15, 2002. The Copyright Law was again amended in 2010 with effect from April 1, 2010 (the "2010 Amendment") and the Implementing Regulations were revised with effect from March 1, 2013. The 2010 Amendment was in response to a 2009 WTO dispute, and attempts to confirm that "illegal" works can obtain copyright protection. In recent years, the PRC National

The current Copyright Law introduces protection for (1) written works, (2) oral works, (3) musical, dramatic, Chinese folk art, choreographic and acrobatic works, (4) works of fine art and architectural works, (5) photographic works, (6) cinematographic works, (7) graphic works, (8) model works and (9) computer software. The Copyright Law does not protect databases, i.e., collections of original information that do not qualify for copyright protection. However, if the means of compilation satisfies the requirement of originality, then such compilation can be protected.

Under the Copyright Law, an author's moral rights of attribution, revision and integrity are perpetual. A citizen's right of publication and the various economic rights are protected for the duration of the life of the author plus 50 years. For works of a legal person or other organization, or works for hire vested in a legal person or other organization, as well as for photographic works and cinematographic works, the right of publication and other economic rights are protected for a period of 50 years from the date of first publication. Registration is not a precondition to copyright enforcement but can provide prima facie evidence of ownership in enforcement actions.

PRC Trade Secrets

A trade secret is defined in both the Law of the PRC against Unfair Competition ("Unfair Competition Law") and the PRC Criminal Code as technical and business information which is private, able to bring economic benefits to the rightful party, is practical, and for which that party has adopted measures to maintain its confidentiality. A non-exhaustive list of measures to maintain confidentiality is set forth in the Several Provisions on the Prohibition of Acts of Infringement of Trade Secrets (the "Trade Secrets Provisions"), effective from November 23, 1995 and amended on December 3, 1998. Such measures include disclosing secrets on a need-to-know basis only, adopting physical preventive measures such as locking, marking information "confidential", requiring access codes and passwords, and requiring confidentiality agreements.

Trade secrets are protected under the Unfair Competition Law. Under the legislation, business operators are prohibited from infringing upon commercial secrets by obtaining the commercial secrets of others by theft, inducement, coercion or other illicit means; revealing, using or allowing others to use commercial secrets obtained by such means; and revealing, using or allowing others to use commercial secrets of others which are in their possession by violation of agreements or other requests for confidentiality by the owners concerned. If a third party knows or should have known of such acts violating the law, but obtains, uses or reveals commercial secrets of others, this will also constitute infringement.

Under a Supreme People's Court Interpretation on intellectual property crimes issued in 2004, the infringement of a trade secret causing loss in excess of RMB500,000 will be regarded as serious and will trigger criminal prosecution under the PRC Criminal Code.

Technology Piracy in the PRC

Despite the adoption of major PRC patent, trademark, copyright and technology transfer laws and their implementing regulations, a dark shadow hangs over much of Chinese intellectual property practice. Counterfeiting of goods and unlicensed use of software and technology is approaching epidemic proportions. Computer software is perhaps the most prominent victim. The official remedies, however diligently applied, seem inadequate to the task of dealing with this problem. Partly, one suspects, there are cultural forces at work. To copy another's work is traditionally a compliment in China.

Partly also, the economics of development fuel piracy in the PRC. It is simply much less expensive to "borrow" from foreigners and (increasingly) domestic entities whatever can be reverse-engineered and imitated. Even "Beijing Jeeps" have reportedly been knocked off by a large number of township enterprises. Although there have been advances in protection of intellectual property and foreigners have successfully availed themselves of Chinese courts (e.g., in 2017 New Balance won a record setting $1.5 million damages award in a Suzhou court), there are no quick solutions to an environment that is fundamentally hostile to intellectual property.

In 2018, for example, a Wisconsin federal jury found China's Sinovel Wind Group guilty under the U.S. Economic Espionage Act of stealing trade secrets, primarily proprietary software controlling wind turbines, from American Superconductor (AS). The theft was undertaken in Austria via a disgruntled AS employee who was royally paid and entertained.

PRC Regulation of Technology Import and Export Contracts

As in many developing countries, there is a fear in China of paying excessive royalties for potentially redundant, outdated or inappropriate technology under oppressive contract terms. Likewise, there is a fear of standardized licensing contracts created by attorneys of foreign licensors. The principal objective of China's technology import regulations is to insure that such contracts do not contain restrictive clauses and to increase the bargaining power of Chinese licensees. Although pure licensing agreements are reasonably common, many technology transfers take place in the context of equity or contractual joint venture investments.

The Regulations on Technology Import and Export Administration, with their detailed implementing rules (the "Regulations"), are the most important example of China's modern approach to licensing agreements. Similar regulations exist in some of China's economic development zones and coastal cities, notably Shenzhen, Xiamen and Guangzhou (Canton), which compete for technology transfers.

Chinese law governs patent, trademark, knowhow and technical service contracts with foreigners. They also apply to technology transfers in connection with foreign investment. Once the parties have reached agreement, all such contracts must be examined and approved by government authorities before implementation. Since 1988, in a welcome reform, any technology transfer contract not disapproved after filing is deemed approved. Most Chinese licensing agreements are essentially installment sales. This is achieved by limiting the licensing agreement to a maximum of 10 years followed by the absence of restraints on the licensee's use of the technology after expiration of the agreement. The result is truly a technology transfer.

Chinese law stipulates that the imported technology must be "advanced," "appropriate" and "necessary" to modernization of China's industrial base. To this end, a feasibility study (which can be conducted by foreign experts) precedes the contract. The licensing agreement must contain certain terms, such as a guarantee by the supplier that the technology is "complete, free of error, effective and can achieve the objectives stipulated in the contract." This is an important representation and probably the most common source of lawsuits and arbitrations initiated by the Chinese in the technology transfer area.

Certain terms cannot appear in the agreement. These include restraints on the Chinese recipient's ability to choose the sources of relevant raw materials, spare parts or equipment. Such restraints are generally called "tying arrangements." However, the Chinese licensee can choose to take such supplies from the foreign licensor. In that case, the supplies must be offered at competitive international prices, itemized in the contract and are subject to special approvals.

Chinese law also prohibits contract terms that are harmful to the public interest, that violate China's sovereignty, or that are unclear, unequal or unreasonable. In general, these regulations are designed to promote economic modernization in China while protecting it from foreign exploitation. In other areas, either by law or practice, greater flexibility has been shown. For example, there is no legally stipulated maximum royalty payment. Royalties of 2% to 5% of net sales value have been routinely approved. Higher royalties get close scrutiny by the examining authorities. Given China's shortage of foreign exchange, barter and countertrade are often substituted for cash royalties.

Chinese law prohibits unreasonable restraints upon the Chinese recipient's domestic or export sales. Nevertheless, as a matter of practice, contract terms which effectively eliminate sales competition with the foreign licensor's products have often been permitted. Once approved and executed, PRC technology transfer contracts are subject to ongoing regulatory approvals. The contract will often stipulate that certification of the delivery of the technology and its integration into the existing Chinese facility is required before payment to the licensor is allowed.

This can get complicated because most technology importation is done by central or regional trading companies, not the end user. These trading companies often lack sufficient knowledge of the application of the technology by a factory hundreds or thousands of miles from their offices. Yet they are the ones who typically must make the necessary certifications. The level of Chinese sophistication about licensing agreements is increasing. They have developed model patent and knowhow licensing contracts with which they frequently initiate negotiations.

In their negotiations, and in the administration of their technology transfer law, the Chinese have so far successfully walked a fine line between providing sufficient incentives to bring foreign licensors into a bargain and discouraging them altogether. However, broad guidelines regulating China-sourced IP transfers to foreign entities, issued in 2018, could lead to less R & D and investment in the PRC by multinational companies seeking global integration of their technology programs.

Made in China 2025

China is already a major technology leader. It has, for example, more supercomputing power than the USA, is ahead in the production of drones for consumers, possesses huge online innovators

(Alibaba, Tencent, Baidu), leads the world in mobile payments systems (We-Chat Pay, Alipay), has outstanding facial recognition systems, exports high-speed rail systems already in place throughout the PRC, is applying gene-editing technology (Crispr) to crops, receives more venture capital than Silicon Valley, and on and on.

The PRC has a "Made in China 2025" program that seeks to make China a global leader in next generation strategic manufacturing and technology industries, including semiconductors, advanced machine tools, medical devices, biopharma, aerospace and aeronautics, advanced information technology, artificial intelligence, green and driverless autos, and robotics. Virtually all these technologies have a military dimension and in varying degrees are presently imported by the PRC.

To achieve its Made in China 2025 goals, local content rules are set at 40% for 2020 and expected to rise to 70% by 2025, abundant state subsidies are upward bound, and protection from foreign competition is anticipated. China takes pride in allocating $300 billion for low cost loans to underwrite the Made in China 2025 program.

Part of this program also includes pressuring foreign and Chinese companies to provide their leading technology. The principal pressure is access to China's large, lucrative and growing domestic market. In other words, this is the price to pay in order to make investments and do business in the PRC. One way to force technology transfers is to mandate use of joint ventures with a Chinese partner. Autos, insurance, cloud computing and telecommunications are subject to such rules.

Another way is mandate research and development inside China, with improvements in licensed technology passing or shared with a Chinese partner. Microsoft, Apple (iCloud) and chip-maker Qualcomm, for example, have "voluntarily" set up joint ventures in China under pressure to make technology transfers.

Made in China 2025 has been repeatedly cited and strongly criticized by the Trump Administration. See Chapter 8.

U.S. SECTION 301 PROCEEDINGS

Section 301 of the Trade Act of 1974 is one of the most politically motivated provisions of U.S. trade laws. Basically, this section applies when U.S. rights or benefits under international trade agreements are at risk or when foreign nations engage in *unjustifiable, unreasonable or discriminatory* act, policy or practice. Thus, Section 301 primarily focuses on the activities of foreign governments.

Although it can be used to protect the United States from foreign imports and technology transfers, as President Trump plans for China (below), Section 301 before the WTO was primarily applied to open up foreign markets to U.S. exports, investments and protection of intellectual property rights. Section 301 of the Trade Act of 1974 authorizes and in some cases mandates *unilateral* U.S. retaliation if another nation is in breach of a trade agreement or engaging in unjustifiable, unreasonable or discriminatory conduct.

Amendments contained in the Trade and Tariff Act of 1984 broadened the original scope of Section 301 to include retaliatory action against foreign country practices in connection with *services*. Special remedies are allowed, including denial of "service sector access authorizations." Presumably, for example, the U.S. Trade Representative (subject to presidential directives) could deny access to foreign banks by withholding licenses from federal authorities.

Section 301 Procedures

Private sector petitions for action under Section 301 are filed with the U.S. Trade Representative, who undertakes appropriate relief after investigation, consultation with the relevant foreign country and other interested parties, and an affirmative determination of a Section 301 "offense." The USTR may self-initiate Section 301 proceedings. Remedies are mandatory (subject to various exceptions) when U.S. trade agreement rights are being denied or an unjustifiable foreign country practice is found. Remedies are discretionary when unreasonable or discriminatory practices are involved.

The remedies available include suspending trade agreement concessions, various import restraints, and bilateral agreements with the offending country. The USTR chooses the remedy subject to presidential "direction." The remedy chosen need not have any connection with the complaints and may last as long as the USTR deems appropriate.

Perhaps the most critical difference between the Section 301 offenses concerns "international legal rights," which is part of the definition of unjustifiable practices. Discriminatory practices are those which deny national or MFN treatment, but there is no reference to doing so inconsistently with U.S. legal rights. Unreasonable practices are expressly not premised on international legal rights, and only need to be "unfair and inequitable." There is a long list of examples of unreasonable practices in Section 301(d) (3)(B).

The statutory definitions of unreasonableness were expanded in 1988. They include inequitable treatment in connection with market opportunities, investment and protection of intellectual property rights. There is no requirement that such behavior violate an international agreement to which the United States is a party. This has the advantage of not linking relief to international dispute settlement procedures. Thus, Section 301 is a statutory provision of remarkable breadth.

WTO Challenge to Section 301

Most Section 301 proceedings prior to the WTO were resolved through negotiations leading to alteration of foreign country practices. Ultimately, if the President or the USTR is not satisfied with any negotiated result in connection with a Section 301 complaint, the United States may undertake unilateral retaliatory trade measures. Unlike subsidy, dumping, Safeguard and market disruption proceedings (see Chapter 4), Section 301 of the Trade Act of 1974 has no origins in or other imprimatur of legitimacy from the GATT or World Trade Organization. Indeed, the unilateral nature of Section 301 is thought by many to run counter to the multilateral approach to trade relations embodied in the GATT and WTO.

Nevertheless, in 1999 the WTO Appellate Body affirmed the legality of Section 301, provided the President does not employ it in a manner inconsistent with the WTO agreements, particularly the Dispute Resolution Understanding. See Chapter 2. The Appellate Body relied heavily on President Clinton's congressionally approved administrative statement that the U.S. would refrain from Section 301 retaliation until the WTO has ruled on disputes falling within its domain. Should some future administration (e.g., the Trump Administration) fail to adhere to this policy, the Appellate Body indicated that Section 301 would violate the WTO Dispute Settlement Understanding.

Super 301

Section 301 received hostile responses from U.S. trade partners, especially after the amendments to Section 301 implemented in 1988 through the Omnibus Trade and Competitiveness Act. These amendments include the so-called "Super 301 procedures" which required the USTR to initiate Section 301 proceedings against "priority practices" in "priority countries" identified by the USTR as most significant to U.S. exports. In May of 1989, the USTR initiated Super 301 procedures against the following:

(a) Japanese procurement restraints on purchases of United States supercomputers and space satellites, and Japanese technical barriers to trade in wood products;

(b) Brazilian import bans and licensing controls; and

(c) Indian barriers to foreign investment and foreign insurance.

Super 301 was timed to dovetail with the Uruguay Round of GATT negotiations scheduled to end in late 1990. Some saw it as a clever U.S. bargaining chip. It was anticipated that intergovernmental negotiations concerning alleged unfair trading practices would be undertaken in the 12 to 18 months that followed. This proved to be true for Japan and Brazil, but not India, which refused to even discuss its Super 301 listing. Settlements were negotiated with Japan and Brazil which significantly opened these markets to U.S. exporters.

The Super 301 procedures and designations created in Section 301 of the Trade Act of 1974 were limited in application to 1989 and 1990. They expired in 1991. Super 301 was perceived to be an acceptable alternative to the "Gephardt Amendment" which would have required 10 percent annual reductions in U.S. trade deficits with countries having excessive and unwarranted trade surpluses. Either way, Japan was clearly the main target of the Gephardt

Amendment, Super 301 and continuing efforts to renew Super 301.

These efforts, a notable rise in Japan's 1993 trade surplus with the United States and the failure of a trade summit early in 1994, all contributed to the revival of Super 301 in 1994 by President Clinton. This revival was undertaken for two years by executive order and (once again) may have forestalled more severe trade sanctions by Congress. The Uruguay Round Agreements Implementation Act in 1995 codified President Clinton's executive order.

Since then, on a few occasions, executive orders have continued to give life to Super 301. As long as Super 301 is an option, it may be used by a U.S. president.

Effect of WTO Dispute Settlement

U.S. adherence to the WTO package of Covered Agreements, including the Dispute Settlement Understanding (DSU), has greatly reduced the frequency with which it unilaterally invokes Section 301. The DSU obligates its signatories to follow streamlined dispute settlement procedures under which unilateral retaliation is restrained until the offending nation has failed to conform to a WTO ruling. See Chapter 2.

Trump, Section 301 and China

Disputes falling outside the scope of the WTO agreements, and disputes with nations that are not

WTO members (Iran), remain vulnerable under Section 301. President Trump, seizing upon the argument that a wide range of China's technology transfer law and practices fall outside the WTO mandate, moved to unilaterally sanction China with dramatic Section 301 tariffs and other trade and investment restraints. He also filed a TRIPS-based patent complaint with the WTO. China threatens to retaliate in what resembles a high-tech focused trade war. See Chapter 8.

For more on the law of technology transfers, see R. Folsom, *Principles of International Trade Law* (West Academic Publishing).

CHAPTER 7
FREE TRADE AGREEMENTS AND CUSTOMS UNIONS

GATT Article 24		Canada, Mexico, U.S. FTAs
GATS Article 5		Pacific Rim FTAs
WTO Enabling Clause		ASEAN
Developing World FTAs		TPP
CETA	EU FTAs	TPP-11

There is a massive movement towards free trade agreements (FTA) and customs unions (CU) throughout the world, though not often of the consequence of that occurring in the European Union and NAFTA 1994. Some of these developments are a competitive by-product of European and North American integration. Others simply reflect the desire (but not always the political will) to capture the economic gains and international negotiating strength that such economic relations can bring. This is particularly true of attempts at free trade and customs unions in the developing world.

The explosion of such agreements, WTO-authorized under GATT, GATS and The Enabling Clause, creates systemic risks for the World Trade Organization's most-favored-nation principles. See Chapter 2.

The Spaghetti Bowl

The WTO reports that all of its members are partners in one or more regional or bilateral trade agreements. Here is a sampling of agreements around the globe: Hong Kong-China, Japan-Singapore, Russia-CIS states, New Zealand-China, Mexico-Israel, Canada-Peru, EU-South Africa, Chile-South Korea, the South Asian Free Trade Area (India, Pakistan, Bangladesh, Nepal, Bhutan, Sri Lanka), and the list goes on. Prof. Bhagwati calls this the "spaghetti bowl". As Prof. Bhala has observed, whether this amounts to competitive trade liberalization or competitive trade imperialism is a provocative question.

One reason for this proliferation is failure of the Doha Round of WTO negotiations. GATT/WTO regulatory failures have also fueled this reality. Yet these "negatives" do not fully explain the FTA and CU feeding frenzy. A range of attractions are also at work. For example, FTAs and CUs often extend to subject matters beyond WTO competence. Foreign investment law is a prime example, and many such agreements serve as investment magnets. Government procurement, optional at the WTO level, is often included in free trade and customs union agreements. Competition policy and labor and environmental matters absent from the WTO are sometimes covered.

In addition, FTAs and CUs can reach beyond the scope of existing WTO agreements. Services are one "WTO-plus" area where this is clearly true.

Intellectual property rights are also being "WTO-plussed" in free trade and customs union agreements.

FTAs and CUs are politically and economically selective. In other words, they avoid not only global most-favored-nation principles, but also domestically "sensitive" national politics and economics. For example, Singapore's absence of farm exports helped make it an ideal U.S. and Japanese free trade partner. The micro-sized economy of Chile contributed to its attraction as a free trade partner with Mexico, China, the European Union, the United States and others. U.S. free trade deals with Jordan, Bahrain and Oman fit economically in a similar fashion, not to mention national security objectives.

Like it or not, the "spaghetti-bowl" maze of FTAs and CUs is driven by powerful negative and positive forces. It is not only the preferred trade medium of today, but also the future. President Trump is driving other countries into FTAs and CUs faster than he is withdrawing the United States from them. See Chapter 8.

Already more than half of world trade is conducted under FTAs and CUs. While international trade lawyers may celebrate full employment, it bears remembering that FTAs and CUs *are* discriminatory. They could render MFN the least favored status in world trade. Such an outcome would be especially harmful to the world's poorest nations, those with whom few WTO partners seek a preferential trade agreement.

GATT ARTICLE 24

Early GATT Regulatory Failure

Article 24 of the GATT (1947 and 1994) attempts to manage the internal trade-creating and external trade-diverting effects of FTAs and CUs. Free trade area and custom union proposals must run the gauntlet of a formal GATT/WTO review procedure during which "binding" recommendations are possible to bring the proposals into conformity. Such recommendations might deal with Article 24 requirements for the elimination of internal tariffs and other restrictive regulations of commerce on "substantially all" products originating in a customs union or free trade area.

Or they might deal with Article 24 requirements that common external tariffs not be "on the whole higher or more restrictive" in effect than the general incidence of prior existing national tariffs. The broad purpose of Article 24, acknowledged therein, is to facilitate trade among the GATT contracting parties and not to raise trade barriers.

It is through this review mechanism that most free trade and customs union agreements have passed *without* substantial modification. The GATT, not economic agreements, has given way.

For example, during GATT review of the 1957 Treaty of Rome creating what we now call the European Union, many "violations" of the letter and spirit of Article 24 were cited. The derivation of the common external tariff by arithmetically averaging existing national tariffs was challenged as more restrictive of trade than previous arrangements. Such averaging on a given product fails to take account of differing national import volumes. If a product was faced originally with a lower than average national tariff and a larger than average national demand, the new average tariff is clearly more "restrictive" of imports than before. Averaging in high tariffs of countries of low demand quite plausibly created more restrictions on third-party trade. If so, the letter and spirit of Article 24 were breached.

Despite these and other arguments, the Treaty of Rome passed through GATT study and review committees without final resolution of its legal status under Article 24. Postponement of these issues became permanent. GATT attempts—through the lawyer-like conditions of Article 24 to maximize trade creation and minimize trade diversion—must be seen as generally inadequate. Treaty terms became negotiable demands that were not accepted.

Attempts at GATT Regulatory Reform

The Uruguay Round, which created the World Trade Organization, presented an opportunity to come to grips with the regulatory failure of Article 24. Agreement was reached in 1994 on an "Understanding on the Interpretation of Article 24," which presently binds the roughly 165 member nations of the WTO. This Interpretation reaffirms that free trade area and customs union agreements *must* satisfy the provisions of Article 24, clarifies the manner in which before and after evaluations of common external tariffs are to be undertaken, limits in most cases interim agreements to 10 years, and details Article 24 notification, report and recommendation duties and processes.

Most importantly, the 1994 Understanding on Interpretation expressly permits invocation of standard WTO dispute settlement procedures (DSU) regarding any Article 24 matters. All that said, the 1994 Understanding did not come to grips with the systemic ambiguities that led to Article 24's early and ongoing regulatory failure.

The failure to launch a new round of WTO negotiations in Seattle (1999), followed by delays and failure of the Doha Round that commenced in 2001, has contributed to the feeding frenzy of CU and FTA agreements. Supported by provisional application of a 2006 Doha Round WTO Transparency Mechanism, hundreds of agreements have been notified to the WTO. A large additional number are believed *not* to have been notified. In general, most of the notified agreements are bilateral, not regional in character.

Meanwhile, the WTO Regional Trade Agreements Committee, working by consensus, has been unable since 1995 to complete even one assessment of a FTA or CU agreement's conformity to GATT Article 24 or GATS Article 5 (below). The same is true for WTO Committee on Trade and Development "review" of Enabling Clause arrangements (also below).

It has been suggested that this record can be explained by the ambiguous relationship between

Committee reports and WTO dispute settlement proceedings. For example, can such reports be used in evidence in WTO dispute proceedings? Can fact-finding by WTO Secretariat and information gathered for WTO regulatory purposes be similarly used? This "dispute settlement awareness" makes WTO members reluctant to provide information or agree on conclusions that could later be used or interpreted in DSU proceedings.

Decades later, the ineffectiveness of GATT/WTO supervision of free trade and customs union agreements continues. At best Article 24 exerts a marginal influence over their contents. Whether the extraordinary proliferation of preferential agreements undermines or supports WTO trade policies is hotly debated.

GATS INTEGRATED
SERVICES AGREEMENTS

Since 1995 "economic integration agreements" (EIAs) covering services are permitted under Article 5 of the General Agreement on Trade in Services (GATS). Such agreements, which can be staged, must have "substantial sectoral coverage," eliminate "substantially" all discrimination in sectors subject to multilateral commitments, and not raise the "overall" level of barriers to trade in GATS services compared to before the EIA. EIAs involving developing nations are to be accorded "flexibility".

Review of GATS Article 5 notifications is undertaken, when requested by the WTO Council for Trade in Services, by the Committee on Regional

Trade Agreements (CRTA). Thus, whereas CRTA examinations of GATT Article 24 agreements are required, such examinations are optional under GATS. Nevertheless, numerous Article 5 examinations have been conducted, including notably the services components of NAFTA 1994, the EEC Treaty (1957) and EU Enlargement (2004), Japan's FTAs with Singapore, Mexico and Malaysia, China's FTAs with Hong Kong and Macau, and various U.S. bilateral FTAs.

None of these examinations have resulted in a final report on consistency with GATS Article 5. This pattern continues the GATT/WTO record of regulatory failure regarding economic integration agreements.

DEVELOPING WORLD INTEGRATION

Developing nations in Africa, the Caribbean, Central America, South America and Southeast Asia (among others) had free trade and customs union agreements in place as early as the 1960s. In 1979, under what is commonly called the Enabling Clause, the GATT parties decided to permit developing nations to enter into differential and more favorable bilateral, regional or global arrangements among themselves to reduce or eliminate tariffs and nontariff barriers applicable to trade in goods.

Enabling Clause

Like Article 24 and GATS Article 5, the Enabling Clause constitutes an exception to MFN trade principles. It has generally been construed to authorize developing world free trade area and customs union agreements. Whether the Enabling Clause was intended to take such agreements out of Article 24 and its requirements, or be construed in conjunction therewith, is unclear. However, the creation of alternative notification and review procedures for Enabling Clause arrangements suggests Article 24 is inapplicable.

Notification to GATT of Enabling Clause arrangements is mandatory. Since 1995, the WTO Committee on Trade and Development (CTD) is the forum where such notifications are reviewed, but in practice not examined in depth. Enabling Clause arrangements should be designed to promote the trade of developing countries and not raise external trade barriers or undue trade difficulties. Consultations with individual GATT members experiencing such difficulties must be undertaken, and these consultations may be expanded to all GATT members if requested.

Unlike GATT Article 24 and GATS Article 5, neither compensation to nonparticipants in CUs nor formal reporting on the consistency with the Enabling Clause of developing nation arrangements is anticipated. The ASEAN-China (2004), India-Sri Lanka (2002), and "revived" Economic Community of West African States (ECOWAS 2005) agreements illustrate notified but unexamined preferential arrangements sheltered by the Enabling Clause.

Africa

A variety of FTA and CU agreements have been formed in Africa. In 1966 the central African countries of Cameroon, Central African Republic, Chad, Congo (Brazzaville) and Gabon formed the Economic and Customs Union of Central Africa (Union Douaniere et Économique de l'Afrique Centrale: UDEAC) to establish a common customs and tariff approach toward the rest of the world and to formulate a common foreign investment code. Implementation has proceeded very slowly.

In 1967 Kenya, Tanzania and Uganda created the East African Community (EAC) in an attempt to harmonize customs and tariff practices among themselves and in relation to other countries. The practical effect of that Community has frequently been negated by political strife, but efforts are underway to revive it with Rwanda and Burundi included. In 1974 six French speaking West African nations formed the West African Economic Community (known by its French initials CEAO). This Community is a sub-group within and pacesetter for ECOWAS, the Economic Community of West African States (now the West African Economic and Monetary Union, WAEMU).

ECOWAS was created in 1975 by Dahomey, Gambia, Ghana, Guinea, Guinea-Bissau, Ivory Coast, Liberia, Mali, Mauritania, Niger, Nigeria, Senegal, Sierra Leone, Togo and Upper Volta to coordinate economic development and cooperation. Some progress on liberalized industrial trade has been made and a Cooperation, Compensation and

Development Fund established. During the 1980s the pace of regionalization quickened. ECOWAS countries agreed upon policies for the Community, especially regarding air transport, communications, agriculture, freedom of movement between Member States, currency convertibility, and a common currency.

In September of 1995, 15 southern African countries, with South Africa under Mandela participating for the first time, targeted free trade under the Southern African Development Community (SADC). A more limited grouping of South Africa, Botswana, Namibia, Lesotho and Swaziland comprise the Southern African Customs Union (SACU), created in 2002 and focused primarily of trade in goods. SACU was created after the South Africa-EU FTA of 1999, which remains in force.

A 20-member Common Market for Eastern and Southern Africa (COMESA) has also been created. In 2015, COMESA, SADC and the EAC agreed to work toward a 26-member free trade area. In 2018, 44 African nations signed the African Continental Free Trade Area agreement, with South Africa and Nigeria, the two largest African economies abstaining.

Islamic World

In 2003, the non-Arab states of Iran, Pakistan, Turkey, Afghanistan and five Central Asian nations joined together in an Economic Cooperation Organization Trade Agreement (ECOTA). In 2004, Jordan, Egypt, Tunisia and Morocco concluded their

Agadir free trade agreement. Neither agreement has matured significantly.

Bahrain, Kuwait, Oman, Qatar, Saudi Arabia, and United Arab Emirates formed the Gulf Cooperation Council (GCC) in 1981. The Gulf Investment Corporation was capitalized in 1984 at 2.5 billion dollars. The GCC implemented a customs union in 2003 with a common external tariff of 5%, and a Gulf Common Market in 2008. Other GCC programs impact government contracts, communications, transportation, real estate investment, and freedom of movement for employment of GCC citizens. Progress on a common currency has been stymied, but some advances have been made on a GCC Uniform Commercial Code and a Commission for Commercial Arbitration. The GCC has a number of FTAs with Middle East and North African (MENA) countries, and notably with Singapore since 2013.

In 2017, a broad economic boycott led by Saudi Arabia of "progressive" Qatar, home to Al Jezeera media, emerged in the Gulf. Qatar, hosting a major U.S. military base, seems to have taken the boycott in stride.

Caribbean

Other FTA and CU groups have been established in Latin America and the Caribbean. Since 1973, the Caribbean countries of Barbados, Belize, Dominica, Jamaica, Trinidad-Tobago, Grenada, St. Kitts-Nevis-Anguilla, St. Lucia, and St. Vincent have participated in the Caribbean Community (CARICOM), an outgrowth of the earlier Caribbean

Free Trade Association. The Grand Anse Declaration commits CARICOM to establishment of its own common market.

Antigua, Dominica, Grenada, Montserrat, St. Kitts-Nevis, St. Lucia, St. Vincent and the Grenadines have formed the Organization of Eastern Caribbean States (OECS) in part "to establish common institutions which could serve to increase their bargaining power as regards third countries or groupings of countries." Some 37 nations signed the Association of Caribbean States agreement in 1994 with long-term economic integration goals.

The longstanding United States economic boycott of Cuba under Fidel Castro has isolated that nation. U.S. policy has not stopped Canada and Mexico from actively trading and investing (tourism especially) in Cuba. And it certainly propelled post-Soviet Cuba into a close relationship with Venezuela under Chavez and Maduro, including a well-known "doctors for oil" agreement. Cuba's larger problem is its regime's isolationist tendencies, fear of "capitalist pollution" and dogmatic ideology. But the winds of change are blowing in Havana, and a dollarized-economy is emerging from the underground. In 2015, the U.S. and Cuba commenced "normalization" of their relations, but a softer embargo remains in place.

Latin America

Numerous countries in Latin America were members of the Latin American Free Trade Association (LAFTA) (1961) which had small success in reducing tariffs and developing the region through cooperative industrial sector programs. These programs allocated industrial production among the participating states. The Latin American Integration Association (LAIA) (1981), the eleven-member successor to LAFTA, is continuing arrangements for intra-community tariff concessions. They agreed to a 50 percent tariff cut on LAIA goods.

Latin America became a central focus in the 1990s of economic integration. Mexico not only signed a free trade agreement with the United States and Canada, it also agreed to free trade with Colombia, Venezuela, Chile, Bolivia, Costa Rica, Nicaragua, Guatemala, Honduras, El Salvador, Peru and Uruguay. Furthermore, Mexico has negotiated free trade agreements with Japan, the European Union, EFTA (European Free Trade Assn) and entered in 2013 into The Pacific alliance with Peru, Chile and Colombia.

Argentina, Brazil, Paraguay and Uruguay signed a treaty establishing the MERCOSUR (Southern Cone) common market in 1991 and Chile and Bolivia joined them as Associates in 1996. MERCOSUR is a moderately well-functioning customs union, not a free trade agreement. Venezuela under Chavez created the Peoples' Trade Treaty in 2007 aligned with Cuba, Bolivia, Nicaragua, Ecuador and others. Venezuela finally obtained membership in MERCOSUR in 2012, only to be evicted on human rights grounds a few years later.

ANCOM ("The Cartagena Agreement") was founded by Bolivia, Chile, Colombia, Ecuador, and Peru in 1969 primarily to counter the economic power of Argentina, Brazil and Mexico and to reduce dependency upon foreign capital and technology. Its Decision No. 24 regulating foreign investment and technology transfers was widely copied during the 1970s. A major boost came in 1973 with the addition of Venezuela, but some of the fragile dynamics of the regional grouping are illustrated by Chile's withdrawal in 1977, Bolivia's withdrawal in 1981 and resumption of membership barely four months later, and Peru's economic (but not political) withdrawal in 1991 and return in 1996.

In 1958 Costa Rica, El Salvador, Guatemala, Honduras and Nicaragua formed the Central American Common Market (CACM), another victim of political strife, but still functioning in a limited way, primarily as a result of the 2005 Central American Free Trade Agreement (CAFTA) with the United States.

All of this activity occurred against the background of the Free Trade Area of the Americas (FTAA) initiative of the United States (below). In 2003 the ANCOM and MERCOSUR groups nominally agreed upon free trade, at least partly to counterbalance United States power in the FTAA negotiations. The United States, pursuing in turn a divide and conquer strategy, has attempted bilateral free trade agreements with all ANCOM members save Venezuela. The U.S. now has FTAs with Chile, Peru, and Colombia.

The Free Trade Area of the Americas (FTAA)

The U.S. "Enterprise for the Americas Initiative" (EAI) under elder President Bush raised hopes of economic integration throughout the Americas against a background of competitive regionalism in trade relations, especially between the European Union and North America. At the Americas Summit in Miami, President Clinton and 33 Latin American heads of state (only Fidel Castro was absent) renewed this hope by agreeing to commence negotiations on a Free Trade Area of the Americas (FTAA). The year 2005 was targeted at the Summit for creation of the FTAA.

Preparatory working groups have regularly met since 1995 to discuss the following topics: (1) Market Access; (2) Customs Procedures and Rules of Origin; (3) Investment; (4) Standards and Technical Barriers to Trade; (5) Sanitary and Phytosanitary Measures; (6) Subsidies, Antidumping and Countervailing Duties; (7) Smaller Economies; (8) Government Procurement; (9) Intellectual Property Rights; (10) Services; (11) Competition Policy; and (12) Dispute Settlement. It is expected that each of these areas would be covered in any FTAA agreement. Formal FTAA negotiations were delayed several times, particularly because of differences between Brazil-led MERCOSUR and U.S.-led NAFTA 1994.

Divisions were particularly evident during the November 2003 FTAA ministerial meeting in Miami. Lowered expectations, known as FTAA-Lite, reflect U.S. refusal to budge on agricultural protection and trade remedies, and Brazilian refusal to fully embrace investment, intellectual property, services and procurement "free trade." Absent successful resolution of these issues in the WTO Doha Round negotiations, an unlikely prospect at this writing, FTAA-Lite, even with different levels of country commitments, seems unlikely.

The absence of U.S. fast track authority (see Chapter 3) and the general perception that political support for free trade in the United States is weak has clearly slowed FTAA developments. MERCOSUR and Brazil in particular seized the opportunity to move towards South American free trade. At this point, MERCOSUR's trade associates include every South American nation. This puts it in a much better position to negotiate terms and conditions with the NAFTA/CAFTA bloc than individual countries or sub-groups within South America.

A CASE STUDY: THE ASSOCIATION OF SOUTHEAST ASIAN NATIONS (ASEAN)

Some interesting moves toward developing world free trade and rule-making have been taken by the Association of Southeast Asian Nations (ASEAN). Its problems, failures and successes are representative of third world attempts at legal and economic integration. ASEAN has its genesis in the 1967 Bangkok Declaration, with common trade rules in various states of growth, implementation and retrenchment. ASEAN has internal tariff preferences, industrial development projects, "complementation schemes," and regional joint ventures, all discussed below.

An important juncture in the integration process is the point in time at which member countries of a regional group accept a supranational mechanism for enforcing the regime's law irrespective of national feelings and domestic law within a member country. In contrast, the ASEAN Secretary-General once remarked that ASEAN's Secretariat was "a postman collecting and distributing letters." The surrender of national sovereignty to ASEAN institutions has been a painfully slow process.

ASEAN Declarations and Summits

ASEAN was formed in 1967 by Indonesia, Malaysia, the Philippines, Singapore and Thailand. Brunei joined in 1984, Vietnam in 1995. Laos and Myanmar (Burma) joined in 1997, and more recently Kampuchea (Cambodia) became a member. Rarely have such culturally, linguistically and geographically diverse nations attempted integration. The Bangkok Declaration establishing ASEAN as a cooperative association is a broadly worded document. Later proposals were made for a formal ASEAN treaty or convention, but were rejected as unnecessary. The Bangkok Declaration sets forth numerous regional, economic, cultural and social goals, including acceleration of economic growth, trade expansion and industrial collaboration.

The Bangkok Declaration establishes several mechanisms, but little supranational legal machinery, to implement its stated goals. An annual

ASEAN Meeting of Foreign Ministers is scheduled on a rotational basis among the Member States. Special meetings are held "as required". The Declaration provides for a Standing Committee composed of the Foreign Minister of the State in which the next annual Ministerial Meeting is to be held, and includes the ambassadors of other ASEAN States accredited to that State. The Declaration also provides for "Ad Hoc Committees and Permanent Committees of specialists and officials on specific subjects". Each Member State is charged to set up a National Secretariat to administer ASEAN affairs within that Member State and to work with the Ministerial Meeting and the Standing Committee.

There have been relatively infrequent meetings of the ASEAN heads of government. This contrasts with the semiannual European "summits" that have kept that group moving forward along the path of integration. The third ASEAN summit was held in Manila in 1987. This summit produced an agreement for the promotion and protection of investments by ASEAN investors (national and most-favored-nation treatment rights are created), made revisions to the basic ASEAN joint venture agreement, and continued the gradual extension of regional tariff and nontariff trade preferences. Goods already covered by the ASEAN tariff scheme were given a 50 percent margin of preference. New items received a 25 percent preferential margin. The nontariff preferences generally co-opt GATT rules, e.g., regarding technical standards and customs valuation.

The fourth ASEAN summit in 1992 committed the parties to the creation of a free trade area within 15 years. Five years were cut from this schedule by agreement in 1994, but operational reality has eluded ASEAN free trade. In 2003, a "watershed" date for complete integration in an ASEAN Economic Community targeted 2020. In 2007, this target date was changed to 2016, a reflection of the fear that ASEAN risks being overwhelmed by the powerhouse economies of China, India and Japan. In 2016, the ASEAN common market was officially launched. Despite the fanfare, its prospects seem limited.

All that said, ASEAN as a group has limited free trade in goods agreements with China, Japan, Korea and India. It is not at all clear to what degree ASEAN exports have increased under these agreements other than by becoming more active suppliers of natural resources and components to these major-economy partners.

ASEAN Trade Rules and Industrial Projects

Between 1967 and 1976, few steps were taken to further the economic cooperation called for in the Declaration. As with most third world regional groups, ASEAN required a period in which its members got to know and trust each other. The annual Ministerial Meetings did facilitate, however, the formation of committees to study economic development projects and economic cooperation, to establish a working relationship with the EU, and to develop close ties with private sector industries within ASEAN Member States.

Early ASEAN economic cooperation focused upon showcase "industrial projects." A "Basic Agreement" and a set of general "Guidelines" govern their creation and operation. ASEAN industrial projects were modeled on the ANCOM "sectoral programs of industrial development" (SPIDs). They are largely government owned industrial development projects. Several of these projects are now in place with the assistance of Japanese financing, notably the ammonia-urea plants in Indonesia and Malaysia. SPIDs are supported by certain monopoly production rights and tariff preferences. Foreign investors may participate in ASEAN industrial development projects through finance, supply, managerial, technical or limited equity relationships.

ASEAN Freer Trade

ASEAN cooperation has accelerated. Rather than focusing upon the creation of common, protective external tariffs, ASEAN has fostered freer trade by instituting preferential tariffs for goods originating in other Member States. Tariff reductions have been negotiated pursuant to the Agreement on ASEAN Preferential Trading Arrangements. The "Manila Agreement" is aimed primarily at encouraging the establishment of preferential tariffs with respect to basic commodities, particularly rice and crude oil, products of ASEAN industrial projects, and products expanding intra-ASEAN trade. Some of the tariff preferences are negotiated on a bilateral basis; others are negotiated multilaterally by the ASEAN states.

By late 1982, tariff reductions had been agreed for approximately 9,000 products, and the scope of the preferences extended well beyond foodstuffs and textiles. Since then, the ASEAN preferential tariff arrangements have been extended to approximately 2,000 additional items each year. Across the board tariff cuts on items of lesser import value have also increased intra-ASEAN trade opportunities. Progress notwithstanding, these efforts stop short of the automatic tariff elimination schedules of the European Union and NAFTA. As ASEAN moves toward freer trade within the bloc, overhead costs for investors, practical sources of supply materials, and product marketing opportunities may undergo substantial change.

The "Framework Agreement on Enhancing ASEAN Economic Cooperation" (1993) as accelerated in 1994 envisions an ASEAN free trade area (AFTA) that will cover goods but not services or unprocessed agricultural products. The ASEAN countries also signed an agreement on Common Effective Preferential Tariffs (CEPT). Under this agreement, internal tariffs on manufactured products were reduced to 20 percent by 1998. To qualify, at least 40 percent of the content of the goods must originate within ASEAN, a relatively "liberal" rule of origin. Vegetable oils, cement, chemicals, pharmaceuticals, fertilizer, plastics, rubber and leather products, pulp, textiles, ceramic and glass products, gems and jewelry, cooper cathodes, electronics and wooden furniture are included in this first round of tariff cuts.

The goal was to have all tariffs on manufactured goods fall to no less than five percent by 2000. Once again this goal proved elusive. Only five percent of ASEAN trade takes advantage of the CEPT. One reason for such a low percentage is unilateral tariff cuts below MFN commitments: Thailand from 41% to 18%, Indonesia from 25% to 8%. Such preference erosion makes it less likely that ASEAN traders will document origin to achieve free trade. There are ongoing efforts to reduce the number of goods excluded from the CEPT.

In common with global trade, as ASEAN tariffs have been eased, nontariff trade barriers (NTBs) have become the chief internal trade problem. These NTBs principally involve safety, health and environmental regulatory rules that keep ASEAN goods from crossing borders, and are often vigorously supported by local interests.

ASEAN's International Impact

ASEAN has entered into negotiations with all of its major world trading partners, dealing with them as ASEAN rather than as individual states. For example, ASEAN negotiated a limited number of preferences for its products entering the EU, and annually negotiates with its biggest trading partners, including the United States. ASEAN has free trade agreements with China, Japan, India, and Australia-New Zealand. These negotiations exemplify ASEAN seeking bargaining strength through unity. However, ASEAN states also pursue individual commercial negotiations with trade partners. Singapore and Thailand, for example, have negotiated or are seeking bilateral free trade agreements with the United States, Japan and others.

There is a voluntary ASEAN Law Association and an "emerging law" within ASEAN as evidenced by the various rules, agreements and guidelines supporting economic cooperation in the region. For example, ASEAN has established certain rules covering the "origin" of products subject to its tariff preferences. Under these rules, products not wholly produced or obtained within ASEAN cannot qualify for preferential tariff treatment unless they are processed so that the total value of the materials originating from non-ASEAN countries or from an undetermined origin does not exceed 50 percent of the FOB value of the products.

However, if the final process of manufacture is performed within ASEAN, the goods will qualify for ASEAN tariff preferences. The value of the non-originating materials is determined CIF at importation. In the case of goods entering another ASEAN nation from Indonesia (the least developed ASEAN nation prior to Vietnam), the non-ASEAN component cannot exceed 40 percent. Reductions in these local content requirements were adopted in 1987. An investor producing goods in an ASEAN country might need to work with these rules so as to qualify for regional tariff reductions.

ASEAN Complementation Schemes

ASEAN has encouraged development in the private business sector by urging the formation of numerous regional "Federations" or "Clubs" in various areas of industry and commerce. Sponsored by the ASEAN Chambers of Commerce and Industry, the Clubs are ASEAN-wide and have been formed to assist with "Complementation Schemes." Complementation involves the reduction, as needed, of trade barriers between Member States so that entire manufacturing processes, such as automobile assembly, make maximal use of ASEAN products. Moreover, each participating country produces a component which can be traded within ASEAN as parts for assembly into a more finished manufacture. Each Club, such as the ASEAN Federation of Cement Manufacturers, plays an initiating role in proposing tariff reductions for products which are of concern to that industry.

Formation of the Clubs, while not envisioned in principal ASEAN Agreements, has been encouraged at the Ministerial Meetings. Club recommendations are approved tentatively by the Committee on Industry, Minerals and Energy of the ASEAN Governments. Recommendations are forwarded from that Committee to the Economic Ministers and Foreign Ministers for final approval.

General Guidelines and a Basic Agreement for ASEAN industrial complementation schemes were completed in 1980 and 1981. The Guidelines have been approved by the Economic Ministers of ASEAN and include "exclusivity" provisions guaranteeing (with limited exceptions) that no similar public or private projects to manufacture a product covered by a complementation scheme will be approved by any Member State of ASEAN. The Guidelines also provide that complemented products will be given priority in other ASEAN countries having foreign exchange controls.

Additional Guidelines deal with the percentage of equity ownership by non-ASEAN nationals, tax incentives, remittances, repatriation of profits and expropriation. In 1983, the ASEAN Foreign Ministers approved an ASEAN auto parts complementation scheme involving local content requirements, exclusivity rights and tariff preferences. Many foreign investors or licensors are potential beneficiaries of this scheme (e.g., a Ford Motor Co. subsidiary has an auto body plant in the Philippines). Despite its origins in the private sector, the success of ASEAN automotive complementation is problematic. The desire to produce "national cars" not "ASEAN cars" is strong and supported by local subsidies. Malaysia, for example, produces the Proton Saga, initially in cooperation with Mitsubishi Motors.

ASEAN Joint Ventures

Since 1982, ASEAN has focused on creating rules for ASEAN Industrial Joint Ventures which involve participation by only two ASEAN Member States, permit foreign equity participation up to 49 percent, contain limited monopoly rights and grant extensive tariff preferences. A set of general Guidelines and a

Basic Agreement on ASEAN joint ventures have been promulgated. ASEAN joint ventures may be proposed through the private sector initiative of industry clubs, few of which seem to have taken up the opportunity as yet. A 1987 revision of the Basic Agreement on joint ventures permits exclusivity privileges and protection against unfair trade practices. ASEAN joint ventures are a unique contribution to regional development and represent an investment alternative holding out the possibility of significant economies of scale.

Eight joint ventures were approved in 1991, including enamel and heavy equipment production by Indonesia and Malaysia, aluminum hydroxide by Indonesia and Thailand and four food products' joint ventures with the Nestlé Co. In general, the ASEAN trade and investment programs have been hard to implement because of tariff exemptions and nontariff trade barriers. The need to solve such problems is heightened by China's rapidly growing economy and foreign investment magnetism.

ASEAN complementation schemes and joint ventures present potential antitrust law problems for U.S. participants insofar as American foreign commerce is affected. For example, if Ford Motor Co.'s participation in the automotive complementation scheme reduces U.S. export or import opportunities, the scheme could fall within the extraterritorial reach of the Sherman Act. If so, United States prosecutors and plaintiffs will surely claim that ASEAN "clubs" amount to government sponsored cartels.

There may also be U.S. customs law problems when and if complemented "ASEAN cars" are exported to the American market. Such cars could, for example, be subject to countervailing tariff duties if it is determined that ASEAN has subsidized their production and the U.S. auto industry is threatened with injury. These potential legal problems may deter involvement in ASEAN joint ventures and complementation schemes by U.S. firms and their business affiliates within the region.

The Asian financial crisis of the late 1990s led to a broad ASEAN Investment Area agreement built around national treatment and MFN treatment principles. The objective is the free flow of investment within ASEAN by 2020.

UNITED STATES, CANADIAN AND MEXICAN FTAs

NAFTA 1994 was a watershed event. In its wake, hundreds of free trade agreements have proliferated around the world, including those of the NAFTA partners.

United States

By 2018, the United States had 12 bilateral free trade agreements, with 20 partners: Australia, Bahrain, Chile, Colombia, Israel, Jordan, South Korea (KORUS), Morocco, Oman, Panama, Peru, Korea, Singapore, the NAFTA 1994 agreement with Canada and Mexico, and the Central America Free Trade Agreement (CAFTA-DR) with the Dominican

Republic, Guatemala, Honduras, El Salvador, Nicaragua and Costa Rica.

The United States free trade agreements since NAFTA 1994 have evolved substantively under a policy known as "competitive liberalization." For example, coverage of labor law has been focused on core ILO principles: The rights of association, organization and collective bargaining; acceptable work conditions regarding minimum wages, hours and occupational health and safety; minimum age for employment of children and elimination of the worst forms of child labor; and a ban on forced or compulsory labor. Coverage of labor and environmental law enforcement is folded into the trade agreement (compare NAFTA's side agreements) and all remedies are intergovernmental (compare private and NGO "remedies" in the side agreements).

Other NAFTA-plus provisions have emerged. These are most evident regarding foreign investment and intellectual property. Regarding investor-state claims, for example, post-NAFTA 1994 U.S. free trade agreements insert the word "customary" before international law in defining the minimum standard of treatment to which foreign investors are entitled. This insertion tracks the official Interpretation issued in that regard under NAFTA.

Further, the contested terms "fair and equitable treatment" and "full protection and security" do not require treatment in addition to or beyond that customary standard, and do not create additional substantive rights. This language is now typically defined in U.S. FTAs:

> "fair and equitable treatment" includes the obligation not to deny justice in criminal, civil, or administrative adjudicatory proceedings in accordance with the principle of due process embodied in the principal legal systems of the world; and

> "full protection and security" requires each Party to provide the level of police protection required under customary international law.

More significantly perhaps, U.S FTA agreements typically contain an Annex restricting the scope of "indirect expropriation" claims:

> Except in rare circumstances, nondiscriminatory regulatory actions by a Party that are designed and applied to protect legitimate public welfare objectives, such as public health, safety and the environment, do not constitute indirect expropriations.

Hence the potential for succeeding with "regulatory takings" investor-state claims has been reduced.

Regarding intellectual property, NAFTA-plus FTAs have moved into the Internet age. Protection of domain names, and adherence to the WIPO Internet treaties, are stipulated. E-commerce and free trade in digital products are embraced, copyrights extended to rights-management (encryption) and anti-circumvention (hacking) technology, protection against web music file sharing enhanced, and potential liability of Internet Service Providers detailed.

Less visibly, pharmaceutical patent owners obtain extensions of their patents to compensate for delays in the approval process, and greater control over their test data, making it harder for generic competition to emerge. They also gain "linkage," meaning local drug regulators must make sure generics are not patent-infringing before their release. In addition, adherence to the Patent Law Treaty (2000) and the Trademark Law Treaty (1994) is agreed. Anti-counterfeiting laws are tightened, particularly regarding destruction of counterfeit goods.

Additional NAFTA-plus FTA changes push further along the path of free trade in services and comprehensive customs law administration rules. Antidumping and countervailing duty laws remain applicable, but appeals from administrative determinations are taken in national courts, not binational panels. Except for limited provisions in the Chile-U.S. agreement, business visas have dropped completely out of U.S. free trade agreements, a NAFTA-minus development.

In sum, except for KORUS (below), the United States has generally used its leverage with smaller trade partners in the Americas to obtain more preferential treatment and expanded protection for its goods, services, technology and investors. It has given up relatively little in return, for example a modest increase in agricultural market openings.

Whether NAFTA 1994 will survive in any recognizable format is not clear at this writing. Of late President Trump has suggested individual bilateral agreements with Canada and Mexico maybe preferable, reflecting again his hostility to multilateral agreements.

Transatlantic Trade and Investment Partnership (TTIP)

The United States and the European Union commenced under President Obama negotiating a Transatlantic Trade and Investment Partnership (TTIP) agreement that could resemble the CETA 2017 agreement between Canada and the European Union (below). Britain's expected withdrawal from the EU casts further doubt on TTIP's prospects, as does the election of President Trump and his Safeguard and national security import tariffs (below). TTIP negotiations remain at a standstill, with the EU less than enthusiastic to move forward.

Mexico

By 2018, Mexico had free trade agreements with Chile, Colombia, Venezuela (dormant), Costa Rica, Bolivia, Nicaragua, Guatemala, Honduras, El Salvador, Peru, Panama, Uruguay, Japan, Israel, EFTA (European Free Trade Assn), and a significantly expanded and revitalized 2018 FTA with the European Union. The latter agreement expansively covers agriculture, procurement, and services, all areas likely to increase EU competition with U.S. sources.

Mexico also participates in the TPP-11 (below) and the Pacific Alliance (below). Manufacturers drawn by NAFTA 1994 to Mexico frequently utilize Mexico's FTAs to engage in additional duty free exports, especially to the EU and Japan.

Pacific Alliance

In 2013, Latin American U.S. trade allies (Colombia, Peru, Chile and Mexico) formed the Pacific Alliance, a free trade deal, which serves as a counterweight to MERCOSUR. This alliance notably provides for visa-free travel among the participants. Canada, Singapore and other nations are considering application.

Canada

By 2018, Canada had free trade agreements with Korea, the EU (CETA 2017 below), Chile, Peru, Colombia, Costa Rica, Israel, EFTA, Jordan, Panama, Honduras, and Ukraine, and was a leader in the TPP-11 agreement (2018, below).

The Canada-EU Comprehensive Economic and Trade Agreement (CETA 2017)

Given the withdrawal of the United States from the TPP, the uncertain future of TTIP negotiations between the U.S. and the EU, and the expected onslaught of FTAs Britain will seek after BREXIT, one the free trade agreement that now stands out as a trade policy model in the developed world is CETA, the Comprehensive Economic and Trade Agreement between Canada and the EU, provisionally in force since September 2017. Together, the EU and Canada represent over $18 trillion economies.

Approximately 98% of the tariffs on trade between the parties were eliminated, with tariffs on autos phasing out over seven years, subject to 50 to 55% Canadian content rules of origin except for a generous 20% content rule applicable to the first 100,000 Canadian auto exports. Considerable agreement on product standards and testing in the country of export was reached, and Canadian firms get to bid on EU contracts on the same footing as EU companies. Free trade in services is based on a "negative list", a first for the EU, and will increase if either party grants broader entry in any other subsequent free trade agreement. Mobility for service providers and business people is extensive, and mutual recognition of professional diplomas and licensing is anticipated.

Both parties have a history of protecting their agricultural and fish/seafood markets. After various transition periods, CETA renders nearly 95% of these markets duty free. There are exceptions for meat quotas on both sides and EU cheese export quotas. The EU obtained greater protection for geographic origin of products (Feta cheese, Parma ham), and increased pharmaceutical patent protection. Healthcare and education, along with cultural industries, are excluded under CETA, and Canada continues to control development of its natural resources.

Foreign investor rights and protections cover the entire EU, another first. After much debate and controversy, an Investment Dispute Court will be created to review arbitral awards. Canada still gets to apply its Investment Act to EU nationals, subject to the "net benefit" to Canada test, but EU investments under $1.5 billion CDN escape review.

There seems little doubt that the trade creation/diversion pattern of CETA will adversely impact the USA.

EUROPEAN UNION FTAs—BREXIT

The European Union is a customs union, not a free trade area. Its trade relations with the rest of the world is exclusively an EU, not a national, competence. The EU has a customs union agreement with Turkey (services excluded). Its other trade agreements are dominated by FTAs, providing access to the world's largest common market.

By 2018, the EU had 40 free trade agreements, including Morocco, Algeria, Tunisia, Libya, Egypt, Israel, Jordan, Lebanon, Norway, Iceland, Serbia, South Africa, Peru, Mexico, Colombia, Central America (6 nations), Chile, Singapore, Vietnam, and South Korea (KOREU). Canada and the EU inked in 2013 an historic Comprehensive Economic and Trade Agreement (CETA, above) that provisionally reached fruition in 2017 under mixed EU agreement procedures requiring national and regional parliamentary approvals. In 2017, Japan and the EU, with $22 trillion combined economies, reached political agreement on a free trade deal that will likely also take years to be realized. This accord is titled the EU-Japan Economic Partnership

Agreement. In 2018, Mexico and the EU, whose economies measure nearly $18 trillion, significantly revised and expanded their existing FTA (see Mexico above).

Agreements with India, ASEAN, MERCOSUR and the Gulf Council may follow. One notable feature of EU FTAs is the inclusion of a Human Rights and Democracy Clause backed up by potential trade sanctions.

An important issue is whether Britain individually after BREXIT in March 2019 can duplicate or substantially retain free trade with current EU partners. Would, for example, Canada, Korea or Japan be willing to give Britain the same terms they gave the much larger and more economically significant European Union? What about developing countries like Vietnam, Chile or Mexico? What about UK Commonwealth countries like South Africa and Singapore?

Would President Trump, who has verbally supported BREXIT, seriously bend his America First policies in negotiating with Britain?

The EU has agreed that during the BREXIT transition period running from March 2019 to January 2021, Britain will benefit from the existing 40 EU FTAs. During that period, the UK may negotiate, sign, and ratify, but not enter into force, FTAs with any partner. Negotiating UK FTAs during this period sounds easier than it is likely to be. Given the complexity of trade deals, and the understandable desire other countries to know exactly the details of the final EU-UK trade relationship, it is hard to imagine agreement on a FTA with Britain prior to 2021.

For more on EU trade law, agreements and BREXIT, see my Nutshell on *European Union Law including BREXIT*.

THE TRANS-PACIFIC PARTNERSHIP (TPP) AND TPP-11

TPP-12

Negotiation of the TPP was led by the United States under President Obama's "pivot to Asia". Late in 2015, a Trans-Pacific Partnership (TPP) agreement was reached among the three NAFTA 1994 nations plus Peru, Chile, Brunei, Singapore, Malaysia, Vietnam, Japan, Australia and New Zealand (but notably not China, India or Russia). These Pacific Rim partners comprise roughly 40% of world trade.

The TPP contained notable developments on freer agricultural and food trade, trade in automobiles and auto parts, bio-similar pharmaceuticals, protection of foreign investment, minimum wages and working hours, independent unions, employment discrimination, forced and child labor, technology protections, anti-corruption obligations, service sector openings, e-commerce, environmental protection and restraints on subsidies for state-owned enterprises (SOEs). It contained minimal currency manipulation rules, a much debated topic. South Korea, Taiwan and Indonesia expressed interest in joining the TPP, which clearly resembled a containment strategy relative to China rising economic power.

As signed by President Obama, TPP ratification in the United States would have been under the fast track procedures, discussed above. President Trump's quick withdrawal from the TPP mooted this possibility. This decision has had broad consequences in the world of international trade. Perhaps most significantly, China, Japan, the EU, Canada and others have moved away from U.S. trade policy leadership and have been seeking and solidifying FTA partners at a rapid pace.

TPP-11

The remaining TPP partners, led by Japan and Canada, signed an altered TPP-11 free trade agreement in 2018 covering roughly 15% of global trade. TPP-11 has been re-named the Comprehensive and Progressive Trans Pacific Partnership (CPTPP). It incorporates most TPP provisions, subject to suspensions and side letters altering TPP-12.

Complete duty free trade in seafood, wine, sheep meat, cotton wool and most manufactured are anticipated under TPP-11. Autos will be subject to a 45% TPP-11 content rule of origin, an advantage expected to favor Japanese exports. Significant intellectual property provisions secured under U.S. pressure, notably eight-year protection for biologic drugs, 70 year copyrights, five-year patent extensions after unreasonable delays in obtaining patents, and eight-year protection of pharmaceutical test data before generic approvals, were dropped.

Canada obtained a cultural industries exclusion, not unlike that of NAFTA 1994. Innovative TPP-12 rules on SOEs were largely retained, including principles of nondiscrimination, adherence to commercial considerations, and limitations on noncommercial governmental assists causing adverse effects and material injury. These rules were diminished for Malaysia in TPP-11. E-commerce trade coverage and protection for digital products drawn from TPP-12 are in TPP-11, but Vietnam has a five-year exception allowing greater control over and taxation of electronic payments along with a national office requirement.

Australia, New Zealand and Canada now have reduced trade barriers on agricultural exports to Japan, which may prove harmful to USA exports of wheat, dairy products, rice and beef. Transparency and anticorruption provisions follow APEC Codes and the UN Convention, with no tax deductions for corrupt payments to public officials. Trader/investor/ professional visas resembling those of NAFTA 1994 are created, but in a change from TPP-12 migration of skilled labor is subject to local market need tests.

Labor and the environment are also part of TPP-11, potentially subject to trade sanctions. On labor, International Labor Organization principles dominate much as under TPP-12, though labor union rights have been delayed for Vietnam. Australia now has reduced trade barriers on agricultural exports to Japan, which may prove adverse to US. exports of wheat, rice and beef. Transparency and anticorruption provisions follow APEC Codes and the UN Convention, with no tax deductions for corrupt payments to public officials.

Trader/investor/professional visas resembling those of NAFTA 1994 are created, but in a change from TPP-12 migration of skilled labor is subject to local market need tests. On the environment, separate agreements concern the Ozone, Ship Pollution, Biodiversity, Emissions, Invasive Species, Endangered Species, and Capture Fisheries. There is a public submission procedure that can trigger review of environmental issues.

Investor-state dispute settlement (ISDS) by arbitration and payment of damages is provided for in a manner not unlike NAFTA 1994 as officially interpreted and altered in subsequent U.S. FTAs (above). The right of member states to regulate in the public interest is made clear. Australia, which refused ISDS under the U.S.-Australian bilateral FTA, joined in TPP-11 ISDS. However, compulsory ISDS between New Zealand and five other TPP-11 nations is not mandatory.

No TPP-11 arbitrations may concern tobacco regulation, a ban originating in TPP-12 after R.J Reynolds abused ISDS remedies by purchasing a Hong Kong distributor in order to challenge Australia's plain packaging cigarette laws under a Hong Kong-Australia bilateral investment treaty (BIT) dating from the British era. This maneuver is a good example of foreign investment "treaty shopping". See R. Folsom, *Foreign Investment Law in a Nutshell.*

PACIFIC RIM FREE TRADE

The Pacific Rim, unlike the European Union or NAFTA 1994, has not developed a functioning regional economic integration agreement with uniform trade, licensing and investment rules.

APEC

The Asia-Pacific Economic Cooperation (APEC) group has somewhat begun to address the Pacific Rim as a whole. The APEC group is comprised of 21 Asia-Pacific nations including the United States, but excluding India. Late in 1994 the APEC nations targeted free trade and investment for industrial countries by 2010 and developing countries by 2020. Nine industries were selected for initial trade liberalization efforts, which are moving at a snail's pace.

Japan

One provocative trade question is the future of Japan. It is not in the interest of any nation that Japan should feel economically isolated or threatened. To some degree, trade in East Asia is growing along lines that follow Japanese investment and economic aid decisions. By 2018, Japan had "Economic Partnership Agreements" (effectively free trade in goods agreements) with Mexico, Chile, Thailand, the Philippines, Malaysia, Vietnam, Switzerland, India, Indonesia, Brunei, Singapore,

Peru, Mongolia and the Association of Southeast Asian Nations (ASEAN). These agreements essentially encircle China. See Chapter 8 regarding Trump and Japan.

Japan in 2018 also signed a comprehensive free trade agreement with the EU, and led the creation of TPP-11 (both above).

Russia

By 2018, Russia had an FTA with eight formerly Soviet satellite countries under the Commonwealth of Independent States (CISFTA). The CISFTA members are Russia, Ukraine, Moldova, Tajikistan, Armenia, Kazakhstan, Kyrgyzstan and Uzbekistan, with Ukraine suspended after Russian annexation of Crimea and occupation of parts of eastern Ukraine. Since 2015, Russia, Kazakhstan, Belarus, Armenia and Kyrgyzstan have joined together in the Eurasian Economic Union (EAEU), strategically linking China's "One Belt" land bridge program with Europe. See Chapter 8. The EAEU has a FTA with Vietnam and is exploring others.

Russia, with considerable Siberian energy development finance from China, is busy developing a Northern Sea Route to exploit reduced artic ice. This strategic, cost-saving initiative connects China/Japan/Korea with Europe.

India

By 2018, India had free trade agreements with ASEAN, Sri Lanka, Malaysia, the Gulf Cooperation

Council (GCC), Singapore, Korea, Japan, Afghanistan, Chile, and led the seven-nation South Asian FTA. India's major trade concern is being surrounded by China, notably via China's OBOR links with Bangladesh, Nepal, Pakistan, the Maldives and Sri Lanka.

South Korea

By 2018, hustling Korea had free trade agreements with ASEAN, India, Australia, Canada, the United States (KORUS I and II), China, Chile, Colombia, EFTA, the European Union (KOREU), Turkey, Vietnam, Peru, and Singapore. At President Trump's insistence, the KORUS agreement was re-negotiated in 2018. See Chapter 8.

China

As a counterbalance to the U.S.-led APEC and TPP, China has been promoting a Regional Comprehensive Economic Partnership (RCEP) with 16 nations including the 10 ASEAN nations, Australia, India, Japan, New Zealand and South Korea, but not the United States. Unlike the wide-ranging TPP and TPP-11, RCEP focuses primarily upon tariff reductions on trade in goods. Early signs after President Trump withdrew from the TPP suggest China may seek to utilize RCEP to integrate much of the Pacific Basin, minus the United States, with its economy. RCEP is moving quickly on a foreign investment pact.

The role of China in Pacific Rim integration is critical. China is pushing for dominant influence in the Pacific Rim economic sphere. Hong Kong's return in 1997 and Macau in 1999 moved in this direction. China has cultivated trade and investment relations with Taiwan, South Korea and, to a lesser extent, Japan. China also has free trade deals that rival and/ or overlap with those of Japan, notably with ASEAN, Australia and South Korea.

China and Japan are clearly rivals for economic leadership of the region. By 2018, China had free trade agreements with its own Hong Kong and Macau Special Administrative Regions, Chile, Pakistan, Costa Rica, Peru, Singapore, New Zealand, Australia, South Korea, Iceland and ASEAN.

Some commentators foresee, as a practical matter, the emergence of a powerful Southern China coastal economic zone embracing Hong Kong, Shenzhen SEZ, Macau, Zhuhai SEZ, and the Chinese province of Guangdong. China's massive One Belt-One Road (OBOR) initiative, while not a free trade agreement, is promoting Chinese alliances and economic interests across Eurasia and in East Africa.

Summary Perspective

As America retreats from free trade, witness TPP, TTIP and NAFTA, the world is not standing by. The European Union, Canada, Japan, China, Mexico and others have stepped forward to fill the void.

CHAPTER 8
TRUMP AND TRADE

AMERICA FIRST and:
The TPP, WTO, Europe, Korea, China, and Japan

For the first time in many years, international trade was a major issue in a U.S. Presidential election. In 2016, Donald J. Trump made it so. He campaigned and tweeted against trade deficits, currency manipulation, NAFTA 1994 as "the worst trade deal ever", and the signed but not ratified twelve-nation (minus China) Trans-Pacific Partnership (TPP). He also criticized just about every U.S. trade agreement, the WTO and KORUS I, the U.S.-Korea 2012 bilateral Free Trade Agreement.

Rallying the oft-forgotten losers under U.S. trade policy, he swept into office in 2017 as the world took a deep breath and wondered what might come.

AMERICA FIRST TRADE

Excluding NAFTA, which will be covered in a revised, future Nutshell, below are major Trump Administration trade policy issues and actions that have emerged to date. All have been taken under an America First mantra:

Trump and TPP

Negotiation of the TPP was led by the United States under President Obama's "pivot to Asia". Late in 2015, a Trans-Pacific Partnership (TPP) agreement was reached among the three NAFTA nations plus Peru, Chile, Brunei, Singapore, Malaysia, Vietnam, Japan, Australia and New Zealand (but notably not China). The TPP contained notable trade law developments. See Chapter 7. South Korea, Taiwan and Indonesia expressed interest in joining the TPP, which clearly resembled a containment strategy relative to China rising economic power.

President Trump quickly withdrew from the Trans Pacific Partnership (TPP), essentially making a gift of trade leadership in Asia to China. President Xi Xinping at Davos accepted this gift, noting ongoing negotiations for its competing trade alliance: The Regional Cooperation and Economic Partnership (RCEP) comprised of the ASEAN states, South Korea, Japan, China and India, but not the United States.

As signed by President Obama, TPP ratification in the United States would have been under the fast track procedures. President Trump's quick withdrawal from the TPP mooted this possibility. This decision has had broad consequences in the world of international trade. Perhaps most significantly, as noted in Chapter 7, many nations have pursued free trade partners elsewhere around the globe.

Trump and TPP-11

The remaining TPP partners, led notably by Japan and Canada, signed an altered TPP-11 free trade agreement in 2018 covering roughly 15% of global trade. TPP-11 has been re-named the Comprehensive and Progressive Trans Pacific Partnership (CPTPP). This agreement borrows substantially from TPP-12, minus provisions closely associated with the United States, and subject to a variety of country-specific alterations. See Chapter 7.

South Korea, Taiwan, Thailand, Colombia and even the United Kingdom have expressed interest in joining TPP-11.

Trump and the World Trade Organization

The Trump Administration launched an extensive review of U.S. participation in the World Trade Organization (WTO), the ultimate rules-based multilateral agreement embraced by approximately 165 countries and customs territories. See Chapter 2. Special attention was given to WTO "most-favored-nation" trade principles, trade remedies and dispute resolution. That report was also highly critical of WTO procedures, specific trade remedy decisions, and especially "activism" on the part of the WTO Appellate Body.

In what amounts to a hostile act, the United States has refused to allow renewal or new appointments to the WTO Appellate Body (AB), shrinking its membership from seven to four. What was normally a 90-day process is taking many months. By the Fall of 2018, there will be only three AB members, the minimum quorum necessary for it to conduct proceedings. Late in 2019, unless the United States permits new AB members, the Appellate Body will cease to function with only one member. Work-around alternatives that would result in voluntary arbitrations by disputing members as an alternative to Appellate Body are under study, with the U.S. of course not expected to volunteer.

It is not at all clear why the U.S. is engaged in this hostile act, particularly given its numerous successes in WTO dispute settlement proceedings. See Chapter 2. At the same time, the Trump Administration seems to be trying to benefit from WTO dispute settlement. In 2018 it filed a complaint with the WTO alleging patent violations of TRIPS by China (see Chapter 6).

Trump and Europe

At over $1 trillion a year, the trading relationship between the United States and the European Union is the largest in the world, accounting for over one-third of global trade. Europe had a trade in goods surplus in 2016 of approximately $270 billion, while the U.S. had a trade in services surplus of $55 billion. Viewed individually for 2017, net U.S. goods and services trade with Britain generated a slight surplus, a slight deficit with France, a small deficit with Italy and a notable deficit of $68 billion with Germany. EU job and technology creating investment in the U.S. amounted in 2016 to about $200 billion, with each side having over $5 trillion invested in the other.

For decades, though not without disputes taken to the WTO, the United States and Europe have maintained a critically important strategic and economic partnership. NATO, for example, counts 22 of the 28 EU states as members. All this suggests that America First policies and tariffs of the Trump administration place much at risk.

The U.S.-EU negotiations for a Transatlantic Trade and Investment Partnership (TTIP) initiated by President Obama are on a very back burner. After considerable delay, Canada and the EU implemented their Comprehensive Economic and Trade Partnership (CETA) in 2017, and Mexico has re-negotiated its year 2000 EU free trade deal. See Chapter 7.

The EU free trade initiatives with Canada and Mexico are in part driven by the prospect of a NAFTA re-negotiation failure. These agreements will allow duty free trade in autos, avoiding an EU tariff of 10%, Canadian tariff of 6.1%, and Mexican tariff of about 7%. Absent re-negotiation of NAFTA 1994 with reasonable auto rules of origin, U.S. car exporters, including U.S.-based European and Asian firms, will have to pay these tariffs to their competitive disadvantage.

Subjecting the European Union to U.S. national security tariffs on steel and aluminum (below) has generated retaliation. President Trump's rejection of the Paris accord on climate change, the Iran nuclear agreement, and his G7 plus Russia goals also signal the potential for a dramatic shift in European-U.S. relations. Perhaps, a G6 group will emerge minus the USA.

Trump and KORUS I and II

In August of 2017, the Trump Administration commenced re-negotiation of the 2012 U.S.-South Korea free trade agreement (KORUS I), expressing concerns about the modest U.S. trade deficit in goods with Korea, while ignoring a sizeable trade surplus in services for a net deficit in 2017 of about $10 billion. Several major Korean firms announced plans to invest in the United States, and Korea pulled its WTO Appellate Body member back home to negotiate with the Trump Administration. These negotiations were notably NOT undertaken under U.S. fast track trade promotion procedures (see Chapter 3). They were held instead via the Joint Committee process under KORUS I.

Then North Korea shot a missile over Japan and exploded a thermonuclear bomb. The United States, at a hefty price, promised South Korea major defense armaments and reduced but did not remove pressure to re-negotiate the KORUS I agreement.

The arrival of U.S. defensive radar and missile systems in South Korea, and the promise of more to come, caused China to organize a painful boycott of South Korean goods and tourism. South Korea and China have a free trade in goods agreement, and a number of prominent Korean companies (Lotte supermarkets, KIA cars) have production and distribution centers in the PRC. Hyundai sales in China dropped 34%. In 2018, having made its point, China lifted the boycott, but its impact lingers.

KORUS I re-negotiations were ongoing at U.S. insistence, but moving slowly in early 2018. The main issues were Korean auto exports to the USA under a 55% KORUS I origin rule, resulting in roughly a $15 billion auto trade surplus. Korea's exports were in no way matched by U.S. auto exports, despite a generous Korean 25,000 entry waiver of its strict car safety and pollution rules. U.S. exports of agricultural, meat and food products to Korea were also contentious on both sides. The Trump Administration's unilateral 25% steel tariffs of 2018 (below) threatened to hurt sizeable Korean exports, and were hard to explain to such a steadfast U.S. ally.

In the afterglow of the 2018 Winter Olympics held in South Korea, President Trump and North Korea's Kim Jong Un agreed to meet. KORUS I re-negotiations accelerated. Late in March the two sides announced a deal. The U.S. got a meaningless doubling to 50,000 cars of its quota to enter Korea without meeting local safety and environmental standards. The U.S., which had promised to lift in 2021 its 25% tariff on Korean pick-up trucks and cargo vans, none ever having been shipped to the USA, obtained an extension to 2041.

Korea got a permanent exemption from the 25% Trump steel tariffs (below), subject to a quota limit of 70% of the average Korean steel exports to the USA in 2015–2017. Korea is expected to easily make up for these lost exports in other markets, but pay attention to trade diversion restraints by other "collateral damage" countries, and WTO challenges to this bilateral voluntary export restraint (VER, see

Chapter 4). The Korean steel industry parcels out the quotas among 54 categories of producers, some of which maxed out almost immediately in 2018.

Both sides agreed not to revise existing, contentious KORUS I agricultural trade rules. Increased transparency revisions on Korean customs procedures, and relaxed Korean pharmaceutical access and pricing rules, were also agreed. A "robust" currency accord banning competitive devaluations and exchange rate manipulation via market interventions, a concern of the U.S. about Korea, is part of the deal.

All in all, a largely cosmetic, mutually face-saving revision of KORUS I was achieved. Call it KORUS II, but President Trump held back signing this "strong card" pending talks with North Korea. Furthermore, the President's threat to globally impose 25% "national security" tariffs on autos and auto parts places Korea's duty free access to the U.S. market at risk. See below.

Trump and Japan

Japan has run a major trade surplus with the United States for decades, lowered somewhat by a U.S. trade surplus in services to a net deficit of $56 billion in 2017. Needless to say, this deficit collides with President Trump's America First trade policies. The Japanese, post President Trump's withdrawal from the TPP, rapidly undertook an extensive FTA with the European Union and led the way to the TPP-11 agreement. See Chapter 7.

Since the arrival of President Trump, Japan has openly declined to negotiate a bilateral FTA with the United States. This refusal helps explain why Japan did not receive a temporary exemption from the Trump steel and aluminum tariffs (below).

Trump and China

Few countries took more abuse than China in the U.S. Presidential election race of 2016, particularly for its massive trade surplus in goods and services with the United States, $337 billion in 2017. Roughly 20% of all U.S. imports come from China, and several studies affirm China's adverse impact since joining the WTO in 2001 on U.S. manufacturing jobs.

Upon taking office, President Trump proceeded to question U.S. adherence to the "One China" policy which suggests that Taiwan is not independent from the PRC. It was only after President Trump reaffirmed this Policy that President Xi Xinping visited him in Florida for what seemed to be an amicable meeting. Subsequently, President Trump withdrew, contrary to numerous prior tweets and pronouncements, assertions that China was a currency manipulator. Perhaps he realized that China had in recent years spent about $1 trillion from its reserves keeping the Yuan up in the market.

President Trump then waited for China's support against North Korea, which has been mostly limited to U.N.-derived trade sanctions. Relatively minor foreign trade and investment law changes were made by China, and its control and militarized "development" of the South China Sea advanced.

China-United States trade relations took a stormy tumble in March of 2018 when the Trump Administration announced its intention to impose approximately $50 to $60 billion tariffs on Chinese exports, file a patent practices complaint against China at the WTO (see Chapter 6), and implement stringently restrictive policies against Chinese investments in the United States, especially in the tech field, via more stringent U.S. foreign investment export controls.

China retaliated almost immediately with a list of $50 to $60 billion tariffs it threatened to impose on U.S. exports. The President responded by ordering the USTR to come up with an additional potential list of $100 billion more U.S. tariffs on Chinese goods. See below.

China Investment Patterns and Issues

China's 25% WTO-negotiated tariff on cars combined with the world's fasting growing auto market makes the PRC a must-be-there market. Virtually all major auto producers have invested in China, with Volkswagen and General Motors leading in sales, and China's Geely rising rapidly after its purchase of Volvo and its owner's personal acquisition of nearly 10% of the shares of Daimler. At this point, having abandoned India and Europe, about 40% of GM's *global* auto sales are in China, with Ford roughly making 20% of its world-wide sales in the PRC. In 2017, a joint venture between General Motors and the City of Shanghai became the first exporter of cars to the USA, Made-in-China Buicks, and they have been selling well!

The Trump administration seems oblivious as China continues to build its One Belt One Road (OBOR) program linking the Eurasian continent by land and sea, which includes creation of what amounts to a Digital Silk Road. Trains are already running from Xian in Western China to Rotterdam in Holland. Many OBOR loans are financed via the China-led Asian Infrastructure Development Bank, which President Obama declined to enter, but almost all other major countries joined. OBOR loans are not subject to international dispute settlement, but rather to vague Chinese investment courts. Early signs are that foreclosure on OBOR loans gives China the ability to take control of infrastructure in Eurasian nations, such as strategic ports in Sri Lanka and possibly Piraeus in Greece.

Chinese investments in the USA, which had been growing rapidly, tightened under Chinese capital export controls and aggressive U.S. national security CFIUS reviews. This has been especially the case when state-owned Chinese enterprises are involved, and even resulted in the blocking of the hostile purchase attempt by *Singapore's* Broadcomm of San Diego-based Qualcomm (a high-tech 5G chip wizard). Broadcomm's connection to China was not obvious.

China, in turn, delayed its review of Qualcomm's proposed acquisition of NXP, an auto and security chip leader. The NXP deal is thought to be critical to Qualcomm's future, and would reduce its heavy dependence on China revenues. The Trump

Administration also blocked the acquisition of Moneygram by China's Ant Financial. The longstanding U.S.-China bilateral investment treaty (BIT) negotiation has stalled.

For more coverage, see my *Foreign Investment Law Nutshell*.

Trump Tariffs

President Trump has imposed a range of new tariffs, that is to say taxes, on U.S. imports since taking office. See generally Chapter 4 on trade remedies. These include:

Softwood Lumber and Paper

Picking up a decades-long dispute, the Trump Administration quickly levied 20% CVD tariffs against Canadian softwood lumber. U.S. timber companies are smiling while U.S. home builders face rising costs, mostly passed on to home buyers. Canada covered the losses to its lumber companies, and expects to win as it has in the past on NAFTA and WTO appeals.

A 22% antidumping tariff on Canadian magazine paper was levied by the Trump Administration in 2018, then withdrawn by request of the complaining firm, Ohio's Verso Corp., after it settled with Canadian exporters for a $42 million share of the AD tariffs that will be refunded by U.S. Customs to them.

Clothes Washers

In 2018, President Trump dusted off a little-used WTO-approved Safeguard remedy allowing temporary trade restraints when imports surge causing serious damage or its threat. See Chapter 4. A three year 20 to 50% Safeguard tariff has been imposed since 2018 on clothes washers from any source except Canada, plus up to a 50% tariff on washer parts, an anti-screwdriver assembly plant tactic. Developing countries eligible for U.S. GSP tariff treatment representing less than 3% of U.S. washer imports are also exempt, a provision not benefiting Thailand at over 3% for example.

"Country hopping" in Asia by Korea's LG and Samsung companies, the main culprits in this scenario, had previously avoided country-specific U.S. AD tariffs. Whirlpool USA, the complainant, is increasing production, while the two Korean companies, after raising their prices in the U.S., say they will build plants in the USA.

When utilizing Safeguard tariffs, the U.S. must consider "compensating" the exporting countries and the EU, all of which are seeking such relief. Those same parties have filed WTO challenges asserting the illegality of this Trump Administration Safeguard tariff, and enacted comparable Safeguard tariffs to protect their markets from diversionary sales from other exporting countries hit by the Trump tariffs.

Solar Panels

The Trump Administration has imposed a four year 30%, declining to 15%, Safeguard tariff on solar panels from any source (except over 3% GSP developing nations). These tariffs mostly target China's large volume, subsidized low price exports that have helped create a large number of solar panel installation jobs in the USA, along with plenty of renewable energy. Korea, Malaysia, Thailand and Vietnam also notably export solar panels to the U.S., some of their production a result of country hopping Chinese investments. Compensation claims and illegality challenges by exporting nations are again pending at the WTO.

The solar complaint was filed by two bankrupt U.S. producers, one Chinese owned, the other German owned, after a rash of U.S. solar panel companies left the market. The solar panel Safeguard tariffs will generally increase solar panel costs and reduce installation jobs. That said, JinkoSolar of Shanghai announced plans in 2018 to build solar panels in a new Jacksonville Florida plant to supply Florida Power and Light with some seven million panels over four years, provided Asian made solar cells are admitted to the USA. Other investors, mindful of Trump's tariffs and immediate tax write-offs, have also announced plans to expand solar panel operations in America.

Steel and Aluminum

Unilaterally invoking in 2018 what many call a "nuclear" trade remedy option, the Trump

Administration adopted a 25% "national security" tariff on steel imports for an indefinite duration. On aluminum imports there is a 10% national security tariff. The Department of Commerce Reports on invocation of these tariffs cite the "welfare" of these U.S. industries as "critical" to "minimum operations of the economy and government". Seeking to ensure that 80% of U.S. capacity is being used, both tariffs were proclaimed under a long dormant provision of Section 232 of the Trade Expansion Act of 1962. See Chapter 4.

Other countries, fearing diversion of steel and aluminum no longer gaining entry to the U.S., are scrambling to impose their own trade restrictions on these metals.

U.S. officials also assert that China exports steel to Vietnam, Korea, Malaysia and other Asian countries where minimal galvanizing, re-rolling and color-coating of rolled steel are said to constitute a "substantial transformations". See Chapter 4. Such products are then labeled as originating from those Asian nations, thus escaping U.S. tariffs and import controls. In addition, outright customs fraud by brazen freight forwarders is alleged as Asian countries repack, relabel and transship Chinese goods destined for the USA.

Contrary to other Trump Administration officials, U.S. Defense Department Secretary Mattis maintained that these import tariffs actually "impair" national security, and warned of a "negative impact" on key allies. The Economist magazine, noting that the vast majority of U.S. steel and aluminum imports are for civilian purposes, scathingly referred to the Trump administration claim of acting in the name national security as "spurious".

Canada at about 17% is the number one source of U.S. steel imports, followed by Brazil, Korea, Mexico, Russia, Turkey, Japan, Germany, Taiwan and in tenth place, China. Canada supplies nearly 50% of all U.S. imports of aluminum, followed by Russia and the United Arab Emirates. China, already under AD and CVD steel and aluminum U.S. tariffs, is a minor exporter of steel and aluminum goods to the USA, though critics maintain its overcapacities drive down market prices.

The many United States manufacturers using steel and aluminum in their goods, from cars to high-tech components to aluminum cans, have argued these tariffs will raise costs and consumer prices, and result in large job losses. For example, layoffs arrived swiftly at the American Keg Company, the only U.S. producer of stainless steel beer kegs. That said, a few new and previously closed U.S. steel mills have announced plans to advance production with small increases in jobs. Bottom line: Many more U.S. jobs are at stake among fabricators of goods using imported steel and aluminum than among producers of those metals.

Steel import tariffs have been imposed by every U.S. President since Ronald Reagan, including Barack Obama. Steel exports almost always increase from exempt countries, frequently for example Mexico and Canada. One study estimates that when

President George W. Bush imposed 30% steel import Safeguard tariffs in 2002, overall about 200,000 steel-related jobs were lost, a decidedly America Last outcome. See Chapter 4.

Canada and Mexico were exempted from the steel and aluminum tariffs, which took effect March 23, 2018, pending the outcome of NAFTA's re-negotiation. Korea, the EU, Brazil, Argentina, and Australia got temporary "exemptions" to May 1, 2018 from the Treasury Department. Japan, under continuing pressure to negotiate a bilateral FTA with the U.S., did not.

Korea's exemption is scheduled to become permanent under KORUS II, subject to export quotas of dubious WTO legality (above). The remaining May 1st exemptions were extended to June 1, 2018. Take it or leave it agreements with Australia, Brazil and Argentina followed the KORUS II pattern, though Brazil's steel makers chose export quotas while its aluminum sector agreed to the 10 % U.S. tariff.

That left the Canada, Mexico and the EU in flux, all promising to retaliate if U.S. steel and aluminum tariffs ultimately applied to its exports. June 1st arrived and the Trump Administration announced steel and aluminum "national security" tariffs against these longtime trade, military and political allies. They in turn responded with WTO complaints and announced equivalent value "rebalancing tariffs" on U.S. exports to take effect by July 1, 2018 (below).

Steel and aluminum prices in the United States have risen significantly. Specific high-need steel and aluminum imports may be permitted by Department of Commerce, and thousands of petitions have been filed by U.S. importers. These petitions can be opposed by U.S. firms arguing they can provide the goods in question, opening up potentially anti-competitive forces.

Responses to Trump's Steel and Aluminum Tariffs, Are Autos Next?

Retaliatory "rebalancing" tariffs against the U.S. steel and aluminum tariffs are underway or expected, with U.S. agricultural exports a prime target. India, Japan, Russia, Turkey, and others are retaliating in addition to the EU, Mexico, Canada and China (below).

The EU vocally created a 10-page target $3.4 billion rebalancing list that included politically precise retaliation targets: U.S. made jeans (California), Harley Davidsons (Wisconsin), boats (South Carolina), orange juice (Florida), peanut butter (Georgia), bourbon whiskey (Kentucky), cranberries (Wisconsin and Massachusetts) and corn (Iowa).

Mexico's list of retaliatory U.S. exports includes steel, cheese, Tennesse Whiskey, pork, apples, grapes, cranberries, lamps and potatoes. Mexico, by the way, is the biggest U.S. apple export market. Canada's $12.8 billion list covers U.S. steel, aluminum, sailboats, beer kegs, yogurt, chocolate (hello Hershey), orange juice and other products. Insulted at the idea that it is a national security risk to the USA, the Trump team might wish to recall that

Canada buys even more U.S. farm goods than China. Canada has also been planning new pipelines to ship its oil and gas to Asia.

With less noise volume, citing U.S. "wanton destruction" of the WTO trading system, China undertook a review of its huge U.S. sorghum, soybean and hog imports, creating near-panic conditions in the U.S. farm belt. U.S. colleges and universities, increasingly dependent on high-paying Chinese students to make ends meet, are shaking their heads in concern. Boeing, the number one consumer of aluminum in America, is worried about potential lost sales if China retaliates, and so is Boeing's extensive workforce. Farm and earth moving machinery makers John Deere and Caterpillar joined the crowd of U.S, industry opponents. These fears carried over to the pending China-specific Section 301 tariffs (below).

Fortunately, China's retaliation to the U.S. steel and aluminum tariffs was measured: $3 billion new 15% to 25% rebalancing tariffs on roughly 128 commodities including U.S. fruit, nuts, pork, ginseng, ethanol, wine, scrap aluminum and steel pipe exports, approximately matching the $3 billion in U.S. Safeguard tariffs applicable to Chinese exports of steel and aluminum. The pork tariffs at 25% hit Trump country states like Iowa, North Carolina and Indiana especially hard. As the steel and aluminum tariffs have cascaded through U.S. metal manufacturers' supply chains, costs and prices have risen. Some firms are moving production out of the USA to lower cost centers abroad.

In turn, President Trump in June of 2018 ordered a report on the national security implications of U.S. imports of automobiles, trucks and auto parts. About a quarter of all the cars sold in the USA are imported, with Mazda, Suburu, Jaguar, VW and BMW high on the list of companies with minimal or no U.S. production. By country, Japanese, Canadian and Mexican auto exports are at greatest risk. The President has threatened market bending and inflationary 25% auto tariffs.

U.S. invocation of the national security nuclear option, largely (but arguably not entirely) a self-judging blank check under GATT/WTO and nearly all free trade agreement rules (see Chapters 4 and 7), provoked a poignant reaction from Mario Draghi, head of the EU Central Bank: "If you put tariffs against your allies, one wonders who the enemies are."

Murmurs of "trade wars", described by President Trump as "good, and easy to win", are everywhere. Indeed, just when the United States, Japan, Korea, Canada and the EU should be uniting their strength to counter China as a trade and technology superpower, President Trump is making that extremely difficult. Why is an excellent question.

The U.S. Section 301 Report on China

After a lengthy study by the USTR of China's trade and technology acquisition practices, generally treated as not falling within WTO jurisdiction, President Trump invoked another dormant U.S. unilateral trade remedy, Section 301 of the Trade Act of 1974 (see Chapter 6). Section 301 focuses on "unreasonable', "unjustifiable" and "discriminatory" trade practices of foreign countries. The President has broad powers to respond with tariffs and trade restraints against "actionable" Section 301 conduct. See Chapter 5. In addition, expanded restrictions on Chinese tech and other investments and acquisitions in the USA were recommended in the USTR's report.

Apart from outright IP, trade secret and confidential business information theft, often via state-sponsored hacking, the USTR report zeroed in on forced or pressured technology transfers (TT) inside China. One such technique is associated with China's mandatory joint venture rules (autos, insurance, cloud computing, telecommunications) as a condition of access to China's vast market.

Forced disclosure of software source codes and data localization rules under China's recent Cybersecurity Law were noted in the USTR report. So was mandatory R & D in China, technology R & D and acquisition inside the USA, Europe and elsewhere, the Made in China 2025 ultra-high-tech program, and Chinese control of licensing and improvement technology. See Chapter 6. The report also cited TT undertaken "voluntarily" by Microsoft, Qualcomm, Apple and others.

A Tech-Driven Tariff War

The Warm-Up. Chinese exports were hit early in 2018 when the Trump Administration slapped Safeguard tariffs on solar panels and clothes washers (above). China filed a WTO challenge to these tariffs but did not directly retaliate. It did, however, launch an antidumping/anti-subsidy investigation regarding U.S. sales of sorghum, a feed grain heavily exported to China.

President Trump subsequently added to the pressure on China by imposing "national security" tariffs on steel (25%) and aluminum (10%). See above. To this, China immediately responded in a measured, reciprocal manner with $3 billion in 15% and 25% "Safeguard" tariffs on U.S. exports, the total amount roughly corresponding to its lost exports of steel and aluminum. These China's tariffs apply to 128 U.S. products, including U.S. fruits, nuts, wine, ethanol, ginseng, seemless steel pipes, pork and pork products, and recycled aluminum. In addition, food products from the USA have encountered tedious Chinese customs examinations, as have Ford autos.

China also filed a WTO complaint based on the view that the U.S. steel and aluminum tariffs are really Safeguards. The U.S. is defending on national security grounds, which it believes are not justiciable by the WTO, a debatable position. See Chapter 2.

Round One. Citing the USTR tech transfer report and the massive U.S. trade deficit with China, trade relations took a stormy tumble in March of 2018. The Trump Administration announced its intention to impose approximately $50 to $60 billion Section 301 tariffs of 25% on some 1300 Chinese exports, file a patent practices complaint against China at the WTO, and implement stringently restrictive policies against Chinese investments in the United States, especially in the tech field. That tariff amount roughly corresponds to what the Trump Administration claims Chinese "cheaters" have gained through technology theft and forced technology transfer practices.

The list of China imports targeted for these tariffs includes aircraft engines, vessels, heavy machinery, industrial robots, lithium-ion batteries, semiconductor production equipment, flat screen televisions, printers, household appliances, midsize cars, electric vehicles, printing equipment, base metals, medicines (insulin), medical equipment (defibrillators, pacemakers, replacement joints), machine tools, electrical equipment, chemicals, and select information and communication technology items. About 47% of all the TVs sold in the USA are imported from China, 83% of PC monitors, 34% of lithium batteries and substantial printer ink and cartridges. Prices on these and other listed items will rise noticeably. All totaled the U.S. list comprises about 10% of the roughly $500 billion Chinese exports in 2017 to the USA.

China's dependency on exports have dropped dramatically over the past decade from 35% to 19% of its GDP. This diminishes the impact and force of Trump's China tariffs. Less obviously, Asian (notably Japanese and Korean) suppliers of components that are incorporated into Chinese exports to the U.S. will also be collaterally hit if these tariffs materialize.

The threatened Section 301 China tariffs were careful to try to reduce their punishing impact on retailers and consumers, especially shoppers in lower/middle end markets like Walmart and Target.

China supplies roughly 42% of the clothing and 72% of the footwear sold in the United States. These items were not on the initial Section 301 China tariff list. Other items not on the initial list include: furniture, personal computers, laptops, and travel gear.

Round Two. Absent a deal, China will certainly retaliate, as it did in response to the U.S. "national security" steel and aluminum tariffs (above). Within 24 hours of the announcement of the list of President Trump's Section 301 China tariffs, the PRC released a 25% retaliatory tariff list on 106 U.S. exports valued at $50 to $60 billion, including: Soybeans, corn, wheat, beef, orange juice, chemicals, smaller aircraft (think Boeing), larger passenger vehicles and SUVs (think U.S.-made BMWs and Mercedes Benz), electric vehicles (think Tesla), auto parts, propane and cotton. All totaled the list comprises about 38% of U.S. exports in 2017 to the PRC. American farmers and ranchers let it be known they are not at all happy with their potential losses. Nearly 60% of U.S. exports of soybeans go to China, which immediately commenced restricting U.S. soybean shipments.

Simultaneously, China, having dramatically accelerated its antidumping/anti-subsidy investigation, announced 178.5% tariffs targeting roughly $1 billion annual sorghum exports from the USA. A "shot over the bow" you could say.

Round Three. Within 24 hours of publication of China's proposed retaliatory list and sorghum announcement, President Trump ordered the USTR to come up with a second list for an additional $100 billion U.S. tariffs on Chinese goods. China vowed absolutely, "no options ruled out", to retaliate again if and when this happens. Combined, $150 billion in Chinese tariffs on U.S. exports would exceed the entire value of the $137 billion U.S. exports to China in 2017.

Unable to fully go tit-for-tat on tariffs, China is likely to consider other retaliatory measures: Perhaps a government encouraged "people's boycott" of travel to the USA and a boycott of American goods, including Made in China U.S. brands (Apple, Ford, Chevrolet, KFC, Starbucks, Nike, P & G cosmetics and skin care). China has a history of "people's wars" against Japan in 2012 over a territorial dispute, the Philippines in 2016 after losing a South China Sea arbitration, and South Korea in 2017 when U.S. missiles were installed. Or, in many opaque ways, the PRC could just simply make life difficult for U.S. firms operating in the Middle Kingdom. Already, as the USTR's report noted, the PRC has restrained the use of VPNs (virtual private networks) by foreign businesses seeking to avoid government monitors and blocked website access via its Great Firewall.

China could also engage in geopolitical retaliation. It could, for example, step up pressure on Taiwan or expand upon its militarization of the South China Sea. China's ultimate trade war weapon is the $1.2 trillion in U.S. Treasuries it owns. Even a small reduction or threatened diminishment in those holdings would drive up U.S. interest rates and rock Wall Street. It would also undermine China's U.S. bond portfolio.

Round Four. China's response to Round Three was initially conciliatory. In a public lecture, stressing a "new phase of opening up", President Xi Xinping indicated that China's 25% tariff on auto imports would be reduced, along with an extensive list of other less significant tariff reductions and relaxation of the sorghum antidumping tariffs, though when and by how much was unclear. U.S.-based BMW and Mercedes Benz lead auto exports to China, well ahead of Ford, Fiat-Chrysler and Tesla. But Europe and Japan (think Lexus), as WTO members, would also benefit from reduced Chinese auto tariffs.

President Xi also suggested that maximum foreign shareholdings in Chinese enterprises and mandatory joint ventures would be relaxed, quota controls over imported films relaxed, protection of intellectual property increased, and that greater foreign access to China's financial sector was planned. Shortly thereafter, all foreign auto companies were allowed to wholly own their operations starting in 2022, and for electrified car plants as of 2019. Tesla may invest, but not many existing automobile joint ventures in China are expected to convert to wholly owned subsidiaries.

The Trump Administration's response was not conciliatory. The President repeatedly sent his top trade staff to China, and vice-versa top Chinese staff came to the USA, for dialogues in May and June. Each side has presented argumentative, conflicting positions. The Trump team promoted such non-starters as immediate abandonment of the Made in

China 2025 program, while Chinese officials pushed cessation of U.S. allegations about forced technology transfers, another non-starter. See Chapter 6.

At one point, it looked like a deal had been reached with China buying $70 billion U.S. farm, energy and manufactured goods if the U.S. would drop its tariff threats. Of course such a deal would have bypassed major U.S. concerns about technology transfers, subsidies and IP rights. In any event, by June of 2018 no agreement was reached on any topic.

Shortly thereafter, the PRC announced a $47 billion fund to boost semiconductor production in China. This decision no doubt reflects China's concern about the U.S. export ban of chips to ZTE, China's global "national champion" cell phone producer. See Chapter 5. President Xi, pouring even more resources into technology development, exhorted his people to cast aside reliance on outsiders.

Round Five. After a public notice and comment period of about 60 days running to late May in 2018, absent a last minute negotiated settlement with China, $34 billion unilateral Section 301 tariffs on roughly 800 Chinese goods were announced in mid-June by the United States. These tariffs are scheduled to take effect July 6, 2018. Responding to the PRC's Made in China 2025 plan (see Chapter 6), the U.S. tariffs focus primarily on tech-oriented products, including semiconductors, information and communications equipment, nuclear reactors, aircraft engine parts, ball bearings, autos, motorbikes and heavy machinery. An additional $16 billion U.S. tariffs on Chinese exports is expected after public review.

China, asserting the United States has "launched a trade war", immediately responded with $34 billion in "rebalancing 25% tariffs" taking effect July 6 on hundreds of U.S. exports. These tariffs are centered on U.S. soybeans, corn, sorghum, wheat, seafood, chicken, beef, and pork, along with SUVs, propane, cigars and whiskey. An additional $16 billion Chinese tariffs on chemicals, energy and medical equipment will match the balance threatened by the United States.

The U.S. stock market took a dive.

Round Six. Trump and Trade may represent a "tipping point" in global relations. Trump tariffs against the goods of steadfast allies lacks strategic thinking in a world where the PRC will soon have the world's biggest economy. To quote Nebraska Senator Ben Sasse: "This is dumb".

Playing a long game, China seems to perceive that its one-party, authoritarian state can endure more trade war punishment than the U.S. democracy.